Lexicalization Typology and Event Structure Templates:
Toward Isomorphic Mapping between Macro-event and Syntactic Structures

Lexicalization Typology and **Event Structure Templates**:

Toward Isomorphic Mapping between Macro-event and Syntactic Structures

Takanori Demizu

KAITAKUSHA

Kaitakusha Co., Ltd.
5-2, Mukogaoka 1-chome
Bunkyo-ku, Tokyo 113-0023
Japan

Lexicalization Typology and Event Structure Templates: Toward Isomorphic Mapping between Macro-event and Syntactic Structures

Published in Japan
by Kaitakusha Co., Ltd., Tokyo

Copyright © 2015
by Takanori Demizu

All rights reserved. No part of this publication may be reproduced, stored in a retrieval system, or transmitted, in any form or by any means, electronic, mechanical, photocopying, recording, or otherwise, without the prior permission of the copyright owner.

First published 2015

Printed and bound in Japan
by ARM Corporation

Cover design by Shihoko Nakamura

Acknowledgements

This book is a slightly revised version of my doctoral dissertation submitted to the Graduate School of Letters at Ritsumeikan University in 2013.

First of all, my greatest gratitude goes to Masaki Sano, my supervisor. Since I began writing this dissertation, he has kindly read the entire manuscript and made a number of helpful suggestions. Without his tremendous help, my dissertation would not have been completed.

I am grateful to Yo Matsumoto, who has kindly served as a member of my dissertation examining committee, and has given me valuable comments and criticisms at the dissertation defense.

My special thanks are due to all members of *Rokko Eigogaku Kenkyuukai* "the Rokko English Linguistics Circle" for helpful suggestions, comments and criticisms, in particular, Kenji Kashino, Koji Yoshida, Kairi Igarashi and Yasuomi Kaiho, to name but a few.

I would like to express my deepest gratitude to the late Tokumi Kodama, Professor Emeritus at Ritsumeikan University, who was also a member of my dissertation examining committee. He had guided me academically since I was an undergraduate student, and had considerably influenced the direction my dissertation has taken. On March 11th, 2014, he passed away, and his untimely demise came as a bolt from the blue. I wish he had lived to see the publication of this book, which owes so much to his aphoristic advice. But at least it was a consolation that I was able to submit my dissertation before his passing.

Tokumi Kodama was the linguistics teacher who inspired me the most. When I first met him at Ritsumeikan University in 1993, I was twenty years old and he was in his late fifties. I chose to be in his linguistic seminar, because I was more and more interested in linguistics rather than in literature. And I had acquired a wealth of knowledge about linguistics and received scads of advice on the direction of my research from him since then. Even after his retirement from Ritsumeikan University, he had offered me numerous suggestions and comments constantly at the meetings of *Rokko Eigogaku Kenkyuukai*. He first introduced lexical semantics to me in his graduate seminar. And I read about Talmy's typology and how motion events are lexicalized in one of his papers for the first time. Looking back over the past twenty years, I realize that much of my linguistic knowledge can be traced back to my study under him. And from now on, I will continue my linguistic research by utilizing the linguistic expertise I had developed under him. He is my eternal mentor. He had always cared about me and encouraged me in my dissertation project. To live up to his expectations, I did everything I could. But I was a bit slow to finish my dissertation and just managed to "deliver the goods" a few months before his death. I wish I were not a procrastinator but a more disciplined researcher!

Last but not least, I would like to thank the Faculty of Humanities and Sciences at Kobegakuin University, at which I have worked for seven years. The faculty manages the Society of Humanities and Sciences, or *Jinbun Gakkai* in Japanese, and this book was partially funded by a grant from the society.

Needless to say, all remaining inadequacies and inconsistencies are my own responsibility.

Contents

Acknowledgements ⋯⋯⋯⋯⋯⋯⋯⋯⋯⋯⋯⋯⋯⋯⋯⋯⋯⋯⋯⋯⋯⋯⋯⋯⋯⋯⋯⋯ v
List of Abbreviations ⋯⋯⋯⋯⋯⋯⋯⋯⋯⋯⋯⋯⋯⋯⋯⋯⋯⋯⋯⋯⋯⋯⋯⋯⋯⋯ xi

Chapter 1   Introduction ⋯⋯⋯⋯⋯⋯⋯⋯⋯⋯⋯⋯⋯⋯⋯⋯⋯⋯⋯⋯⋯⋯⋯ 1

Chapter 2   Talmy's Motion Typology and Its Criticism ⋯⋯⋯⋯⋯⋯ 9
  2.1. Talmy (1985) ⋯⋯⋯⋯⋯⋯⋯⋯⋯⋯⋯⋯⋯⋯⋯⋯⋯⋯⋯⋯⋯⋯⋯ 10
    2.1.1. Motion Events and External Events ⋯⋯⋯⋯⋯⋯⋯⋯⋯⋯⋯ 10
    2.1.2. Motion Events and Three Lexicalization Types ⋯⋯⋯⋯⋯ 13
    2.1.3. First Lexicalization Type: Motion + Manner/Cause ⋯⋯⋯ 14
    2.1.4. Second Lexicalization Type: Motion + Path ⋯⋯⋯⋯⋯⋯ 16
    2.1.5. Third Lexicalization Type: Motion + Figure ⋯⋯⋯⋯⋯⋯ 19
  2.2. Talmy (2000) ⋯⋯⋯⋯⋯⋯⋯⋯⋯⋯⋯⋯⋯⋯⋯⋯⋯⋯⋯⋯⋯⋯⋯ 21
    2.2.1. Macro-events and Framing Events ⋯⋯⋯⋯⋯⋯⋯⋯⋯⋯⋯ 21
    2.2.2. Functions of Framing Events over Macro-events ⋯⋯⋯⋯ 24
    2.2.3. Functions of Framing Events over Subordinate Events ⋯⋯ 27
    2.2.4. Subordinate Events as Co-Events ⋯⋯⋯⋯⋯⋯⋯⋯⋯⋯⋯ 28
    2.2.5. Dichotomy and Concept of Satellites ⋯⋯⋯⋯⋯⋯⋯⋯⋯ 31
    2.2.6. Satellite-Framed and Verb-Framed Languages ⋯⋯⋯⋯⋯ 34

2.2.7. What Expresses Co-Events in Verb-Framed Languages? ········ 39
　2.3. Criticism against Talmy's Typology ···································· 43
　　2.3.1. Kopecka (2006) ··· 44
　　2.3.2. Broader Definition of Satellites ································ 47
　　2.3.3. Reconsideration of Dichotomy ································ 49
　　2.3.4. Satellite-Framed Expressions in Verb-Framed Languages ······· 50
　　2.3.5. Verb-Framed Expressions in Satellite-Framed Languages ······· 55
　　2.3.6. New Proposal ·· 60
　2.4. Recapitulation ··· 64

Chapter 3　Event Structure Templates and their Development············· 65
　3.1. Aspectual Classification of Verbs ····································· 66
　　3.1.1. Vendler (1957) ·· 66
　　3.1.2. Three Temporal Features ······································· 70
　　3.1.3. Three Important Situation Types ······························ 72
　3.2. Lexical Decomposition in Generative Semantics ···················· 76
　3.3. Lexical Decomposition in Recent Studies ··························· 80
　　3.3.1. Two Components of Verb Meaning ···························· 80
　　3.3.2. Similar Distinctions Proposed by Other Authors ·············· 82
　　　3.3.2.1. Pinker (1989) ·· 82
　　　3.3.2.2. Grimshaw (2005) ······································ 83
　　　3.3.2.3. Goldberg (1995) ······································· 85
　　3.3.3. Summary ·· 86
　3.4. Representations of the Two Components ···························· 87
　　3.4.1. Primitive Predicates vs. Constants ···························· 87
　　3.4.2. Manner vs. Result Verbs ······································· 90
　　3.4.3. Structure vs. Constant Participants ···························· 95
　　3.4.4. Simple vs. Complex Event Structures ······················· 103
　3.5. Revision of Notions of Manner and Result ························ 108
　　3.5.1. Divergence from Aspectual Definition ······················· 108
　　3.5.2. Nonaspectuality of Lexical Decomposition ·················· 109
　3.6. Two Pieces of Evidence against Aspectual Characterization ········ 111
　　3.6.1. Evidence #1: Object Determines Telicity ···················· 112
　　3.6.2. Evidence #2: Telicity does not Equal Result ················· 113
　　　3.6.2.1. Evidence #2(1): Result Verbs are not Necessarily Telic···· 113

  3.6.2.2. Evidence #2(2): Telic Verbs do not Necessarily Encode Result ··· 115
 3.7. Alternatives to Aspectual Definition··································· 122
  3.7.1. Scalar vs. Non-Scalar Changes ································ 122
  3.7.2. Three Types of Scalar Changes································ 124
  3.7.3. Non-Scalar Changes ·· 128
  3.7.4. Revision of Event Structure Templates····················· 130
 3.8. Summary and Implications ··· 131

Chapter 4 Event Structure Templates, Event Coidentification, and Macro-event ··· 135

 4.1. Unergative vs. Unaccusative Verbs ··································· 136
 4.2. The Origin of Research into Motion Verbs ······················ 141
  4.2.1. Three Types of Motion Verbs································· 142
  4.2.2. Motion Verbs and Unaccusativity ··························· 143
  4.2.3. Lexical Subordination and *Run* Verbs····················· 147
  4.2.4. Arguments against Lexical Subordination Analysis ············· 151
  4.2.5. First Alternative and its Problems···························· 154
 4.3. Event Coidentification as Second Alternative···················· 157
  4.3.1. What is Event Coidentification?······························ 157
  4.3.2. Event Coidentification and Semantic Representation ············· 160
 4.4. Event Coidentification and Event Structure Templates················· 162
  4.4.1. Event Structure Template of Goal Prepositional Phrases ······ 162
  4.4.2. Event Coidentification and Scalarity························ 169
  4.4.3. Coidentified Event Structure Template···················· 172
 4.5. Event Coidentification and Macro-events ························· 174
  4.5.1. Parallelism between Talmy's and Levin & Rappaport Hovav's Analyses ··· 175
  4.5.2. How to Solve Problems with Mapping?··················· 179
 4.6. Advantages of our Approach ·· 184
 4.7. Conclusion ·· 187

Chapter 5 English Examples and Translations ··················· 189

 5.1. When Verb *walk* Takes no Prepositional Phrase··············· 191

5.2. When Verb *walk* Takes Goal Prepositional Phrase ·············· 201
5.3. When Verb *walk* Takes Directional Prepositional Phrase ············ 213
5.4. When Verb *walk* is Followed by Particle *away* ···················· 220
5.5. Conclusion ·· 225

Chapter 6 Conclusion ·· 227

References and Works Cited ·· 233

Index ·· 239

List of Abbreviations

Acc	Accusative
Aux	Auxiliary
Dat	Dative
Gen	Genitive
Nom	Nominative
Perf	Perfective
PRF	Perfective
PL	Plural
SG	Singular
Top	Topic

Chapter 1

Introduction

Perhaps it is best to begin by considering what the motion as we know it is. When we are asked to name the most important element in motion events, the moving entity will occur to us first of all. There is nothing wrong with it. Yet, a linguistically truer answer would be the path the moving entity takes. In linguistics, the term "motion" usually refers to a change in position from one place to another, and does not include a change in posture in one place. In other words, the path is assumed to be an indispensable part of motion events as defined by linguists. Then why is the path thought to have special significance in motion events? And what are the basic determinants of motion events other than the moving entity and the path?

The configuration of motion events has posed riddles to linguists, most notably semanticists, though it might seem a mere trifle to those uninitiated in linguistics. The lexical semantics of motion events first came into the spotlight in 1985, with the appearance of an article titled "Lexicalization patterns: semantic structure in lexical forms." The article was written by Leonard Talmy, a cognitive linguist who has played a prominent role in the study of semantic typology. In it, he claims that languages are classified into three types according to what semantic element their verb roots characteristically "lexicalize" together with Motion. The classification is dubbed "lexicalization types," and a multitude of linguists have used his theory to analyze many different types of languages and produced a cornucopia of important findings. After that, perhaps because of the relative infrequency of the third lexicalization pattern, Talmy embarked on an effort to overhaul and reorganize his classification system, and consequently Talmy (1991) replaced the three lexicalization types with the famous dichotomy between satellite-framed and verb-framed languages.

Talmy's theory will remain a landmark study of the lexicalization of motion verbs, and no one can probably cast doubt on his prowess as a typological linguist. Without the groundwork he laid, the great advances in linguistic research on motion events made in the 1990s and thereafter would not have been possible. But Talmy seems to present a slightly oversimplified view of typological behavior. In particular, Talmy (1991, 2000) astutely analyze the two distinct lexicalization patterns displayed by a multiplicity of verbs; however, perhaps as a result of his sole commitment to the simple dichotomy, he tends to elide exceptions that undermine the division in favor of characteristic examples corroborating it. Talmy also fails to provide a persuasive rationale behind the distribution or packaging of information in verb meaning.

More recently, some linguists have tried alternative approaches to the problem. In particular, Beavers et al. (2010) have attempted to refute Talmy's view, arguing that "no single parameter governs the options for how motion is encoded across languages" (Beavers et al. (2010: 332)). This means that Talmy's dichotomy is not unimpeachable. In order to invalidate Talmy's theory, they point out its problems and deficiencies. However, though we accept some of their arguments, we reject their main contention that we should do away with Talmy's bipartite classification altogether. Then where do we stand on this issue? We must approach it from a different standpoint.

Accordingly, what we propose in chapter 2 is a substitute for the simple either-or categorization into satellite-framed and verb-framed languages—an effort to obtain the advantages of Talmy's classification without belying the linguistic truth. More specifically, we argue that satellite-framed lexicalization is a highly irregular manner of encoding motion events, and that it is made possible by an add-on to the regular mapping system used for verb-framed lexicalization. As we will see in sections 2.3.4–2.3.6, in verb-framed languages, satellite-framed expressions are not permitted, even though they have lexical resources such as manner verbs and adpositional phrases denoting the path to a goal. By contrast, in satellite-framed languages, verb-framed expressions are possible whenever lexical resources are available. Given these observations, we argue that an absence of satellite-framed lexicalization in verb-framed languages is attributed to grammatical constraints, while a dearth of verb-framed expressions in satellite-framed languages is ascribable to lexical gaps.

Chapter 3 constitutes a chronology of event structure templates proposed by two lexical semanticists, that is, Beth Levin and Malka Rappaport Hovav. But here one might wonder what event structure templates are. They are semantic representations of event structure in terms of lexical decomposition, and can be exemplified as below:

(1) a. [x ACT$_{<MANNER>}$] (activity)
    b. [x <*STATE*>] (state)
    c. [BECOME [x <*STATE*>]] (achievement)
    d. [[x ACT$_{<MANNER>}$] CAUSE [BECOME [y <*STATE*>]]]
                                                           (accomplishment)
                                        (Rappaport Hovav and Levin (1998: 108))

Here the predicates ACT, BECOME and CAUSE represent the structural part of verb meaning that is relevant to argument realization and semantic classes of verbs, whereas the roots, which are written in italicized capitals and put in angle brackets, encode the idiosyncratic aspect of verb meaning that distinguishes the verb from other members of the same class. The theory based on event structure templates made a meteoric appearance on the linguistic scene when they published a seminal paper, Rappaport Hovav and Levin (1998).[1] Of course, some of the ideas incorporated in event structure templates had already appeared in an inchoate form in their earlier studies, for example, Rappaport and Levin (1988), Levin and Rapoport (1988) and Levin and Rappaport Hovav (1991, 1992, 1995). But event structure templates are a much more advanced method of defining the lexical meaning of verbs. More specifically, they are an elaborate system of semantic representation that amalgamates lexical conceptual structures (sometimes abbreviated

---

[1] In fact, the draft of this paper was already circulated among linguists in 1996.

as LCSs) with argument structures.

Since the publication of Rappaport Hovav and Levin (1998), they have developed their theory and applied it to a wide assortment of verbs. At first, event structure templates were directly related to aspectual notions such as telicity and durativity, and so they were labeled with Vendlerian aspectual classes. However, a couple of problems cropped up when they used event structure templates for the analysis of some classes of verbs. For example, they associated change of state verbs with the accomplishment event structure template (1d). But it was shown that the verbs dubbed "degree achievements" by Dowty (1979: 88), which are assumed to be change of state verbs, exceptionally allow both telic and atelic interpretations. In addition, further research revealed that some accomplishment verbs, for instance *read a book*, do not encode a change of state. Considering these aspectual irregularities, Levin and Rappaport Hovav stopped characterizing event structure templates aspectually. In the 2000s and 2010s, they turned to new, powerful concepts which promised to end their dependence on unreliable aspectual criteria and contribute to rapid progress in understanding event structure. To be more specific, in Rappaport Hovav (2008) and Rappaport Hovav and Levin (2010), they introduced scalar and non-scalar changes as alternatives to aspectual notions such as telicity and durativity.

Given these, chapter 4 examines the details of how our revised view on Talmy's typology of motion events is associated with the recast theory of event structure templates based on scalarity. After introducing the Unaccusative Hypothesis proposed in the framework of relational grammar, we redefine event structure templates in terms of the hypothesis. Grounded in this hypothesis, Levin and Rappaport Hovav (1992), one of their earlier papers written before the advent of event structure templates, divide motion verbs into three categories, and two of them are the *run* verbs or "verbs of manner of motion," on the one hand, and the *arrive* verbs or "verbs of directed motion," on the other. They observe that the former verbs are basically unergative and the latter are unaccusative, but when the former are accompanied by a goal prepositional phrase, they become unaccusative. In order to explain this effect produced by the addition of a goal phrase, they propose the mechanism of lexical subordination. But this proves to be incompatible with the Argument-Per-Subevent Condition, which is imposed on event structure templates.

Then we review the process of event coidentification, which is proposed by Levin and Rappaport Hovav (1999) and Rappaport Hovav and Levin (2001) in order to allow the semantic amalgamation between manner of motion verbs and goal prepositional phrases without violating the Argument-Per-Subevent Condition. Regrettably, they do not base the process on event structure templates, and so we try to associate it with scale-based event structure templates. On the assumption that goal phrases have the same event structure template as verbs of directed motion, we characterize event coidentification as the amalgamation of a scalar change into a non-scalar change, and point out that this is comparable to what Talmy (2000: 219) calls the "structurer" function, that is, one of the semantic effects that framing events exert on subordinate events. In satellite-framed languages, but not in verb-framed languages, this process copies a scale from scalar to non-scalar changes, and makes it possible to map the augmented ex-subordinate event straightforwardly onto syntactic structure.

Finally, in chapter 5, we bolster up our argument by citing examples of the manner of motion verb *walk* that have been culled from a variety of novels written in English, together with their Japanese, French, German and Chinese translations. In doing so, we will confirm the characteristics of satellite-framed and verb-framed encoding options. For example, when the verb *walk* is followed by a goal phrase in English, the manner of motion is often left out and only the path is verbalized as a verb of directed motion in Japanese and French.[2] This is exemplified below:[3]

(2) a. Hooper ... *walked to the cage*. (P. Benchley, *Jaws*: 240)
   b. Fuupaa-ga ...   *ori-ni*   *chikazui-ta* (325) [Japanese]
      Hooper-Nom   cage-to   approach-Past
      'Hooper *approached* the cage.'
   c. Hooper   *s'approcha*   *de*   la   cage. (247) [French]
      Hooper   oneself-approached   of   the   cage
      'Hooper *approached* the cage.'

---

[2] For further details of motion expressions in Japanse, see Matsumoto (1996) and Kageyama and Yumoto (1997).

[3] As is also noted in chapter 5, the number in parentheses in translations refers to the number of the page on which the example is found.

Here the verb *walk* is followed by the goal prepositional phrase *to the cage* in the original English text. But in Japanese and French, the same motion is described by the verbs semantically equivalent to the English verb *approach*. As a result, the manner of motion "walking" is not expressed in the Japanese and French versions. Since these languages are verb-framed languages that lack satellite-framed encoding options, the manner of motion has to be denoted by an adverbial or gerundive type constituent, but this is stylistically awkward and therefore not preferred.

Furthermore, we will look at examples of *walk away*. Intriguingly, even in satellite-framed languages like German and Chinese, the motion is sometimes denoted by a verb of directed motion.

(3) a. "Thank you, I don't drink." Jill smiled and *walked away*.
(S. Sheldon, *A Stranger in the Mirror*: 210)

b. »Herzlichen Dank, ich trinke nicht.« Jill lächelte und
sincere   thanks   I   drink not   Jill smiled and
verschwand. (181) [German]
disappeared
'"My sincere thanks, I don't drink," Jill smiled and *disappeared*.'

c. "谢谢   您,   我   不   喝   酒。"   吉尔   微微
xièxie   nín   wǒ   bù   hē   jiǔ   Jí'ěr   wēiwēi
Thank   you   I   not drink alcohol Jill   slightly
一   笑   就   走   了。 (188) [Chinese]
yī   xiào   jiù   zǒu   le
as-soon smile   as   leave Perf.
'"Thank you, I don't drink alcohol." Jill *left* as soon as she smiled slightly.'

Here the verb phrase *walk away* in English is translated as the German verb *verschwinden* "to disappear" and as the Chinese verb 走 *zǒu* "to leave." It is noteworthy that both verbs in the translations are categorized as verbs of directed motion, which typify verb-framed motion encoding. This shows that verb-framed expressions are possible even in satellite-framed languages as long as they have semantically compatible verbs of directed motion in their lexicon, and in turn that verb-framed encoding is ubiquitous and satellite-framed lexicalization is just an add-on to it. But these alone are certainly not the whole story. We will cover a lot of ground, including cases where *walk* takes no prepositional phrase, cases where *walk* is followed by a directional prepositional phrase, and so on.

Linguistics is the intellectual instrument which has been created for rendering clear the important aspects of language that would remain obscure without it. In the eyes of those who do not have special knowledge of linguistics, motion events might be everyday experiences that would arouse no particular interest. But they have stimulated intellectual creativity in linguistic buffs and have contributed substantially to the current semantic theories.

Before moving on, I would like to add a few personal notes. In retrospect, I got interested in motion events in the late 1990s, when I was a graduate student at Ritsumeikan University. At that time, I was poring over Rappaport Hovav and Levin (1998), and the following footnote piqued my curiosity.

(4) The directed motion use of verbs of manner of motion, as in *Pat ran to the beach*, also involves an activity-to-accomplishment shift; however, a causative analysis seems inappropriate for such derived accomplishments even though they also consist of a process and a result. If so, the account we present in this section of the accomplishment uses of verbs of surface contact may not extend to verbs of manner of motion. We leave the exact representation and derivation of the accomplishment uses of verbs of manner of motion as a topic for further research.
(Rappaport Hovav and Levin (1998: 121, note 17))

This was a starting point for my research into motion verbs, and I stumbled across Kageyama (1996) and Kageyama and Yumoto (1997), which also deal with the semantics of motion events. But I was dissatisfied with their analysis by lexical conceptual structures and so read a paper that proposes two improvements to their theory at the 25th annual meeting of the Kansai Linguistic Society in 2000. And this was the first time I made a presentation at a linguistic conference. The paper was published as Demizu (2001) in the proceedings of Kansai Linguistic Society (KLS). Since then, fourteen years have already passed. Therefore, it was an amazing twist of fate that I chose the same topic when I decided to write a dissertation.

But this book has given this old topic a real new twist. Recently, I have been trying to relate cognitive linguistic approaches with event structure templates used in lexical semantic approaches. And Demizu (2013) is also one of the results of this line of research. In this book, I do my best to produce a happy marriage between lexical semantics based on event structure and Talmy's cognitive linguistic approaches. I leave it to the readers to judge whether this attempt is successful or not. In any case, I hope that learned readers will find in this book something other than linguistic gobbledygook, and that my efforts will not go unnoticed nor unrewarded.

Chapter 2

Talmy's Motion Typology and Its Criticism

In this chapter, we will examine the details of Talmy's typology of motion verbs. Leonard Talmy, a cognitive linguist, is famous for his pioneering research on motion verbs, and a legion of his followers have applied his theory to manifold languages, yielding a wealth of cross-linguistic findings.

Recently, however, there has been a "growing recognition that most languages straddle more than one of the previously proposed typological categories" (Beavers et al. (2010: 331)). Then what should we do about the Talmyan typological system? Should we defend it, abandon it, or overhaul it? Beavers et al. suggest doing away with it, but is their strategy a reasonable one? It seems that it is excessively radical, nullifying Talmy's creative endeavor.

The purpose of this chapter is to reconsider Talmy's typological system by meticulously examining his claims. The argument will proceed as follows. Section 2.1 describes the three lexicalization types of motion verbs established by Talmy (1985). Section 2.2 is concerned with how Talmy (2000) revises and generalizes his previous theory. In particular, we will examine a variety of newly introduced concepts, such as macro-events, framing events and framing functions, and the dichotomy between satellite-framed and verb-framed languages. Section 2.3 considers recent criticisms against Talmy's system. More specifically, we reconsider the definition of Talmyan satellites, and examine how to modify Talmy's typology. Section 2.4 is the recapitulation.

2.1. Talmy (1985)

This section provides a broad outline of the lexicalization patterns in motion verbs exposed by Talmy (1985). Talmy is renowned for his introduction of a language typology of motion events, or "three lexicalization types for verb roots" (Talmy (1985: 61)).

2.1.1. Motion Events and External Events

Before exploring his typology, let us examine how Talmy (1985) defines "motion." As we can easily see from its dictionary definitions, the word "motion" in a generally accepted sense is used to express the process of moving, but he interprets the term more broadly so as to embrace not only movements, but also stasis or the state of not moving or not changing. This is why Talmy (1985: 61) begins his argument on motion by making it clear that he deals with "a situation containing movement or the maintenance of a stationary location alike as a 'motion event'." However, since we are concerned with discernible lexicalization patterns of motion verbs in a strict sense, we concentrate on movement, to the exclusion of stasis or a condition in which there is no movement.

First of all, Talmy defines the linguistic notion of motion as follows:

(1) The basic motion event consists of one object (the 'Figure') moving or located with respect to another object (the reference-object or 'Ground'). It is analyzed as having four components: besides 'Figure' and 'Ground', there are 'Path' and 'Motion'.

(Talmy (1985: 60–61))

The first thing we notice is that motion events are made up of four components, namely Figure, Ground, Path and Motion. This suggests that motion events fail to materialize when any of the components is lacking. We also notice that he clarifies the relationship between the Figure and the Ground, stating that the former is located in relation to the latter. In other words, the

Ground is used as a reference point to specify the position of the Figure.

As is familiar to linguists, the terms "Figure" and "Ground" are borrowed from Gestalt psychology, and in the usual sense, the figure refers to an object in the foreground of our perception, while the ground denotes the background from which the figure appears to stand out. But when it comes to motion events, Talmy uses them differently and provides his own definitions:

(2) [T]he Figure is a moving or *conceptually* mov*able* object whose path or site is at issue; the Ground is a reference-frame, or a reference-point stationary within a reference-frame, with respect to which the Figure's path or site is characterized. [italics in original]
(Talmy (1985: 61))

His definition of Figure roughly corresponds to the theta role of theme in generative grammar, since the term "theme" refers to "the entity which is conceived as moving or undergoing transitions," and for motion verbs, "the entity which is in motion" (Gruber (1976: 38)). Moreover, when the Figure moves, its path consists of an ordered set of the sites or points located in relation to the Ground, and this reminds us of a scale or a scalar change. In fact, the connection between paths and scales will be discussed in more detail in sections 3.7.2, 4.4.1 and 4.4.2.

Talmy (1985) then elaborates on the two other components of motion events, that is, Path and Motion:

(3) The 'Path' (with a capital P) is the course followed or site occupied by the Figure object with respect to the Ground object. 'Motion' (with a capital M) refers to the presence *per se* in the event of motion or location (only these two motion states are structurally distinguished by language). (Talmy (1985: 61))

Here we notice that Talmy (1985) clarifies two points regarding the Path: (i) it is the route traveled by the Figure, and (ii) it is defined or determined relative to the position of the Ground. Motion is thought to be the inner or intrinsic core of the whole event, but Talmy says nothing more than that; and we can only conjecture that Motion might be the element that makes the event what it is, or to put it differently, gives the event the quality of being an event. This point is illustrated more explicitly in Talmy (2000), as we will see in section 2.2.1.

Let us next turn to the marginal status assigned to Manner in Talmy (1985):

(4) In addition to these internal components a Motion event can have a 'Manner' or a 'Cause', which we analyze as constituting a distinct external event.   (Talmy (1985: 61))

Here Talmy discusses Cause along with Manner, but to avoid unnecessary complexity, we do not deal with Cause in this book.

Most importantly, Talmy analyzes Manner as external to motion events. Above all else, the expression "a Motion event can have a 'Manner'" is worthy of notice. His use of the modal auxiliary "can" denotes the possibility, but not the necessity, of the existence of Manner. This means that motion events are sometimes but not always associated with Manner. Or to put it another way, Manner is not an obligatory element for motion events. In addition, Talmy states clearly that Manner is considered to be not only an external, but also a distinct event. Looking back now, this clear and strict separation between Path, one of the four components intrinsic to motion events, and Manner, a possible but not necessary concomitant, is Talmy's significant contribution to the semantic analysis of motion verbs.

The composition of motion depicted by Talmy (1985) can be diagrammed as follows:

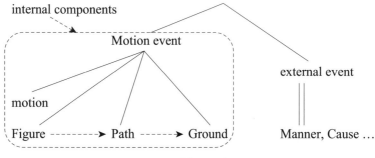

Figure 1

Here we notice that the details of motion events, namely the internal components, are laid out in Talmy's description, whereas the specifics of external events are not revealed. In this connection, it is instructive to note the term "event," which is used by Talmy in order to characterize both the internal components of motion and the external elements like Manner. In linguistics, the concept of events is inseparable from that of participants, that is, entities involved in events. Semantically, motion events are ordinarily associated with two participants: a mover or theme and a direction or path. In addition, the former clearly corresponds to the Figure and the latter the Path in Talmy's analysis. Therefore, Talmy can be said to provide an adequate explanation of the internal components of motion events.

On the other hand, Manner is also regarded "as constituting a distinct external event," but what are the components of the external event? Though Talmy does not elaborate any further, it seems reasonable to assume that at least one participant, namely an agent, is necessary in order to bring about the Manner event. Moreover, this participant must be coreferential with the theme or the Figure, since Manner modifies the movement of the Figure. Then how should we represent the association between the two participants? Unfortunately, Talmy's theory provides no conceptual apparatus for explaining how these two events are semantically unified, and this will be discussed in more detail in section 4.3.2 and thereafter. Instead, we will look at how Talmy associates this semantic configuration of motion events with his famous three types of lexicalization patterns.

2.1.2. Motion Events and Three Lexicalization Types

Let us turn to his lexicalization typology of motion verbs. Talmy (1985: 61-74) classifies languages into three types according to what semantic element their verb roots "lexicalize" together with Motion, with the caveat that languages exhibit their distinctive behavior in their "most characteristic expression of Motion" (Talmy (1985: 62)). But the adjective "characteristic" and its adverbial form "characteristically," which recur in his description of the motion typology, can be understood in numerous ways. In order to resolve this potential ambiguity, Talmy defines his use of the adjective "characteristic" as follows:

(5) (i) It is *colloquial* in style, rather than literary, stilted, etc. (ii) It is *frequent* in occurrence in speech, rather than only occasional, (iii) It is *pervasive*, rather than limited, that is, a wide range of semantic notions are expressed in this type.   (Talmy (1985: 62))

The definition of this word has more significance when we consider some motion verbs in English, and we will explore the motivation behind his decision to interpolate the adjective "characteristic" at the end of section 2.1.4.

We will now examine the three lexicalization types in more detail. Before doing so, though, a note is in order on Talmy's use of the term "conflation." The verb *conflate* usually means putting two or more things together and as a result forming one new thing. Talmy uses this term to refer to the process in which Motion and another semantic element are combined and turn into a semantic amalgamation, which is in turn verbalized into a single motion verb. When Motion is expressed by a verb, each lexicalization type differs in what semantic element is semantically combined, or "conflated" in Talmy's term, with Motion, and the difference is dubbed "the type of conflation pattern" (Talmy (1985: 63)).

2.1.3. First Lexicalization Type: Motion + Manner/Cause

Let us begin by looking at the first type of conflation pattern, for which Talmy (1985: 62) offers the following explanation:

(6) In a motion-sentence pattern characteristic of one group of languages, the verb expresses at once both the fact of Motion and either its manner or its cause.   (Talmy (1985: 62))

This type is exemplified by the English sentence *He walked into the room*, in which the verb *walk* denotes both Motion and the Manner "by putting one foot in front of the other." Talmy (1985: 62) goes on to say that languages showing this type of conflation pattern are "Chinese and apparently all branches of Indo-European except (post-Latin) Romance." English is an Indo-European language of the Germanic branch, and so it fits into this lexicalization pattern.

In order to illustrate the point, Talmy represents "[t]he semantic-to-surface relationship" as follows:

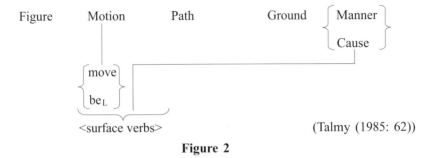

Figure 2

This figure shows that Motion is conflated with Manner or Cause, and that the resultant complex is expressed by a single surface verb.

Let us now consider the characteristics of the surface verbs produced by this type of conflation. The conflation of Motion and Manner generates verbs that encode a manner of motion such as *walk* and *run*. Because of this semantic attribute, they are called "manner of motion verbs" in Rappaport Hovav and Levin (1998: 102, 2010: 27). As Talmy (1985: 62) observes, the languages that follow this lexicalization pattern have "a whole series of verbs in common use that express motion occurring in various manners," that is, manner of motion verbs. Talmy (1985: 63-64) includes the verbs under the rubric of "move + Manner," and subclassifies them as "self-agentive." In order to explain their meaning, Talmy (1985: 64) offers an "unconflated" paraphrase of the English sentence *I ran down the stairs*:

(7) (I ran down the stairs =)
    I went down the stairs, running [the while]   (Talmy (1985: 64))

Here the motion event is expressed by the main clause *I went down the stairs*, whereas the Manner "running" is described by the gerundive subordinate clause. Or to put it differently, the main clause specifies the four essential ingredients of motion events: the Figure (*I*), the Ground (*the stairs*), the Path (*down*) and Motion (*went*). The Manner expression is given a lower status in the paraphrase, subordinate to the main clause denoting the motion event. This syntactic subordination of the Manner description in the para-

16 *Lexicalization Typology and Event Structure Templates*

phrase reflects Talmy's view that Manner is distinguished and detached from motion events and is itself an external event attached to them.

2.1.4. Second Lexicalization Type: Motion + Path

The second type of conflation pattern is described as follows:

(8) In the second typological pattern for the expression of Motion, the verb root at once expresses both the fact of Motion and the Path.

(Talmy (1985: 68))

This kind of conflation is illustrated by the English sentence *She entered the room*, where the verb *enter* lexicalizes both Motion and Path. According to Talmy (1985: 69), "[l]anguage families that seem to be of this type are Semitic, Polynesian, and Romance," and in Talmy (2000: 49), a revised version of Talmy (1985), Japanese, Korean, Turkish, Tamil, Nez Perce and Caddo are newly added to the list.

Talmy schematically represents this conflation pattern as below:

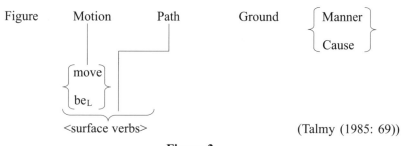

(Talmy (1985: 69))

Figure 3

Here Motion is semantically combined with Path to form a single surface verb. By comparison with Figure 2, we can see that Motion is conflated with a much "nearer" semantic element, namely Path, in Figure 3. We can speculate that, by positioning Path next to Motion, and Manner on the extreme left, Talmy probably shows that Motion is conceptually more closely related to Path, one of the internal components, than to Manner, an external event. But Talmy does not make explicit the meaning of their position, leaving it to the intuitive judgment of the readers. We will take up this problem again at the end of section 2.1.5.

As discussed earlier, English does not characteristically show this second type of conflation pattern, but rather the first type. Then why does English have several Path-encoding verbs like *arrive* and *enter*? Talmy himself gives a historical explanation for the existence of such verbs in English, and we will confirm this just below. However, we will consider a more underlying reason in section 2.3.5, which impels us to reconsider Talmy's analysis.

Let us return to the semantic properties of the verbs that lexicalize both Motion and Path. The verb *enter* and its ilk, such as *arrive*, *ascend*, *fall*, *leave* and so on are called "verbs of directed motion" in Rappaport Hovav and Levin (1998: 102) and "Inherently directed motion verbs" in Rappaport Hovav and Levin (2010: 27). Talmy (1985: 69) states that languages exhibiting this type of conflation pattern have "a whole series of surface verbs that express motion along various paths," that is, inherently directed motion verbs.

In languages that follow this pattern, Manner is not easy to express within the sentences that describe motion events. The reason is explained by Talmy (1985: 68-69) as follows:

(9) If Manner or Cause is expressed in the same sentence, it must be as an independent, usually adverbial or gerundive type constituent. In many languages—for example Spanish—such a constituent can be stylistically awkward, so that information about Manner or Cause is often either established in the surrounding discourse or omitted altogether. (Talmy (1985: 68-69))

As Talmy remarks, Spanish motion verbs lexicalize Path, and so they do not semantically combine Manner with Motion. As a result, the Spanish sentence **La botella flotó a la cueva* "The bottle floated into the cave" is not acceptable, because it does not conform to the characteristic lexicalization pattern of Spanish. To be more specific, the verb *flotar* "to float" conflates the Manner "floating" with Motion in this sentence, and Path, which should be conflated with Motion in Spanish, is expressed by the prepositional phrase *a la cueva* "to the cave." In order to encode both Motion and Manner within one sentence in Spanish, we can certainly add an extra gerundive clause, such as *flotando* "floating" in (10), to express Manner. But this results in a stylistically cumbersome sentence.

(10) La botella entró a la cueva (flotando)
 the bottle moved-in to the cave (floating)
 'The bottle floated into the cave' (Talmy (1985: 69))

Here the gerundive *flotando* is shown in parentheses probably because it is omitted when the Manner can be inferred from the surrounding context.

A similar stylistic awkwardness is observed in Japanese, which also exhibits this type of conflation pattern. The following serves as an example:

(11) Taro-wa heya-ni (aruite) hait-ta.
 Taro-Top room-to (walking) enter-Past
 'Taro entered the room (, walking [the while]).'

In Japanese, which does not conflate Manner with Motion, we need an additional gerundive phrase to express Manner together with Motion. Under ordinary circumstances, we usually walk in order to move to another room in the house, and the manner of motion can be inferred from common knowledge. For this reason, the manner of motion "walking" often remains unexpressed in Japanese. If we take the trouble to describe the inferable Manner by a gerundive phrase *aruite* 'walking' as in (11), the whole sentence sounds redundant and consequently awkward. On the other hand, English, which follows the first conflation pattern and combines Manner with Motion, can express a manner of motion "at no extra cost," and in most cases, actually expresses it within one clause.

Thus far, we have looked at the second conflation pattern, in which Path is conflated with Motion. But intriguingly, English, which in principle exhibits the first conflation pattern, has no dearth of verbs that follow the second conflation pattern, most notably the above-mentioned verb *enter*. In fact, the literal translations of (10) and (11), that is, the sentences *The bottle entered the cave* and *Taro entered the room*, are perfectly acceptable, though not colloquial, in English. Talmy (1985: 72) explicates this kind of exceptionality as follows:

(12) English does have a certain number of verbs that genuinely incorporate Path, as in the Spanish conflation type, for example: *enter, exit, pass, rise, descend, return, circle, cross, separate, join*. And these verbs even call for a Spanish-type pattern for the rest of the sentence. [...] But these verbs (and the sentence pattern they call for) are not the most characteristic of English. In fact, the majority (here all except *rise*) are not original English forms but rather borrowings from Romance, where they are the native type.

(Talmy (1985: 72))

By shifting responsibility for their existence onto their origin in Romance, Talmy seems to deftly circumvent the difficulties caused by the "uncharacteristic" verbs mentioned in (12). In addition, the exceptionality of these verbs is thought to be the very rationale behind his use of the adjective "characteristic." This issue is further explored in Talmy (2000: 52–53), which we will see in section 2.3.5.

2.1.5. Third Lexicalization Type: Motion + Figure

In the third conflation pattern, Figure is conflated with Motion. Talmy (1985: 73) says that "Atsugewi, a Hokan language of northern California" is a language of this ilk, but English does have the few following examples that conform to this type:

(13) a. It rained in through the bedroom window. [nonagentive]
     b. I spat into the cuspidor. [agentive]

(Talmy (1985: 73))

Here the Figures, which refer to moving entities such as "rain" and "spit," are described by the verbs together with Motion. In other words, these sentences describe that the Figures "rain" and "spit" move, by incorporating them into verb roots denoting Motion.

The schematic representation of this conflation pattern is as follows:

20 Lexicalization Typology and Event Structure Templates

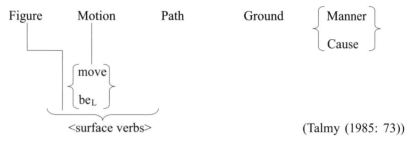

(Talmy (1985: 73))

Figure 4

As Talmy (1985: 75–76) describes, this conflation type is quite exceptional and "least extensive," observed exclusively in a few languages such as "Atsugewi (and apparently most northern Hokan) and Navajo." Owing chiefly to the scarcity of typological candidates, this conflation pattern is thought not to be adopted as one of the typological classes in later papers.

Before summarizing the main points of this section, let us finally point out the drawbacks of Talmy's schematic representations of the three conflation patterns. At first sight, these graphic representations of conflation seem adequate and effective in capturing the distinctive characteristics of each type of conflation, but we argue that they are unacceptable for two reasons.

First, the representations do not elucidate the relationships between Figure, Ground and Path. In particular, as explained in section 2.1.1, Figure is located with respect to Ground in motion events, and Path is defined by this process. But the representations do not clarify the central roles the three elements play in motion events. Second, Talmy considers Manner and Cause to be external events, and differentiates them from the four internal components, but the representations do not reflect this difference. Indeed Manner and Cause are on the far right, but this says nothing explicit about their relations to the internal components of motion events. For these reasons, we are not completely satisfied with the way he represents conflation types. In section 2.2.6, given the refinements added in Talmy (2000), we will offer our own representations of conflation patterns.

In summary, this section has given an overview of three types of conflation pattern discerned in motion verbs. It is Talmy (1985) that has first propounded the idea of three lexicalization patterns in motion verbs. The first pattern is the conflation of Manner with Motion, typified by English. The second pattern is the conflation of Path with Motion, observed in Japanese and Romance languages like Spanish. The third and infrequent pattern is the conflation of Figure with Motion, which is exemplified by a few languages such as Atsugewi and Navajo, and not used as a lexicalization type in his later papers. The advent of Talmy's typology has changed forever the way motion verbs are analyzed, and therefore his contribution is of paramount importance in lexical semantics.

2.2. Talmy (2000)

Talmy (1985) is predominantly concerned with the lexicalization of motion, making only a passing reference to "change of state" as a metaphorical extension from motion. By contrast, in his much revised and expanded version of Talmy (1991), Talmy (2000: 213-228) fits the lexicalization patterns of motion and change of state into a much bigger picture.

2.2.1. Macro-events and Framing Events

Talmy (2000: 213) associates motion and change of state with three more different types of events, namely "events of 'temporal contouring,' 'action correlating,' and 'realization'." We do not go into detail about the events other than motion, but at least we need to introduce a general term for all the five types of events in order to fully understand his theory. He defines the term "macro-event" as follows:

(14) [...] there is a fundamental and recurrent category of complex event that is prone to conceptual integration and representation by a single clause, a type here termed a **macro-event**.

(Talmy (2000: 216))

A macro-event, as Talmy (2000: 216) describes, is created from "the conceptual integration or conflation" of several events, each of which can be denoted by a separate "unconflated" clause. It is a combination or an agglomeration of heterogeneous events and is represented by a single clause that has more semantic content than each unconflated clause.

Among the events that constitute a macro-event, the event which plays a central role in the macro-event is dubbed "a framing event" (Talmy (2000: 217)). Talmy (2000: 218) states that the framing event is made up of four components, in a similar vein to Talmy (1985). Talmy (2000: 218) expounds on each component, and we will scrutinize his statements, comparing them with what Talmy (1985) has remarked.

Let us start with the first component, "a figural entity," which is called Figure in Talmy (1985):

(15) The first component is a **figural entity**. The figural entity is generally the component on which attention or concern is currently most centered. (Talmy (2000: 218))

What interests us here is that its status as the center of attention, which is connoted by the term "Figure," is made more apparent and explicit than in (1).

Next comes a ground entity, which is equivalent to Ground in Talmy (1985).

(16) The second component is a **ground entity**. This component is conceptualized as a reference entity, with respect to which the condition of the figural entity is characterized. (Talmy (2000: 218))

Here the phrase "conceptualized as" deserves some attention, because it adds a cognitive flavor to the definition, which is not so conspicuous in (1).

So far, we have seen how Talmy (2000: 218) defines the first two components of the framing event which correspond to Figure and Ground in Talmy (1985). The definitions are much the same as before, except that they take on more cognitive characteristics. On the other hand, the concepts of the other two components have undergone substantial revision.

Let us now turn to the third component, "a process," which is analogous to Motion in Talmy (1985) but is more generalized in order to encompass all the five types of events.

(17) The third component is a process by which the figural entity either makes a transition or stays fixed with respect to the ground en-

tity. This will be called the **activating process**, because it is the component conceived as contributing the factor of dynamism to the event. (Talmy (2000: 218))

Here we notice that the process, which of course includes Motion, is regarded as lending "dynamism," or energy, to the whole event and is therefore dubbed "the activating process." The term "dynamism" is not used in Talmy (1985) and is thought to be added to make it clear that Motion, or the activating process, gives the event the quality of "dynamism," namely being an event.

The activating process is further explained as follows:

(18) The activating process generally has only two values: **transition** and **fixity**. Thus, for example, in the domain of "Motion," these two values are realized as 'motion' and 'stationariness,' while in the domain of "state change," they are realized as 'change' and 'stasis'. (Talmy (2000: 218))

We can easily see that the two values of the activating process, that is, "transition and fixity," are more refined and sophisticated versions of "movement" and "the maintenance of a stationary location" in Talmy (1985: 60). This means that motion or movement is reinterpreted more generally as transition, or a change from one state to another.

The last component is named "an association function," under which Path in Talmy (1985) is subsumed.

(19) Finally, the fourth component is an **association function** that sets the figural entity into a particular relationship with the ground entity. (Talmy (2000: 218))

What has to be noticed is his use of the term "function." In mathematics, functions express a relationship between one variable and another, in which the one changes along with the other. In brief, both variables change. In the case of Path, however, the position of the Figure changes with respect to the fixed position of the Ground, which plays a role of the reference point. Path, therefore, does not agree completely with a function in mathematics, but the two bear some similarity in that the value of the one element is in some sense determined by that of the other. Therefore, in cognitive terms, Path can be metaphorically interpreted as a mathematical function.[1]

Of all the four components, Talmy (2000: 218) states, the association function plays the most important role in the framing event, relating the figural entity with the ground entity. Ultimately, it is the "portion of the event that most determines its particular character and that distinguishes it from other framing events." This is why Talmy considers the association function, sometimes accompanied by the ground entity, to be the most important or central part of the framing event, hence the name "core schema."

Talmy elaborates on the association function and the core schema by using a motion event as an example:

(20) Here, both the figural entity and the ground entity are each a physical *object*. The activating process, here of the transition type, constitutes *motion*. And the association function that relates the figural entity to the ground entity constitutes the *path*. The core schema here will then be either the path alone or the path together with the ground object. (Talmy (2000: 218))

Since we are concerned specifically with motion verbs, we should keep in mind that the path and the optional ground object constitute the core schema of motion.

So far, we have examined the amended definitions of the four components in framing events, which subsume motion events. We have seen that the definitions are generalized to include other four types of macro-events, and couched in more cognitive language.

2.2.2. Functions of Framing Events over Macro-events

From the components of the framing event, we now move on to the concept of "framing event." In particular, we consider the rationale for coin-

---

[1] This implies the possibility that we can analyze Path more systematically than in Talmy (2000), for example, by introducing the concept of scalarity. We will further consider the possibility in sections 4.4.1 and 4.4.2.

ing the term in order to characterize the main event in macro-events. Let us start by looking at his explanation:

(21) Relative to the whole [macro-event], the main event provides or determines certain overarching patterns. Thus, the main event can be said to perform a *framing* function in relation to the macro-event. Hence, our term for it is the **framing event**.
(Talmy (2000: 219))

Here, Talmy defines a framing function as providing or determining patterns, without further elaborating on why he has chosen the verb "frame." But we can speculate that this is probably because the main event "frames" or organizes the whole macro-event by providing or determining the general framework, or in his terms, "certain overarching patterns."

Talmy assumes that the conceptual framework "the framing event provides for the whole macro-event" has four facets, which we will examine in turn. The first two aspects specified by the framing event are temporal and spatial ones. Talmy (2000: 219) enunciates his interpretation of them as follows:

(22) The framing event thus determines at least the overall temporal framework and thereby determines the aspect of the sentence that expresses the macro-event. It also generally determines the overall spatial framework where a physical setting is involved—or some analogous reference frame where another conceptual domain is involved.
(Talmy (2000: 219))

Here Talmy states explicitly that the framing event organizes the macro-event temporally and spatially. This is a reasonable assumption since time and space are the two essential elements of our perceptions of the world.

The third facet provided by the framing event reflects its syntactic and semantic characteristics.

(23) Further, the framing event determines all or most of the argument structure and semantic character of the arguments overall within the macro-event, as well as determining all or most of the syntactic

complement structure in the sentence that expresses the macro-event. (Talmy (2000: 219))

A macro-event, as mentioned above, is represented by a single clause, and the resultant clause possesses syntactic and semantic properties. What Talmy states here is that the framing event specifies all or most of the properties that the clause exhibits. Firstly, the framing event determines the syntactic structure of the clause, for example, what kind of complement the clause takes. In addition, it determines the semantic properties of the arguments, including what types of participants the macro-event selects. That is, it imposes selectional restriction on the macro-event. In a nutshell, the framing event specifies the macro-event syntactically and semantically.

The last aspect contributed by the framing event constitutes the gist, or what Talmy calls "the upshot," of what is expressed by a macro-event.

(24) In addition, the framing event constitutes the central import or main point—or what will here be termed the **upshot**—relative to the whole macro-event. That is to say, it is the framing event that is asserted in a positive declarative sentence, that is denied under negation, that is demanded in an imperative, and that is asked about in an interrogative. (Talmy (2000: 219))

Interestingly enough, the upshot is usually the content of a clause that affirms or denies the fact, and therefore it can be partly equated with the proposition, that is, the objective meaning of statements. This means that what the framing event contributes to the macro-event has a propositional quality. In brief, the framing event determines the macro-event propositionally.

To sum up, we have looked at the four facets of the framing function that the framing event exerts over the whole macro-event: (i) temporal, (ii) spatial, (iii) syntactic and semantic, and (iv) propositional. In order to relate two events and reinterpret them as a single new event, semantic facets like these always seem to be involved. In fact, similar notions are introduced as the conditions imposed on "event coidentification," which is proposed by Levin and Rappaport Hovav (1999: 213) and Rappaport Hovav and Levin (2001: 782) in order to explain the syntactic and semantic characteristics of such sentences as *Kim ran into the room*. We will briefly mention "event coidentification" in section 2.4 and delve deeply into this issue in section 4.3.1.

2.2.3. Functions of Framing Events over Subordinate Events

Moreover, Talmy (2000: 219) goes on to argue that the framing event has influence over the subordinate event as well, or in his own words, it "can also manifest certain framing functions relative to the subordinate event." He mentions two framing functions the main event has over the subordinate event, which we will consider in turn.

The first framing function is to make the subordinate event dependent on or subservient to the macro-event. This can be simply called "subordination."

(25) First, the framing event can anchor the subordinate event within, or link that event to, the overarching conceptual framework that it determines. (Talmy (2000: 219))

Here the adjective "overarching" and the verb "determine" are noteworthy. These words are used to describe the element to which the subordinate event is linked, and interestingly enough, the same words are also used by Talmy in order to characterize the function the framing event exercises over the macro-event. More specifically, as we have seen at the outset of section 2.2.2, the framing event "determines certain overarching patterns" of the macro-event. This means that "the overarching conceptual framework that it [i.e. the framing event] determines" refers indirectly to the macro-event. Taken together, Talmy suggests here that the subordinate event is anchored within, namely subordinated to, the macro-event.

The second function of the framing event is to coerce the subordinate event into having the same structure, which is dubbed "structuring."

(26) Second, the framing event can bear to the subordinate event the relation of "structurer" in a cognitive process of conceptual structuring. In particular here, the framing event can act as an abstract structure conceptually imposed on the subordinate event acting as a "substrate." (Talmy (2000: 219))

Here Talmy states that the structure of the framing event is superimposed or overwritten onto that of the subordinate event. Talmy also asserts that the subordinate event acts as a "substrate," which means an underlying layer or a base. But what does the subordinate underlie? Talmy does not make it explicit, but it can be surmised from the first function that the subordinate event constitutes the base of the macro-event, and not the framing event.

What is more, Talmy argues that the structure of the framing event is "abstract," and what does this mean? Talmy goes on to enlarge on what this means.

(27) Generally in this relationship, the semantic character of the framing event is more that of an abstract schema, while that of the subordinate event tends to be more substantive or perceptually palpable. For this reason, the content of the subordinate event is often more vivid than that of the framing event and thus might draw much or at times even more attention to itself; in this respect it might seem semantically more primary than the framing event.

(Talmy (2000: 219))

To put it simply, Talmy states that the framing event is semantically more schematic and contains less information than the subordinate event. It is true that the framing event wields considerable semantic and conceptual influence over the subordinate event as well as the macro-event, but it does not have rich semantic content, in spite of its privileged status in the macro-event. In marked contrast, the subordinate event has more concrete meaning, which makes it more salient than the framing event, despite its subordinate and underlying status. What does this incongruity between their semantic salience and their status in macro-events mean? In fact, this has a direct bearing on the process of event coidentification, and we will consider it in section 4.5.

2.2.4. Subordinate Events as Co-Events

Up to this point, we have identified the distinctive characteristics of the framing event, or the main event in macro-events. Let us now move on to the characteristics of the subordinate event, the event other than the framing event in macro-events. At the beginning, Talmy remarks the aspectual unboundedness or atelicity of the subordinate event:

(28) As to its intrinsic properties, the kind of event that constitutes the subordinate event within a macro-event is probably most frequently and perhaps prototypically an aspectually unbounded activity.

(Talmy (2000: 220))

At first sight, his statement does not seem worthy of special mention, but it is reasonable to emphasize that the subordinate event, on which the framing event imposes an abstract structure, has no temporal bound initially, since a bound, or to put it differently a scale, can be regarded as a kind of abstract structure and is therefore reasonably provided by the framing event.

Talmy then delineates the essential function of the subordinate event, that is, the supporting function of the framing event, describing the circumstantial situation.

(29) ... the subordinate event can be held to constitute an event of **circumstance** in relation to the macro-event as a whole and to perform functions of **support** in relation to the framing event. In these supporting functions, the subordinate event can be seen to fill in, elaborate, add to, or motivate the framing event.

(Talmy (2000: 220))

As discussed in section 2.2.3, the semantic structure of the framing event is a skeletal framework, and so the subordinate event plays a role in fleshing out the schema. Here we should note the word "support." In Talmy (1991: 484), the subordinate event is termed "the supporting event." Talmy (2000: 220), however, renames it the "co-event," since the degree of subordination involved is not the same in all the supporting functions. He chooses the word "co-event" because the prefix *co-* "ranges from subordinateness, as in 'co-pilot,' to coequality, as in 'co-author.'" (Talmy (2000: 220)).

In order to further elucidate the roles of support, he mentions the following particular supportive relations:

(30) These include Precursion, Enablement, Cause, Manner, Concomi-

tance, Purpose, and Constitutiveness. The most frequent among these are Cause and Manner. (Talmy (2000: 220))

Manner, with which we are primarily concerned, is cited as one of the most common supporting functions, which seems to point to the significance of this explanation. Most importantly, this statement, together with (29), makes the status of Manner in the whole event much clearer than in Talmy (1985). More specifically, Talmy (1985: 61) argues that Manner is "a distinct external event" Motion events can optionally have, but he reveals nothing more than that there. Here Talmy (2000) further makes it clear that Manner is subordinate to the macro-event as a whole and supports the framing event.

To illustrate his point, Talmy draws the following diagrams that depict the configurations of his macro-event and framing event:

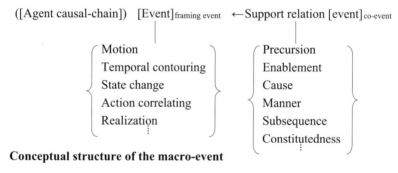

Conceptual structure of the macro-event

Figure 5

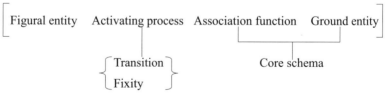

Conceptual structure of the framing-event

Figure 6

(Talmy (2000: 221))

These diagrams are far more desirable than the previous figures by Talmy (1985), because Figure 6 clarifies the relationships between Figural entity (Figure), Ground entity (Ground) and Association function (Path) in it, and Figure 5 shows that Manner is an external Co-event that supports the framing Motion event.

However, there remain some inadequacies in the above figures. First, although he introduces the concept of subordination in order to characterize external events, Figure 5 does not schematically represent the hierarchical structure formed by all the ingredients of macro-events. Second, the two figures show nothing about the internal structure of co-events. As explained at the end of section 2.2.3, the framing event "structures" the subordinate event, that is, the internal structure of the framing event is imposed on that of the co-event. Given these facts, we propose the following hierarchical representation of the components put forward by Talmy (2000):

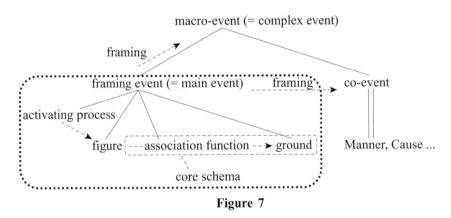

Figure 7

Here the framing event is marked by the rounded rectangle of dotted lines, and it is the essential part of the whole macro-event. The co-event is external to the framing event and subordinate to the macro-event. The framing event exerts several framing functions on the macro-event and the co-event, and this is shown by the two dashed arrows with the label "framing."

2.2.5. Dichotomy and Concept of Satellites

In Talmy (2000), the three lexicalization types proposed by Talmy

(1985) have been superseded by the dichotomy between verb-framed and satellite-framed languages. Talmy (2000) redefines the classification and argues that it is determined by whether or not the core schema in the framing event is expressed by, or more precisely mapped onto, the main verb. As we have seen at the end of section 2.2.1, the core schema is "either the path alone or the path together with the ground object." Therefore, the category of verb-framed languages corresponds to the second lexicalization type in Talmy (1985), that is, the conflation of Motion and Path. In contrast, the group of satellite-framed languages parallels the first lexicalization type, namely the conflation of Motion and Manner. Talmy (2000) modifies the three-way classification in Talmy (1985) into the dichotomy by discarding the third and uncommon pattern, that is, the conflation of Figure with Motion, which is exemplified by Atsugewi and a few languages. The dichotomy is employed to analyze many different languages by a multitude of linguists and, as a result, makes Talmy's typology of motion verbs familiar and popular among linguists.

At the beginning, Talmy (2000) elaborates on the dichotomy of languages he proposes as follows:

(31) [T]he world's languages generally seem to divide into a two-category typology on the basis of the characteristic pattern in which the conceptual structure of the macro-event is mapped onto syntactic structure. To characterize it initially in broad strokes, the typology consists of whether the core schema is expressed by the main verb or by the satellite. (Talmy (2000: 221))

The adjective "characteristic," used in Talmy (1985: 62) to exclude exceptional verbs, is utilized again, and his use of the same adjective implies that his definition of the word in Talmy (1985) is implicitly inherited here.

In addition, we notice the unfamiliar technical term "the satellite," placed in juxtaposition with "the main verb." As a matter of fact, the term "satellite" has already been introduced in Talmy (1985: 102) to refer generically to "certain immediate constituents of a verb root other than inflections, auxiliaries, or nominal arguments." The term "satellite" is coined by Talmy in order to "[capture] an observable commonality" (Talmy (2000: 222)) shared by multifarious grammatical forms attached to the main verb, and is defined more accurately as follows:

(32) the **satellite to the verb**—or simply, the **satellite**, abbreviated Sat—is the grammatical category of any constituent other than a nominal or prepositional-phrase complement that is in a sister relation to the verb root. (Talmy (2000: 222))

Here we notice that Talmy uses syntactic categories and configuration as criteria to determine whether a particular constituent is a satellite or not. At first glance, Talmy's definition of the term "satellite" seems flawless, but it is actually beset with three problems.

Let us first pay attention to the syntactic explanation that "that is in a sister relation to the verb root." Here Talmy does refer to syntax to characterize satellites, but deplorably, he does not expound on the syntactic structure of the main verb and the satellite, making his argument less convincing. Moreover, no evidence is advanced to suggest that satellites are sister to the main verbs. In short, his definition is obscured by the paucity of syntactic argumentation. Instead, he just enumerates a variety of examples of the satellite.

(33) The satellite, which can be either a bound affix or a free word, is thus intended to encompass all of the following grammatical forms: English verb particles, German separable and inseparable verb prefixes, Latin or Russian verb prefixes, Chinese verb complements, Lahu nonhead "versatile verbs," Caddo incorporated nouns, and Atsugewi polysynthetic affixes around the verb root.
(Talmy (2000: 222))

Here we can observe that Talmy cites a miscellaneous assortment of syntactic elements as examples.

Behind this enumeration lurks a second problem. Here English and French verb prefixes are not given as examples, but they are semantically and syntactically analogous to German inseparable verb prefixes. This means that if we regard German inseparable verb prefixes as satellites, we should also put English and French verb prefixes into the same category. Otherwise, we should include none of these verb prefixes in satellites. Presumably this inconsistency between German on the one hand and English and French on the other leads to the confusing and somewhat counterintuitive analysis by Kopecka (2006), which we will look at in section 2.3.1.

Thirdly, more noteworthy is the exclusion of prepositional phrases from satellites. The complication is that most verb particles in English have the same form and meaning as prepositions, which head prepositional phrases; nevertheless the former are included in, and the latter are excluded from, the category. A comparison between *John ran down* and *John ran down the stairs* illustrates the point. The two sentences can describe the same situation, with only the latter specifying the ground entity. Talmy sidesteps the problem by admitting that the core schema can sometimes exceptionally be described by a preposition alone.

(34) Although the core schema in satellite-framed languages is largely expressed by the satellite alone, it is also often expressed by the combination of a satellite plus a [preposition], or sometimes by a preposition alone. Such a "preposition" itself can consist not only of a free adposition, but also of a nominal inflection, or sometimes of a construction containing a "locative noun." (Talmy (2000: 222))

In English, however, the core schema is "largely" expressed by prepositional phrases, which questions the validity of defining satellites as above.

In sum, we have observed that Talmy's definition of satellites runs up against three problems. In order to satisfactorily solve the problems, we need to reconsider the idea of satellite; in fact, Kopecka (2006) and Beavers et al. (2010) each propose their own alternative definition of satellites. We will examine them more closely in sections 2.3.1 and 2.3.2. There we will reject Kopecka's proposal and accept the revision recommended by Beavers et al. (2010).

2.2.6. Satellite-Framed and Verb-Framed Languages

Having looked at the definition of satellites and its inadequacies, we now turn to Talmy's bipartite typological classification based on the lexicalization of the core schema. The first group includes English and is characterized as follows:

(35) [L]anguages that characteristically map the core schema onto the satellite will be said to have a **framing satellite** and to be **satellite-framed** languages. Included among them are most Indo-European minus Romance, Finno-Ugric, Chinese, Ojibwa, and Warlpiri.

(Talmy (2000: 222))

Needless to say, "Indo-European minus Romance" includes Germanic and Slavonic languages, such as English, German, Russian and so on. Among the languages we are concerned with, English, German and Chinese are categorized into this group. Next we will examine the second group, which includes Japanese and Spanish and is defined as follows:

(36) Languages that characteristically map the core schema into the verb will be said to have a **framing verb** and to be **verb-framed** languages. Included among such languages are Romance, Semitic, Japanese, Tamil, Polynesian, Bantu, some branches of Mayan, Nez Perce, and Caddo. (Talmy (2000: 222))

As is commonly known, Romance means languages that come from Latin, for example French or Spanish. Among the languages that fall into this category, we are mainly concerned with Japanese and French.

Talmy goes on to describe that how the co-event, for example a manner, is expressed together with the framing event within one sentence. In satellite-framed languages, the main verb, such as *walk* in English, denotes the co-event.

(37) Languages with a framing satellite regularly map the co-event into the main verb, which can thus be called a **co-event verb**.

(Talmy (2000: 222))

On the other hand, in verb-framed languages, grammatical forms other than the main verb describe the co-event.

(38) On the other hand, languages with a framing verb map the co-

event either onto a satellite or into an adjunct, typically an adpositional phrase or a gerundive-type constituent. Such forms are accordingly called a **co-event satellite**, a **co-event gerundive**, and so on. (Talmy (2000: 222))

Here Talmy seems a bit evasive about the grammatical status of what expresses the co-event. But as we will see in section 2.2.7, Talmy (2000: 224) illustrates the point by giving examples of Spanish.

To recapitulate briefly, Talmy represents the differences between verb-framed and satellite-framed languages by the following diagrams:

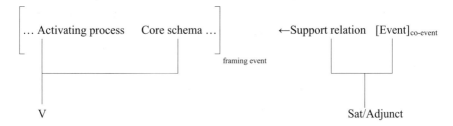

Syntactic mapping of macro-event in verb-framed languages

Figure 8

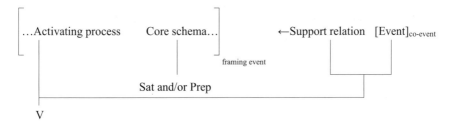

Syntactic mapping of macro-event in satellite-framed languages

Figure 9

(Talmy (2000: 223))

These representations are better than the three schematic representations of conflation patterns in Talmy (1985), in that the framing events are given in square brackets, which visually show that they are separated from the co-events. However, as already remarked with respect to Figure 5 in section 2.2.4, they likewise remain inadequate since they do not reflect the hierarchical structure within which the co-event is subordinate to the macro-event, and not to the framing event.

Given the arguments above, we now provide our own hierarchical representations of how languages map the core schema onto syntactic structures. At the end of section 2.2.4, we have already represented the hierarchy on which the relationships between the framing event, the macro-event and the co-event are based. Therefore, we can combine the hierarchical structure with the syntactic structure in which it is realized, and associate the whole macro-event with the syntactic configuration.

Let us first look at the graphical representation of the mapping characteristics of verb-framed languages. For the sake of simplicity, instead of Japanese or French examples, we use the English sentence *John entered the room (, walking)*, which uncharacteristically conforms to the verb-framed pattern. In this sentence, the core schema or the path is lexicalized into the verb *enter*, and the co-event of Manner is optionally described by the gerundive clause *walking*. The whole framing event is expressed by the matrix clause *John entered the room*, to which the gerundive clause is subordinate. This syntactic relationship is thus analogous or isomorphic with the configuration of macro-events proposed by Talmy (2000). This isomorphism between the syntactic and macro-event structures can be diagrammed as below:

38   *Lexicalization Typology and Event Structure Templates*

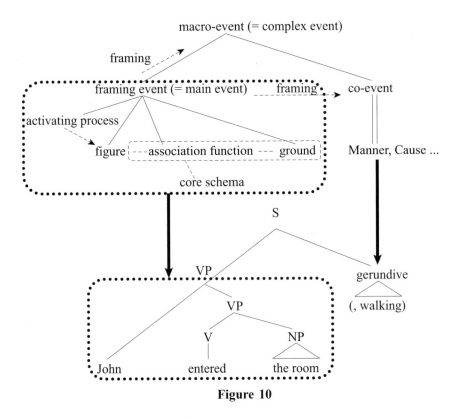

Figure 10

Here the privileged framing event is mapped onto the main clause, and the co-event, which is subordinate to the macro-event, is denoted by the subordinate gerundive clause.

However, the same parallelism is not true of the typical lexicalization pattern of satellite-framed languages. Take the English sentence *John walked into the room* for example. In this sentence, the path and the ground are expressed by the prepositional phrase *into the room*, and the Manner co-event is lexicalized by the verb *walk* in the matrix clause. Moreover, the figure in the framing event is denoted by the subject in the main clause. This means that, during the process of mapping, the framing event appears to be divided into two parts, which in turn are lexicalized into different parts of the sentence. As a result, the syntactic structure does not reflect the structure of macro-events depicted in Talmy (2000). This discrepancy between the syntactic and macro-event structures can be diagrammed as below:

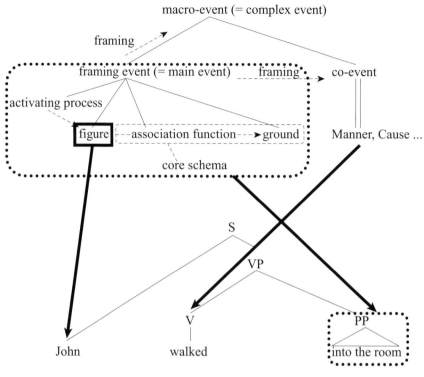

Figure 11

This irregularity in mapping suggests the possibility that satellite-framed languages have a special conceptual apparatus that allows the deviations of syntax from the semantic configuration. Then we wonder what the special mechanism is. We argue that it is the mechanism "event coidentification" formulated by Levin and Rappaport Hovav (1999) and Rappaport Hovav and Levin (2001) that enables such a complicated mapping. We will delve deeply into this issue in section 4.5.2.

2.2.7. What Expresses Co-Events in Verb-Framed Languages?

As we have seen in section 2.2.6, Talmy (2000: 222) states that the co-event is mapped onto several syntactic categories in verb-framed languages. In order to buttress his argument, Talmy (2000: 224) gives two examples from Spanish, each of which contains a different syntactic category describing the co-event, and we will consider them in turn, along with their Japanese counterparts. Talmy begins his discussion by explaining why the co-event is mapped onto different syntactic forms.

(39) In verb-framed languages, the constituent that expresses the co-event exhibits a certain characteristic. The degree of its syntactic integration into the main clause of the sentence can range over a gradient. (Talmy (2000: 224))

Here Talmy argues that the constituents denoting the co-event vary in the degree to which they are integrated into the matrix clause, meaning that satellites and adjuncts are at opposite ends of the spectrum.

First, Talmy looks at the least integrated end of the spectrum, taking examples from Spanish.

(40) The least integrated end of the gradient is represented, for example, in Spanish and Japanese. Thus, certain end-of-sentence gerundives in Spanish and certain -*te* constructions in Japanese—in both cases, expressing a co-event—may be interpreted syntactically as adverbial subordinate clauses. They do not function as satellites. By this interpretation, the overall construction is a complex sentence composed of two clauses and could therefore not represent a macro-event. (Talmy (2000: 224))

Here Talmy uses the expression "the least integrated end of the gradient" to refer to the most adjunct-like type of constituent. Talmy asserts that end-of-sentence gerundives and -*te* constructions do not fall in the category of co-event satellites, since they are adjunct subordinate clauses. More specifically, when a sentence contains an adjunct clause, it is generally presumed to be made up of two clauses, namely the main and subordinate clauses, and therefore does not fit the definition of macro-events. As we have seen at the outset of section 2.2.1, a macro-event is a conceptually integrated event that is represented by a single clause. Then it automatically follows that a sentence composed of two clauses does not express a macro-event. Talmy illustrates the point by giving the following example in Spanish:

(41) La botella salió de la cueva flotando.
'The bottle exited from the cave, floating.' (Talmy (2000: 224))

According to Talmy, this Spanish sentence consists of two clauses, that is, *La botella salió de la cueva* "The bottle exited from the cave" and *flotando* "floating." Since macro-events are mapped onto single clauses, the gerundive *flotando* is not a satellite of macro-events, but an adjunct-like gerundive clause. One problem is that Talmy does not give an example of a Japanese *-te* construction. But we can easily provide a corresponding example by translating the Spanish example above into Japanese.

(42) Bin-wa nagare-te dookutsu-kara de-ta.
bottle-Top float-TE cave-from exit-Past
'The bottle exited from the cave, floating.'

Similarly to the previous Spanish example, this Japanese sentence comprises two clauses, namely *Bin-wa dookutsu-kara de-ta* "The bottle exited from the cave" and *nagare-te* "floating." Here the expression *nagare-te* constitutes an adjunct clause, and so cannot be regarded as a satellite.

Talmy then argues that both Spanish and Japanese have constructions that possess more satellite-like properties.

(43) But both languages also have constructions in which a verb (sometimes with additional constituents) referring to the co-event is in direct construction with the main verb—that is, with the framing verb (see Aske 1989, Matsumoto 1991). With this syntactic pattern, the whole sentence now can be interpreted as a single clause, and hence as representing a macro-event. (Talmy (2000: 224))

Talmy (2000: 224) takes the following Spanish example, with the caveat that the "gerundive verb here may nevertheless be considered to represent only a midway integration into the framing clause because its gerundive grammatical form still points to a separate-clause origin."

(44) La botella salió flotando de la cueva.
'The bottle exited floating from the cave.' (Talmy (2000: 224))

Here the gerundive *flotando* "floating" occurs between the verb *salió* "exited" and the prepositional phrase *de la cueva* "from the cave." According to Talmy, this gerundive is syntactically constructed with the main verb *salió* rather than the whole main clause *La botella salió de la cueva*. This means that the gerundive and the main verb constitute a single clause together with the prepositional phrase.

The Japanese translation of this Spanish example does exhibit similar satellite-like characteristics.

(45) Bin-wa   dookutsu-kara   nagare-de-ta.
     bottle-Top   cave-from   float-exit-Past
     'The bottle exited floating from the cave.'

In a similar way to the Spanish counterpart, the phrase *nagare* is attached directly to the verb *de-ta*, without the intervention of the *te-* form, and the whole sentence constitutes a single clause.

As examined in section 2.2.6, Talmy mentions an adpositional phrase, as well as a gerundive-type constituent, as a typical example of an adjunct into which the co-event is mapped. But he does not cite an example of the former, since his examples in Spanish are both gerundives. Then what can be an example of an adpositional phrase? We assume that the following examples in French and Japanese may be conceived of as containing an adpositional phrase.

(46) a. Jean   a traversé   la chaussée   à pied.
        Jean   traversed   the road   on foot
        'Jean crossed the road on foot.'
     b. Taro-wa   toho-de   shadoo-wo   oodanshi-ta.
        Taro-Top   foot-with   road-Acc   cross-Past
        'Jean crossed the road on foot.'

Here the French phrase *à pied* "on foot" is composed of the preposition *à* "at, to" and the noun *pied* "foot," and so constitutes a prepositional phrase, which is a kind of adpositional phrase. The Japanese phrase *toho-de* "on foot" can be decomposed into two parts, *toho* "walking," a two-word noun that is originally Chinese, and the postposition *de* "with," which denotes a means. The two parts make up a postpositional phrase, which is also a sort of adpositional phrase. The same semantic content is also expressed by a gerundive in French and a *-te* construction in Japanese as follows:

(47) a. Jean a traversé la chaussée en marchant.
　　　　Jean traversed the road in walking
　　　　'Jean crossed the road, walking.'
　　b. Taro-wa arui-te shadoo-wo oodanshi-ta.
　　　　Taro-Top walk-TE road-Acc cross-Past
　　　　'Jean crossed the road, walking.'

Adding everything up, it has been observed that constituents expressing the co-event in verb-framed languages show a wide range of the degree of integration into the matrix clause, and that satellites and adjuncts represent both ends of the spectrum.

To summarize, we have looked at how Talmy (2000) revises and generalizes his previous theory. First, we have introduced the generic term "macro-event" proposed by Talmy (2000), under which the term motion is subsumed. Next, we have explored the framing event and its ingredients and functions, and then we have examined the subordinate or co- event and its characteristics. Given these observations, we have looked at how Talmy (2000) modifies the three-way classification in Talmy (1985) into the dichotomy between verb-framed and satellite-framed languages. In addition, we have offered our own hierarchical representations of how satellite-framed and verb-framed languages map the framing event onto syntactic structure. Finally, we have considered what syntactic categories can express co-events in verb-framed languages.

2.3. Criticism against Talmy's Typology

Thus far, we have looked at Talmy's typology of event conflation or integration, with special reference to motion verbs. After examining the initial tripartite typology of event conflation in Talmy (1985), we have surveyed the famous dichotomy between satellite-framed and verb-framed languages posited by Talmy (2000), citing a few examples in English, Japanese, Spanish and French.

It is well known that the dichotomy has been espoused by many linguists and applied to diverse languages, amassing a cornucopia of linguistic findings. Some important questions, however, remain unanswered: Can we reliably distinguish satellites from prepositions? What can be satellites in verb-framed languages? Is Talmy's dichotomy or binary opposition between satellite-framed and verb-framed languages viable? These conundrums are discussed below.[2]

2.3.1. Kopecka (2006)

Kopecka (2006) reconsiders the definition of satellites, and newly adds French prefixes to the list of satellites. For justification of her approach, Kopecka refers to Latin, whose verb prefixes are included in the list of satellites we have investigated in section 2.2.5. Kopecka (2006: 86) argues that prefixes in French are "inherited from Latin," and therefore they, as well as Latin prefixes, should be regarded as examples of satellites. On the basis of this assumption, she argues that French, as well as Germanic and Slavonic languages, displays satellite-framed behavior.

(48) [A]lthough the fact of encoding Path in the verb is well attested, French (and possibly other Romance languages as well) can also express this notion in a prefix, leaving the slot of the verb root free to encode Manner, a characteristic typically assigned by the typology to Germanic and Slavonic languages.... (Kopecka (2006: 84))

Here Kopecka maintains that Path, or the core schema in the framing event, is indeed expressed by a prefix, which is supposedly a satellite in her analysis, and that concomitantly, the verb root, or more precisely the main verb if we accept her definition of satellites, lexicalizes Manner. Given these assumptions, Kopecka asserts that French as well as German and English ex-

---

[2] Actually, Matsumoto (2003: 408) proposes a broader reformulation of Talmy's dichotomy. In particular, he argues that satellite-framed and verb-framed languages should be redefined as nonhead-framed and head-framed languages. However, since we believe that a broader definition of satellites, which includes not only particles but also prepositions, satisfactorily solves the problem, we do not adopt his proposal here.

hibits satellite-framed characteristics.

Furthermore, Kopecka (2006: 87) characterizes the function carried out by French prefixes as follows:

(49) With respect to the specific role of prefixes associated with verbs of motion, they determine the spatio-temporal frame of the process expressed by the verb and indicate one of the three phases of motion on the axis of Path: initial (departure from the source), medial (course of the journey) or final (arrival at the goal).

(Kopecka (2006: 87))

Here Kopecka states that some prefixes in French "determine the spatio-temporal frame of the process expressed by the verb." This function is almost identical to the first two facets of the conceptual framework that the framing event provides for the whole macro-event, and we have looked at them in section 2.2.2. This suggests that some French prefixes serve the function of the framing event, and therefore should be considered to be framing satellites, which in turn shows that French does have a satellite-framed aspect.

In order to vindicate her statement, Kopecka categorizes the prefixes into three groups according to their temporal distribution, and the classification is presented in the following table:

Table 1 Spatio-temporal semantics of French prefixes

initial phase or source	medial phase or journey	final phase or goal
em-/en- (Lat. inde) 'away, off'	tra-/trans- 'across, through'	a(d)- 'to, toward'
dé(s)- 'from, off, apart'	par- 'by'	entre-/inter- 'between, among'
é-/ex- 'out of'	sous- 'under'	em-/en- (Lat. in) 'in, into'
		re- 'back'
		sur- 'on, on top of'

(Kopecka (2006: 88))

Verbs with the prefixes in the table are illustrated by the following examples:

(50) a. L'oiseau s'est **en**volé du nid. [initial phase]
'The bird flew away from the nest.'
b. Les enfants ont **par**couru le parc. [medial phase]
'The children ran all over the park.'
c. Oscar a **en**foui le trésor dans le sable. [final phase]
'Oscar buried the treasure in the sand.'

(Kopecka (2006: 88))

Here the prefixes are boldfaced, and they are characterized as follows:

(51) *en-* (Lat. inde) 'away' indicates the departure from the source [(50a)], *par-* (by, over) indicates the course of a journey [(50b)] and *en-* (Lat. in) 'in' indicates the arrival at the goal [(50c)].

(Kopecka (2006: 88))

By giving glosses of English particles to French prefixes, Kopecka seems to imply that both of them carry out a similar role and should be therefore subsumed under the same category.

At first glance, her explanation seems convincing and plausible, but we are opposed to her suggestion, because we encounter difficulties when we take account of other French examples and similar English examples. The problem is that Kopecka deals exclusively with the cases in which the prefixes are applied to manner verbs, such as *voler* "to fly," *courir* "to run" and *fouir* "to dig." However, the same prefixes are contained in more basic motion verbs in French such as *arriver* "to arrive" and *entrer* "to enter," and also in their English counterparts like *arrive* and *enter*.

(52) a. Jean est **ar**rivé à la gare. [French]
'Jean arrived at the station.'
b. John **ar**rived at the station. [English]
(53) a. Jean est **en**tré dans la maison. [French]
'Jean entered the house.'
b. Jean **en**tered the house. [English]

If we followed her suggestion and categorized these prefixes as satellites, we would have to say that English verbs that contain one of these prefixes and denote Path, as well as their counterparts in French, exhibit a satellite-framed lexicalization pattern. But such characterization reveals nothing conducive to the typological analysis of motion events, since it just blurs the typological distinction and throws Talmy's accepted theory into a state of total chaos.

In summary, her argument that French has "the typologically mixed nature" (Kopecka (2006: 84)) has been based entirely on the status of French prefixes as satellites. In the penultimate section of her paper, Kopecka states that in addition to satellite-framed behavior, French can conflate Figure and even Ground to motion.

(54)　French also displays the properties of a satellite-framed language, by expressing Path in a prefix. Furthermore, the process of prefixation allows not only the Manner of motion but also the Figure and even the Ground to be expressed in the verb, through the formation of verbs encoding externally caused motion.

(Kopecka (2006: 97))

Since prefixes are richer in meaning than particles and prepositions, this might be the inevitable conclusion, but we argue that her strategy diverges from Talmy's original and primary aim, playing havoc with the meaningful typological distinction.

2.3.2. Broader Definition of Satellites

Beavers et al. (2010) also reconsider the concept of satellites, and in addition they renounce the use of Talmy's binary typological distinction. We will address these two issues in turn.

First, let us look at their critical examination on candidates for satellites. Beavers et al. (2010: 337) start the discussion by arguing that "the English elements that Talmy labels satellites are not always sisters to the verb, at least not to the exclusion of the ground." Talmy's definition of satellites, as we have already seen in section 2.2.5, is not entirely satisfactory, in that it refers to the syntactic relation "in a sister relation to the verb root" but is not supported by further syntactic argumentation. In order to prove the inadequacy of Talmy's definition of satellites, Beavers et al. (2010: 338) use the *it*-clefting constituency test to the sentence *I ran out of the house*, and confirm that the combination of the satellite *out* and the prepositional phrase *of the house* is a constituent, while the satellite *out* alone is not.

(55) a. ?It was out of the house that I ran, not into the house.
b. *It was out that I ran of the house, not in.

(Beavers et al. (2010: 338))

They attribute the slight oddness of (55a) to the fact that prepositional path phrases prefer to follow verbs, but the lower acceptability is not a serious problem here. Beavers et al. (2010: 338) go on to underscore the significance of their findings as follows:

(56) By this diagnostic, *out of the house* is a constituent. Thus, *out* alone is not a sister to the verb root; rather, *of the house* is a complement of *out*, and the entire PP *out of the house* is a sister to *run*, effectively nullifying the distinction between satellites and prepositions.

(Beavers et al. (2010: 338))

Here we have to agree with Beavers et al. in thinking that the distinction between satellites and prepositions cannot survive intact.

Beavers et al. (2010: 338) further point out that the core schema is sometimes expressed by a prepositional phrase alone. As we have seen at the end of section 2.2.5, this very fact is admitted by Talmy himself as well, but he circumvents the problem by appealing to exceptionality. According to Beavers et al. (2010: 338), the problem is further exacerbated by the fact that prepositions and prepositional phrases are neither satellites nor verbs under Talmy's definition. This is elucidated as follows:

(57) [F]or Talmy [*John ran in*] and [*John ran to the store*] represent typologically distinct methods of encoding path: as a satellite and as non-verb non-satellite, suggesting that in addition to V[erb]-framed and S[atellite]-framed languages, there might also be A(dposition)-framed languages, something surely not intended. Thus, we suggest that PP not be excluded from the notion of satellite, thereby recognizing a wider range of path encoding options than under a

strict interpretation of Talmy's typology.

(Beavers et al. (2010: 338))

In brief, if we were wedded to Talmy's deficient definition of satellites, we would need to identify a third lexicalization type, that is, adposition-framed languages. But this move just makes the classification system more entangled.

Based on the linguistic data above, Beavers et al. (2010: 339) reach the following conclusion, with which we totally agree:

(58) Thus, in what follows, we employ the term 'satellite' in a broader sense: any constituent that is sister to or adjoined to the verb (root).

(Beavers et al. (2010: 339))

To sum up, we have considered the proposal by Beavers et al. (2010) concerning the revision of the concept of satellites. As a result, we have decided to accept it and assume that satellites refer to any constituent that is sister to or adjoined to the verb, or to put it differently, any constituent that is attached to the verb.

2.3.3. Reconsideration of Dichotomy

Let us now turn to their reconsideration of Talmy's motion event typology. Beavers et al. (2010) propose that we scrap Talmy's dichotomy between satellite-framed and verb-framed languages and ascribe the observed differences in lexicalization to the following three factors:

(59) (i) the motion-independent morphological, lexical, and syntactic resources languages make available for encoding manner and path of motion, (ii) the role of the verb as the single clause-obligatory lexical category that can encode either manner or path, and (iii) extra-grammatical factors that yield preferences for certain options.

(Beavers et al. (2010: 331))

Beavers et al. (2010: 331) justify the abolition of the dichotomy on the grounds that "most languages straddle more than one of the previously proposed typological categories: a language may show both verb- and satellite-framed patterns," but their position seems untenable for several reasons.

In the rest of this section, we will review a few facts that Beavers et al. (2010) cite as grounds for their refusal of the dichotomy. We will further argue that it is more reasonable to assume that verb-framed expressions are possible in all languages, whereas satellite-framed options are additionally available in some languages.

2.3.4. Satellite-Framed Expressions in Verb-Framed Languages

The first evidence they cite in order to falsify Talmy's dichotomy is the fact that supposedly satellite-framed expressions are observed in Italian and French, which are verb-framed languages. At the outset of the paper, Beavers et al. (2010: 333) exemplify Talmy's two way typology as follows:

(60) a. *S(atellite)-framed*: Manner is encoded as a MAIN VERB; path must be a satellite.
John limped into the house.   (English; also Russian, German)
   b. *V(erb)-framed*: Path is encoded as a MAIN VERB; manner must be a subordinate adjunct.
Je   suis   entré   dans   la maison   (en boitant).
I   am   entered in   the house   in limping
'I entered the house (limping).'
               (French; also Spanish, Turkish, Japanese, Hebrew)
                                            (Beavers et al. (2010: 333))

Concomitantly, it is a well-known fact that prepositional phrases denoting a path do not occur with manner verbs in verb-framed languages like French, and Beavers et al. (2010: 341) illustrate this point by giving the following examples:

(61) a. Je   suis   allé   à   la librairie.
I   am   gone   to   the bookstore
'I went to the bookstore.'

b.??J'ai boité à la librairie.
I-have limped to the bookstore
'I limped to the bookstore.'　　　(Beavers et al. (2010: 341))

Here the verb *aller* "to go," which encodes a path away from the deictic center, takes a prepositional phrase further specifying the path of motion, namely *à la librairie* "to the bookstore." On the other hand, the verb *boiter* "to limp," which is a manner of motion verb, cannot be followed by the same prepositional phrase. In verb-framed languages, when a path is encoded, a manner must be expressed periphrastically in the form of gerundives, as follows:

(62) Je suis allé à la librairie (en boitant).
I am gone to the bookstore in limping
'I went to the bookstore (limping).'

In this example, the prepositional phrase *à la librairie* occurs with the verb *aller*, and the verb *boiter* takes the gerundive form *en boitant* and modifies the rest of the sentence.

Beavers et al. (2010: 349), however, point out that "there are more and more mentions of what might appear to be instances of the prototypical S[atellite]-framed pattern in V[erb]-framed languages, including French, Italian, and Spanish, all considered 'strongly' V[erb]-framed."[3] Here we focus our attention on French, one of the languages discussed later.

Beavers et al. (2010: 349) argue that the French preposition *dans* "in" can occur with manner verbs, denoting the path to the inside of a place. Or to put what they say another way, the preposition allows a path interpretation even when it appears with manner verbs. They illustrate this point by giving the following examples:

---

[3] Among the languages mentioned, Italian is supposed to show the most satellite-framed behavior, in which "in present-day spoken Italian, a verb-particle construction is gaining ground [...]. An adverbial particle can be used to express a path with manner-of-motion verbs" (Beavers et al. (2010: 348)).

(63) a. Il court dans le jardin.
    he runs in the garden
    'He runs into the garden.'
  b. Allez, courons dans la maison!
    go.2PL, run.1PL in the house
    'Come on, let's run in the house!'
  c.?#Allez, entrons dans la maison en courant!
    go.2PL enter.1PL in the house in running
    'Come on, let's enter the house running!'
                                         (Beavers et al. (2010: 349))

In (63a) and (63b), the preposition *dans* encodes a path, although it occurs with the verb *courir* "to run," which lexicalizes a manner of motion. If the verb *courir* and the preposition *dans* followed the pattern of verb-framed lexicalization, which is characteristic of French, the sentence (63b) should take the form (63c). But Beavers et al. (2010) state the latter sentence is not used by native speakers of French. Comparing (63b) with (63c), they comment that "some French speakers find [(63b)] more natural than [(63c)] in the context of a mother telling her children that they should all go inside (perhaps as it starts to rain)." This means that, in such a context, satellite-framed lexicalization, which is highly uncharacteristic of French, is preferred to verb-framed lexicalization typical of French. From this observation, they draw the following conclusion:

(64) The fact that this option is possible suggests that there is not a complete ban on such constructions in V[erb]-framed languages, as in Talmy's two-way typology. (Beavers et al. (2010: 350))

Their argument seems, at first sight, sufficiently persuasive, but the problem lies in a subtle but crucial difference in meaning or, more accurately, polysemy between the verb *boiter* "to limp" in (61b) and (62) and the verb *courir* "to run" in (63).

Let us look first at the definition of the verb *boiter* by a standard French monolingual dictionary. The dictionary gives two definitions for the verb *boiter*. One of them denotes a manner of motion, and the other is its metaphorical extension. Here we exclusively consider the first one.

(65) Marcher en inclinant le corps d'un côté plus que l'autre, ou alternativement de l'un et de l'autre.
'to walk, inclining one's body on one side more than the other, or alternatively on one side and the other.'
(*Le Nouveau Petit Robert de la langue française, 2008 nouvelle édition* S.V. BOITER; English translation by TD)

Here we can understand that the definition specifies a manner of motion in detail. In particular, the expression *en inclinant le corps* "inclining one's body" explicitly defines the body posture the mover assumes when moving.

In contrast, the verb *courir*, as well as the English verb *run*, has many definitions. We will turn our attention to the meanings that are listed under the rubric "A. (ÊTRES ANIMÉS)," which are considered to describe a rapid movement of animate beings. Among them, we will concentrate on the most relevant meanings:

(66) 1 Aller, se déplacer rapidement par une suite d'élans, en reposant alternativement le corps sur l'une puis l'autre jambe (ou patte) et d'un train plus rapide que la marche.
'to go, to move rapidly by a continuation of momentum, alternatively resting one's body (weight) on one leg then the other and at a pace more rapid than walking.'
[...]
3 (milieu XIIIe) Aller vite, sans précisément courir.
'(the middle of the 18th century) to go quickly without precisely running.'
    Ce n'est pas la peine de courir, nous avons le temps.
    'There's no need to run/hurry, we've got (plenty of) time.'
♦ Aller rapidement (quelque part); atteindre qqch. le plus vite possible.
'to go fast (somewhere); to reach something as quickly as possible.'
    Je prends ma voiture et je cours chez vous.
    'I take my car and I run to your place.'
(*Le Nouveau Petit Robert de la langue française, 2008 nouvelle édition* S.V. COURIR; English translation by TD)

54   *Lexicalization Typology and Event Structure Templates*

We begin by considering the definition 1, which applies to usual running, that is, moving quickly using legs. This is the prototypical meaning of the verb *courir*. Most importantly, this definition contains a full specification of a manner of motion, such as "alternatively resting one's body (weight) on one leg then the other." When used in this meaning, the verb *courir* is considered to be a genuine manner of motion verb.

Now let us turn to the definition 3, which is extended from, or more precisely a "bleached" meaning of, the semantic prototype of *courir*. A brief perusal of the definition shows that it specifies no manner of motion. It is true that the definition does specify the speed of movement, as seen from the expressions *vite* "quickly," *rapidement* "fast" and *le plus vite possible* "as quickly as possible," but it makes no reference to a manner of motion, such as a posture of the mover, a way of moving legs, and so on.

Furthermore, the second example in the definition 3 deserves careful attention, which is repeated here for convenience:

(67)   Je   prends   ma   voiture   et   je   cours   chez vous.
       I   take   my   car   and I   run   to-your-place
       'I take my car and I run to your place.'

The first point to note is that the verb *courir* takes a prepositional phrase denoting a path, namely *chez vous* "to your place." If this usage of the verb *courir* encodes a manner, the sentence does not conform to the Talmyan typology, since such a lexicalization pattern is typically observed in satellite-framed languages, in which French is not included. However, as we have already observed, the verb *courir* in this example does not lexicalize a genuine manner, but encodes a path away from the deictic center (we can surmise this from the verb *aller* "to go" in the definition) together with the rapidity of movement (expressed by the adverb *rapidement* "fast"), and it therefore takes a prepositional phrase further specifying a path, as in the case of the verb *aller* in (61a). The same is true of the verb *courir* in the examples (63).

The second point to observe is that the verb *courir* in (67) describes a rapid movement by car.[4] As we have seen above, the definition of this *courir* does not refer to a manner of motion, or more specifically a way of moving legs. This means that the semantic element of moving legs is not necessarily included in the denotation of this usage. This is why the verb *courir* in this usage can describe rapid travel by car with no leg movements. Even more interestingly, the reflexive verb *se précipiter* "to rush, to dash," which encodes only rapidity and no manner, takes a prepositional phrase denoting a path, as illustrated below:

(68) 2 (se ruer) to rush
      […]
      se précipiter dans les bras de qn
      'to throw oneself into somebody's arms'
      (*Oxford-Hachette French Dictionary* (Fourth Edition) French-English S.V. SE PRÉCIPITER)

These observations suggest that French motion verbs can take a prepositional phrase denoting a path as long as they do not encode a genuine manner of motion, even if they lexicalize the speed of movement.

To summarize, we have examined the French examples that Beavers et al. (2010) give to illustrate that satellite-framed expressions are used in verb-framed languages. Contrary to what they state, we argue that the supposedly satellite-framed examples are in fact not satellite-framed, because their verbs do not encode a genuine manner but a deictic path and the speed of movement. This inevitably leads to the conclusion that satellite-framed expressions are virtually impossible in verb-framed languages.

2.3.5. Verb-Framed Expressions in Satellite-Framed Languages

Conversely, Beavers et al. (2010: 345) also point out that almost all languages, including satellite-framed languages like English, have verbs that

---

[4] As Erteschik-Shir and Rapoport (2004: 223–224, 2005: 81–82) point out, a similar meaning is lexicalized into the English verb *run*. Furthermore, *Genius English-Japanese Dictionary (4th edition)* takes the sentence *Can I take the car to run to the store?* as an example of this meaning. We leave a satisfactory explanation of this polysemy to future research.

lexicalize a path. First, they point out that this is clearly illustrated by the English translation of the French example *Je suis entré dans la maison (en boitant)*, that is, *I entered the house (limping)*. In this English sentence, the verb *enter* encodes a path and does not display satellite-framed behavior characteristically observed in English. Based on this, Beavers et al. (2010: 345) argue that this fact "[calls] into question a clear separation between V[erb]- and S[atellite]-framed languages types." Furthermore, Beavers et al. (2010: 350) present two specific facts in order to further demonstrate "the availability of path verbs in S[atellite]-framed languages." They first refer to English path verbs and then carefully examine Chinese motion expressions. For the sake of explanatory convenience, we will first look at Chinese data, and then consider English path verbs.

In order to further buttress their argument that path verbs are also available in satellite-framed languages, Beavers et al. (2010: 350) show that there are verbs encoding a path in Chinese, which is also categorized into satellite-framed languages. They add that such verbs in Chinese are not so formal or stilted as English equivalents. In Chinese, verbs expressing a manner of motion, such as 走 *zǒu* "to walk" and 跑 *pǎo* "to run," are sometimes followed by verbs denoting a path, for example, 上 *shàng* "to ascend," 进 *jìn* "to enter," 过 *guò* "to pass, to cross," and so on. The following sentence illustrates the use of these verbs.

(69)　他/她　　跳/走/踏-上　　　　　了　　车
　　　　tā　　　tiào/zǒu/tà-shàng　　le　　chē
　　　　3SG　 jump/walk/step-go.up　PRF　vehicle
　　　'(S)he jumped/walked/stepped onto the vehicle.'
　　　　　　(Beavers et al. (2010: 350), Chinese characters added by TD)

In this type of usage, path verbs are not considered to be full-fledged verbs. Instead, they are assumed to be demoted to a lower preposition-like status and called "directional complements." As a result of the relegation, 上 *shàng*, 进 *jìn*, and 过 *guò* roughly correspond to *up*, *into*, and *through* or *across* in English, respectively.

On the other hand, path verbs can occur without manner of motion verbs as in the following example. Since path verbs are supposed to be atypical in satellite-framed languages, Beavers et al. take them as evidence against Talmy's typology.

(70) 他/她　上　　了　　车
　　　 tā　 shàng　le　 chē
　　　 3SG　go.up　PRF　vehicle
　　　 '(S)he boarded the vehicle.'
　　　　　　　(Beavers et al. (2010: 350), Chinese characters added by TD)

Here the path verb 上 *shàng* functions as the main verb of the clause, instead of being affixed to the other main verb as a directional complement as in (69).

Additionally, Beavers et al. (2010: 350) describe the stylistic differences between (69) and (70) as follows:

(71) For example, in scenarios involving boarding or alighting from a vehicle, sentences with path verbs such as [(70)] are just as natural as their counterparts with the manner verb [跳] *tiào* 'jump' in [(69)], and in some contexts are more natural than those with the manner verbs [走] *zǒu* 'walk' and [踏] *tà* 'step', this last having a somewhat literary flavor.
　　　　　　　(Beavers et al. (2010: 350), Chinese characters added by TD)

Here they point out that verb-framed lexicalization options are sometimes less formal than satellite-framed ones in Chinese. Since Chinese is a satellite-framed language, this fact is also unpredictable from Talmy's typology. In brief, though it is classified as a satellite-framed language, Chinese has some path verbs that are neither formal nor stilted, and this constitutes counterevidence to Talmy's (2000) account of lexicalization patterns.

Let us now turn to English path verbs. Beavers et al. (2010: 350) point out that, unlike Latinate path verbs like *enter*, path verbs "such as *rise*, *fall*, and *sink*, seem colloquial and tend not to be replaced by a verb plus satellite collocation." From this observation, Beavers et al. (2010: 350) conclude that satellite-framed languages like English do have verb-framed encoding options, and we agree with them on this point.

Talmy, of course, is also aware that there are exceptionally colloquial path verbs in English; in fact, Talmy (1985: 72) cites the verb *rise* as an exceptional non-Latinate example of a path verb. Furthermore, in Talmy (2000: 21-146), a much revised and expanded version of Talmy (1985), he adds several other verbs to the list, which is shown below:

(72) Important examples are *enter, exit, ascend, descend, cross, pass, circle, advance, proceed, approach, arrive, depart, return, join, separate, part, rise, leave, near, follow.* (Talmy (2000: 52))

Among the examples, as Talmy (2000: 52) says, "the last four verbs listed," namely *rise, leave, near* and *follow*, are exceptionally English native words. But Talmy (2000: 53) argues that the vast majority of them "are borrowings from Romance, where they are the native type." Judging from these remarks, Talmy implies that it should come as no surprise that most English path verbs exhibit verb-framed behavior as motion verbs in Romance do, since they are borrowed from Romance. In other words, Talmy seems to think that the existence of path verbs in English does not pose a serious problem for his analysis, since most of them are loanwords from Romance.

In order to further substantiate his argument, Talmy takes German as an example. More specifically, Talmy argues that German has no verbs that are equivalent to most of the English path verbs on the list above, since, unlike England, Germany has not fallen under the strong influence of French.

(73) By contrast, German, which has borrowed much less from Romance languages, lacks verb roots that might correspond to most of the Path verbs in the list. (Talmy (2000: 53))

By labeling most of the path verbs in English as non-native and alien species, and by stating that they are brought in by a historical coincidence, Talmy tries to effectively exclude English counterexamples to his typology. If there were no corresponding path verbs in German, his argumentation would work well.

A closer examination of German motion verbs, however, demonstrates that we cannot take his statement at face value. The following table enumerates path verbs in English with corresponding verb plus satellite collocations, and their French and German translations.

Table 2

English path verbs	verb + satellite collocations	French translations	German translations
enter	go in(to ...)	entrer	(ein|)treten, betreten
exit	go out (of ...)	sortir	ab|treten
ascend	go upward	monter	auf|gehen
descend	go downward	descendre	unter|gehen, sinken, fallen
cross	go across	traverser	überqueren, kreuzen
pass	go past/across	passer	vorüber|gehen, überschreiten, passieren
circle	move in a circle	décrire des cercles	umkreisen
advance	move forward	avancer	vor|rücken (lassen)
proceed	move forward	avancer	weiter|gehen
approach	move closer	s'approcher (de ...)	heran|kommen (an+Acc), sich nähern (+Dat)
arrive	come (to ...)	arriver (à ...)	(an|)kommen
depart	go away	partir	weg|gehen
return	go back	retourner	zurück|kommen
join	go to the same place	se joindre (à ...)	sich zu|gesellen
separate	go apart	se séparer	sich trennen
part	go apart	se séparer	sich trennen
rise	go upward	monter	auf|steigen, auf|gehen
leave	go away (from ...)	partir (de ...)	(weg|)gehen, verlassen
near	move closer	s'approcher (de ...)	sich nähern (+Dat)
follow	go after	suivre	hinter (+Dat) her gehen, folgen (+Dat)

Indeed, as expected from Talmy's typology, all English path verbs have French corresponding path verbs, except for the verb *circle*. Contrary to our expectations, however, German does have some equivalent path verbs such as *fallen* "to fall," *sinken* "to sink," *folgen* "to follow," *passieren* "to pass," *sich trennen* "to separate, to part" and *sich nähern* "to near."

Maybe we can also include *betreten* "to enter" and *verlassen* "to leave" in the category of path verbs. As we have seen in 2.2.5, German inseparable verb prefixes are semantically and syntactically similar to English and French verb prefixes, which are contained in basic path verbs of both languages, such as *arrive*, *enter* and their French counterparts. Furthermore, German inseparable prefixes like *be-* and *ver-* have lost their clear meaning and can hardly regarded semantically as full-fledged satellites if we consider Talmy's semantic elucidation of his satellites in his papers. Taking these data into account, it is concluded that Talmy's claim that German has no path verbs corresponding to English ones belies the linguistic reality of motion verbs.

All of the data in Chinese, English and German point to the conclusion that verb-framed encoding options are possible even in satellite-framed languages when lexical resources are available. To recapitulate, we have seen the data that Beavers et al. (2010) provide to corroborate their view that verb-framed expressions are possible in satellite-framed languages. We agree with them on this point, and we will give more examples to strengthen the argument in chapter 5.

2.3.6. New Proposal

Let us summarize the main points that have emerged so far. As we see from the French example (61b) ??*J'ai boité à la librairie*, verb-framed languages like French do not allow liberal use of satellite-framed expressions, even though they have lexical resources such as manner verbs and prepositional phrases denoting a path. In other words, a lack of satellite-framed lexicalization in verb-framed languages is generally attributed to grammatical constraints. On the other hand, in satellite-framed languages, such as English, German and Chinese, verb-framed encoding options are possible whenever lexical resources are available, as shown in section 2.3.5. To put it another way, a scarcity of verb-framed expressions in satellite-framed languages is ascribed to lexical gaps, and verb-framed lexicalization itself is not strictly prohibited by the grammatical system of satellite-framed languages. What further follows from this are the following: (i) verb-framed expressions are linguistically more basic than satellite-framed ones. (ii) more basic verb-framed lexicalization options are observed in almost all languages. (iii) satellite-framed conflation is an add-on to basic verb-framed lexicalization ubiquitous in the language system; thus it is possible only in certain languages conventionally characterized as satellite-framed.

More generally, it leads us to the conclusion that the view of satellite-framedness as an "add-on module" is a more reasonable explanation for encoding possibilities in satellite-framed languages, which sometimes exhibit verb-framed characteristics, than the generally accepted theory based on binary opposition. But has no one mentioned this underlying asymmetry between the two lexicalization patterns? In fact, both Talmy (1985) and Beavers et al. (2000) seem to be vaguely aware of the difference in generality and reflect it in their use of quantifier expressions.

First, with an open and empty mind, let us read two statements by Talmy (1985) on the conflation types of English and Spanish.

(74) a. Even a language as seemingly kindred as Spanish *can express virtually none* of the above sentences in the way that English does […].

(Talmy (1985: 63), italics original and underline mine)

b. English does have a certain number of verbs that genuinely incorporate Path, as in the Spanish conflation type […]

(Talmy (1985: 72), underline mine)

Here we must draw attention to the underlined parts. In (74a), the expression "virtually none" suggests that almost all English-like expressions are impossible in Spanish, and so this means that Spanish, a typical example of a verb-framed language, does not tolerate satellite-framed expressions as a rule. In contrast, the phrase "does have a certain number of" in (74b) affirms the existence or availability of Spanish-like expressions in English. That is to say, Talmy here acknowledges that English, a satellite-framed language, allows verb-framed lexicalization to some degree.

The difference in quantification reveals that, whether consciously or unconsciously, Talmy recognizes a crucial difference in the relative frequency of uncharacteristic encoding options between satellite-framed and verb-framed languages. More specifically, verb-framed expressions in satellite-framed languages are much more frequently encountered than satellite-framed expressions in verb-framed languages. That is to say, it seems that, taking all languages together, verb-framed expressions are more prevalent than satellite-framed expressions. Talmy, however, makes no mention of the potential importance of this glaringly obvious asymmetry.

Next, let us turn to how Beavers et al. (2010) inadvertently mention the same difference. Beavers et al. (2010: 350–351) offer the following as a summary of what they have discussed in section 2.3 of the paper:

(75) Many languages exhibit properties of both V[erb]- and S[atellite]-framed languages. <u>Some V[erb]-framed languages allow</u> goal-marking via *until*-markers or applicativization, or even via affixes and particles, i.e. <u>unexpected S[atellite]-framed options</u>. Likewise, <u>most S[atellite]-framed languages have path verbs</u>, thus allowing V[erb]-framed encoding options.

(Beavers et al. (2010: 350–351), underline mine)

Here the contrastive use of the quantifiers "some" and "most" shows their unconscious recognition of the difference in frequency between satellite-framed expressions in verb-framed languages and verb-framed expressions in satellite-framed languages. Nevertheless, Beavers et al. (2010) might be too preoccupied with the justification of the abolition of Talmy's dichotomy to give any serious thought to the fundamental difference between "some" and "most" in their own phrasing, or to put it more plainly, the asymmetry between the two lexicalization patterns.

Then why are verb-framed expressions more common than satellite-framed ones? Is there any rationale behind the observed difference in prevalence between the two lexicalization types? The answers lie in Talmy (1985).

As we have seen in section 2.1.2, Talmy (1985) has classified conflation patterns discerned in languages into three groups: languages conflate with motion (i) a manner or cause, (ii) a path, and (iii) a figure. Let us now turn to an interesting and insightful comment that Talmy (1985: 75) makes on the relationships between the three types of conflation:

(76) Explanation may next be sought in a concept of hierarchy: the different conflation types seem to be ranked in their prevalence among the world's languages, with conflation of Path as the most extensively represented, of Manner/Cause next, and of Figure least so. (Talmy (1985: 75))

Here Talmy arranges them on the scale of commonness across languages. By doing so, he shows that Path is most commonly conflated with Motion. The conflation of Manner/Cause with Motion is the second most frequent pattern, and Figure is most rarely combined with Motion. But the same hierarchical system can be applied to their positions within a single language. For example, the "conflation of Path" or verb-framedness is higher in the rank of availability than the conflation "of Manner/Cause" or satellite-framedness, and English does, but French does not, tolerate the lower ranking encoding options. To put it more generally, satellite-framed languages allow a wider range of lexicalization patterns, or encoding options, than verb-framed languages.

Then why do verb-framed languages not tolerate encoding options which rank low and are thus less extensively available? The answer lies in the configuration of the ingredients in macro-events, in which Manner component is located outside the framing event. In view of this, we assume that the less availability of satellite-framed lexicalization options stems from the extra effort required for satellite-framed encoding.

As we have seen at the end of section 2.2.6, satellite-framed encoding requires a special conceptual apparatus for resolving the structural discrepancy between macro-events and syntax structure. In verb-framed encoding, the structure of macro-events is mapped isomorphically onto the syntactic structure. Conversely, in satellite-framed mapping, there are deviations from isomorphic mapping. More specifically, the Manner co-event is lexicalized by the main verb and the framing event is mapped onto the prepositional phrase attached to the verb. What is more, the figure in the framing event is apparently separated and mapped onto the subject in the main clause. Therefore, satellite-framed languages are assumed to have a mechanism for dealing with such a complicated mapping.

The required mechanism reminds us of an "event coidentification" analysis of the sentence *Kim ran into the room*, which is proposed by Levin and Rappaport Hovav (1999: 213) and Rappaport Hovav and Levin (2001: 782). By this process, what can be construed as two separate events and expressed by two clauses, for example, *Kim ran* and *Kim entered the room*, are "coidentified" and represented as one event, which is in turn encoded by the sentence *Kim ran into the room*. We will consider the compositional process and its significance in chapter 4.

The "coidentification" is a special procedure of semantic composition that requires additional processing effort, and it semantically associates the framing event with the extrinsic manner event. It is this process that makes satellite-framed languages what they are, that is, that enables them to use satellite-framed expressions. This leads ineluctably to the conclusion that only satellite-framed languages have "event coidentification" as a productive system, and thereby have satellite-framedness. Contrastingly, verb framed expressions require no additional "event coidentification" process, and thus are possible in almost all languages.

2.4. Recapitulation

In this chapter, we have looked at Talmy's typological system and its criticisms. In section 2.1, we have considered Talmy (1985), in which his analysis of motion is still in its infancy but reveals interesting findings. In section 2.2, we have looked at Talmy (2000), which replaces his former tripartite typology with the dichotomy between satellite-framed and verb-framed languages. In section 2.3, we have examined recent criticisms against Talmy's theory, and accepted some of them and dismissed the others as unrealistic. Finally, we have referred to the relationship between Talmy's typology and Levin and Rappaport Hovav's theory, the latter of which we will consider in chapters 3 and 4.

Chapter 3

Event Structure Templates and their Development

In the previous chapter, we have looked at how motion events are analyzed under Talmy's typological system. In this chapter, we will turn to the theory of lexical semantics advanced by Beth Levin and Malka Rappaport Hovav. Their theory is based on lexical decomposition in the form of event structure templates.

This chapter is organized as follows. In section 3.1, we will look at the aspectual classification introduced by Vendler (1957), in which verbs are classified according to their time schemata into four types, that is, activities, accomplishments, achievements and states. We will then look into Smith (1997), introducing her visual representation of temporal schemata and some diagnostic tests for telicity. In section 3.2, we will review the lexical decomposition of the verb *kill* in McCawley (1968) and its potential problems. In section 3.3, we will turn to the significant distinction between two components of verb meaning in Rappaport Hovav and Levin (1998). In section 3.4, we will look at their articulate representation of verb meaning, which is based on four dichotomies, that is, (i) primitive predicates vs. constants, (ii) manner vs. result verbs, (iii) structure vs. constant participants, and (iv) simple vs. complex event structures. Sections 3.5 and 3.6 set out the reasons why Rappaport Hovav and Levin reconsider their aspectual characterization of event structure templates. In section 3.7, we will look at how they revise their theory in order to reconcile with it the contrary evidence presented in section 3.6. In section 3.8 we will summarize the arguments in this chapter and then examine wider implications of the revision.

3.1. Aspectual Classification of Verbs

Before proceeding to a discussion of event structure templates, we will examine the aspectual classification of verbs established by Vendler (1957) and espoused by more recent work such as Dowty (1979), Smith (1997), and Rothstein (2004). We turn to the issue of aspect because event structure templates are labeled in aspectual terms in Rappaport Hovav and Levin (1998). This suggests that Rappaport Hovav and Levin first conceived the idea of event structure templates by analogy with the time schemata of aspectual classification. In this section, we will focus on Vendler (1957) and Smith (1997) and will look at them in turn.

3.1.1. Vendler (1957)

Vendler (1957) is best known for the four aspectual classes based on time schemata, namely activities, accomplishments, achievements and states. These aspectual categories are familiar to most linguists and are still widely used in the analysis of verb meaning. At the beginning, Vendler (1957: 143) sketches the background to the study. Since verbs have tenses, their usages naturally reflect some aspects of the concept of time. But it has become clear that the finer, more subtle facets of time are also germane to the usages of verbs in that they draw distinctions among "processes, states, dispositions, occurrences, tasks, achievements, and so on" (Vendler (1957: 143)). He refers to these classes as time schemata, and stresses the importance as follows:

(1) [I]f we focus our attention primarily upon the time schemata presupposed by various verbs, we are able to throw light on some of the obscurities which still remain in these matters.

(Vendler (1957: 143))

The time schemata reflect the inherent temporal properties of the events de-

Chapter 3 Event Structure Templates and their Development

noted by verbs, and thus their systematic examination provides an entirely new paradigm for dealing with verb meaning.

Vendler proposes some diagnostic tests that differentiate between four main types of time schemata. The first test is based on whether or not verbs occur in the continuous or progressive form.

> (2) I start with the well-known difference between verbs that possess continuous tenses and verbs that do not. The question, "What are you doing?" might be answered by "I am running (or writing, working, and so on)," but not by "I am knowing (or loving, recognizing, and so on)."   (Vendler (1957: 144))

Here we should note that Vendler does not use the progressive form in isolation as a test. This diagnostic test divides verbs into two groups, and each group is further subdivided.

First, Vendler subclassifies the verbs that can appear in the progressive into two types according to whether they have an endpoint or not. Vendler (1957: 145) observes that "while running or pushing a cart has no set terminal point, running a mile and drawing a circle do have a 'climax'." To substantiate his claim, Vendler goes on to point out that "[r]unning a mile and drawing a circle have to be finished, while it does not make sense to talk of finishing running or pushing a cart."

Furthermore, Vendler proposes two syntactic frames which distinguish the two subgroups and applies them to the verbs mentioned above.

> (3) Accordingly, the question, "For how long did he push the cart?" is a significant one, while "How long did it take to push the cart?" sounds odd. On the other hand, "How long did it take to draw the circle?" is the appropriate question, and "For how long did he draw the circle?" is somewhat queer.   (Vendler (1957: 145))

The two syntactic frames have the form of interrogative sentences, and can therefore be answered in the following way:

> (4) And, of course, the corresponding answers will be, "He was pushing it for half an hour" and "It took him twenty seconds to draw

the circle" or "He did it in twenty seconds," and not vice versa.

(Vendler (1957: 145))

Here we should notice that Vendler uses adverbials such as *for half an hour* and *in twenty seconds* and the verb of time *take*. Most importantly, these forms can be used as diagnostic tests for a climax in verb meaning even if they are not preceded by the corresponding interrogative sentences. More specifically, without the preceding interrogative sentence, the adverbial *for half an hour* is compatible with verbs that have no endpoint like *push something*, but does not occur with verbs having an endpoint such as *draw the circle*. On the other hand, the adverbial *in twenty seconds* and the construction *it took him twenty seconds to do something* can be used with verbs having an endpoint, but do not appear with verbs without an endpoint.

For this reason, these forms are nowadays more frequently used to identify the aspectual nuances of verb meaning. The two types of adverbials, that is, *for*-adverbials like *for half an hour* and *in*-adverbials like *in twenty seconds*, are particularly preferred by lexical semanticists.

Moreover, Vendler gives each type of verb phrase a different name.

(5) Let us call the first type, that of "running," "pushing a cart," and so forth *activity terms*, and the second type, that of "running a mile," "drawing a circle," and so forth *accomplishment terms*.

(Vendler (1957: 146))

Here Vendler uses the word "term" to designate the whole expression, but Vendler himself and many subsequent studies often call the two types of verb phrases activities and accomplishments for short.

Let us next turn to the verbs that do not occur in the progressive. As Vendler (1957: 146) argues, it is true that "verbs like 'knowing' and 'recognizing' do not indicate processes going on in time." The two sorts of verbs, however, denote rather different situations. More specifically, as Vendler acknowledges, recognizing something occurs at a moment, whereas knowing something obtains for a period. In other words, recognizing is instantaneous or punctual, and knowing is durative. Nevertheless, they are at least similar in that they do not describe a process, which in turn prevents them from occurring in the progressive form.

Chapter 3   Event Structure Templates and their Development   69

Vendler propounds the following diagnostic test that differentiates achievements and states:

(6) "At what time did you reach the top?" ("At noon sharp") and "At what moment did you spot the plane? ("At 10:53 A.M."); but "For how long did you love her?" ("For three years") and "How long did you believe in the stork?" ("Till I was seven"), and not the other way around.   (Vendler (1957: 146-147))

Here Vender uses two kinds of adverbials, namely *at*-adverbials and *for*-adverbials, both of which are sensitive to the durativity of verbs. The adverbial *at noon sharp* only occurs with punctual verbs such as *reach the top* and *spot the plane* and is odd with durative verbs like *love someone* and *believe in the stork*.[1] The adverbial *for three years* is not only compatible with verbs that have no endpoint, but also requires durativity in verb meaning. Consequently, it occurs with durative verbs, but does not appear with punctual verbs.

Vendler gives the two groups of verbs the following names:

(7) [L]et us call the first family (that of "reaching the top") *achievement terms*, and the second (that of "loving") *state terms*. Then we can say that achievements occur at a single moment, while states last for a period of time.

Today, the names of classifications "achievement" and "state" are familiar to lexical semanticists, together with the other two names, namely "activity" and "accomplishment."

So far we have been concerned with the four groups in the classification devised by Vendler (1957), namely activities, accomplishments, achievements and states. First we have seen that the first two categories occur in the progressive form, while the other two do not. We have then examined temporal characteristics that differentiate activities from accomplishments, and achievements from states. The four distinct categories of event sche-

---

[1] For more details of the relationship between *at*-adverbials and aspectual classification, see Filip (1999: 113).

mata are adopted by more recent researchers, such as Dowty (1979), Smith (1997), and Rothstein (2004). Among them, Smith (1997) provides an indepth analysis of Vendlerian classes using three temporal properties, namely "dynamism, telicity, and duration" (Smith (1997: 19)). Moreover, she supplements Vendlerian classification with a fifth class dubbed "semelfactives." In the next subsection, we will examine Smith's analysis with special attention to activities, accomplishments and achievements.

3.1.2. Three Temporal Features

Let us delve deeply into the three temporal features introduced by Smith (1997). Smith applies the three features to five idealized situation types, that is, states, activities, accomplishments, achievements and semelfactives. For the sake of clarity, Smith refers to the features by pairs of antonymous adjectives instead of by positive adjectives. This means, for example, that she states that a situation is static or dynamic rather than saying that it is static or not static.

The first feature is stasis, or the opposition between being static and being dynamic, and is explained as follows:

(8) *[Static / Dynamic]:* The distinction between stasis and motion is fundamental, and bifurcates situation types into the classes of states and events: states are static, events are dynamic. [...] The natural class of events comprises all non-stative situations.

(Smith (1997: 19))

This feature distinguishes states from the other four classes. To put it more clearly, the situations that have stasis are states, and those which lack stasis, or are dynamic, are classified into one of the other four categories.

The second property is telicity, or the opposition between being telic and being atelic. She characterizes the opposition as follows:

(9) *[Telic/Atelic]:* Events may be telic or atelic. Telic events have a change of state which constitutes the outcome, or goal, of the event. When the goal is reached, a change of state occurs and the event is complete. [...] In contrast, atelic events are simply pro-

cesses. They can stop at any time: there is no outcome. In other words, atelic events have arbitrary final endpoints.

(Smith (1997: 19))

Telicity differentiates accomplishments and achievements from activities. For example, Vendler's famous accomplishment *draw a circle* entails the completion of the circle, which constitutes a change of state, and is therefore telic. By contrast, the activity *push a cart* does not encode a change of state, and it is thus atelic. Neither the pusher nor the cart undergoes a change of state, and pushing can stop at any time.

Here we should note that she states that "a change of state occurs", but does not specify which participant is construed as undergoing the change of state. In most cases, an entity undergoing it is denoted by the direct object of the sentence, but there are some interesting exceptions to this tendency, such as the accomplishment *read a book*. We will address the issue later in section 3.6.2.2.

The final feature is durativity, or the opposition between being durative and being instantaneous or punctual. Smith (1997: 19) argues that this notion involves idealization, because "[a]n event such as [win the race] may take several milliseconds, strictly speaking," and these several milliseconds should not be interpreted as temporal duration.

Smith (1997: 20) defines the five aspectual classes in terms of the combination of the three features. The general result is diagrammed below:

(10) Temporal features of the situation types

Situations	Static	Durative	Telic
States	[+]	[+]	[−]
Activity	[−]	[+]	[−]
Accomplishment	[−]	[+]	[+]
Semelfactive	[−]	[−]	[−]
Achievement	[−]	[−]	[+]

(Smith (1997: 20))

Her analysis is revealing in that it throws into sharp relief the commonalities and differences between the situation types, or the time schemata in Vendler's terms.

3.1.3. Three Important Situation Types

Smith (1997: 23-35) delineates the characteristics of each aspectual class. Among the situation types she clarifies, we will concentrate on activities, accomplishments and achievements, since the three types are most relevant to our concern with motion verbs.

Smith begins her discussion by elaborating on activities:

(11) Activities are processes that involve physical or mental activity, and consist entirely in the process. [...] Typical Activities are [stroll in the park], [laugh], [revolve], [think about], [enjoy], [eat cherries]. [...] The termination of an Activity does not follow from the structure of the event. The arbitrary final endpoint of an Activity is a temporal bound, explicit or implicit. Activities *terminate* or *stop*, but they do not *finish*: the notion of completion is irrelevant to a process event. (Smith (1997: 23))

Here she lists miscellaneous verb phrases to illustrate her point, and the example *stroll in the park* includes a manner of motion verb. The enumerated instances are conceptually dissimilar and heterogeneous, but they all describe some kind of process and have three temporal characteristics, namely dynamicity, atelicity, and durativity, in common. This makes it clear that the classification is based entirely on temporal features, to the exclusion of all other semantic factors such as abstractness, animacy, agency and so on. The same is true of the examples of the other situation types.

We next turn to her exposition of achievements, which are punctual events made up only of a change of state:

(12) Achievements are instantaneous events that result in a change of state. [...] Typical examples are [leave the house], [reach the top], [recognize Aunt Jane]. Preliminary or resultant stages may be associated with the event, but they are not considered part of it.
(Smith (1997: 30))

Here we notice that the examples *leave the house* and *reach the top* include a motion verb encoding a path. Smith does not exactly define "preliminary

Chapter 3 Event Structure Templates and their Development   73

stages" and "resultant stages," but she exemplifies the former as follows:

(13) [reach the top] requires a preliminary approach. If a magician whisked Mary to the top of a pyramid, we would not say that she had reached the top. (Smith (1997: 31))

Here she states that the "preliminary approach" to the top is the necessary concomitant of reaching the top, but it is not part of the situation itself. This means that achievements do not have preliminary stages in their time schema or, to put it more broadly, in their event structure.

Finally, we look at the explanation Smith provides for accomplishments.

(14) Typical examples are [build a bridge], [walk to school], [drink a glass of wine]. Accomplishments have successive stages in which the process advances to its natural final endpoint. They result in a new state. [...] The notion of completion is essential: Accomplishments *finish*, or are *completed*, whereas Activities *stop* or *terminate*. (Smith (1997: 26))

Here she defines an accomplishment as a process leading to a change of state. This means that an accomplishment consists of an activity and an achievement, or to put it another way, it is an activity followed by and resulting in an achievement. Here we focus on the example *walk to school*, a manner of motion verb taking a prepositional phrase denoting a goal. Smith (1997: 26) argues that "[i]f you have walked to school and arrived there, the event is complete." In this case, walking is a process and an activity, and arriving at school is an achievement. The composition, or conflation in Talmy's terms, of the two situations is an accomplishment *walk to school*.

Smith presents the following schematic representations of the situation types:

(15) a. Temporal schema of Activities: I......F_{Arb}
                                                                            (Smith (1997: 23))
     b. Temporal Schema of Accomplishments: I.....$F_{Nat\ R}$
                                                                            (Smith (1997: 26))
     c. Temporal Schema of Achievements: ...E_R...
                                                                            (Smith (1997: 30))

Here I is the symbol for an initial endpoint or the beginning of a situation. F_{Arb} and F_{Nat} represent arbitrary and natural final endpoints, respectively. The subscript R designates the result state produced by the change of state that constitutes a natural final endpoint. The dotted line between I and F denotes successive stages of events.

Smith represents the temporal schema of achievements as (15c), but the symbol E is not used in (15a) and (15b), and so it does not contribute to the clarification of their relationship with activities and accomplishments. We should therefore adopt a modified version of the achievement schema shown below:

(16)   Temporal Schema of Achievements: $F_{Nat\ R}$ (Smith (1997: 30))

Here the dots before E in (15c) designating the preliminary stages of achievements have been removed, because the preliminary stages are not considered part of achievements and so should not contained in the schema. The dots after E designating the resultant stages also have been eliminated, because they are entailed by the subscript R symbolizing a result and thus need not be explicitly represented.

Having elucidated the temporal characteristics of the situation types, Smith presents the following standard diagnostic tests for telicity and atelicity.

(17)   The grammatical correlates of telicity involve the notion of completion. Verbs and adverbials of completion (*finish, in an hour*) contrast with verbs of termination and adverbials of simple duration (*stop, for an hour*).   (Smith (1997: 43))

The four diagnostics are grouped into two categories, which we will examine

Chapter 3 Event Structure Templates and their Development

in turn.

The first two diagnostics, that is, the verb *finish* and *in*-adverbials, indicate whether the meaning of verbs has completion or not, or to put it another way, whether verb phrases are telic or atelic. Telic verb phrases pass the diagnostic tests, whereas atelic verb phrases fail them.

(18) Telic verb constellations are compatible with completion; [...]. In contrast, atelic verb constellations are odd with forms of completion, as [(19)] shows:

(19) a. Mary walked to school in an hour. (telic)
b. Mary finished walking to school. (telic)
c. ?Mary walked in the park in an hour. (atelic)
d. ?Mary finished walking in the park. (atelic) (Smith (1997: 43))

Here the verb phrase *walk to school* is telic, while the expression *walk in the park* is atelic. The former occurs with *in an hour* and serves as the complement of the verb *finish*, and is therefore diagnosed as having telicity. On the other hand, the latter is not compatible with *in an hour*, and does not occur as the complement of *finish*, and is thus judged to be atelic.

Smith argues that the other two diagnostics, namely the verb *stop* and *for*-adverbials, show whether verb phrases are atelic or not.

(20) With adverbs of simple duration the situation is reversed. Atelic verb constellations allow them but they are odd with telic constellations. The verb *stop* is good with telic verb constellations, but does not indicate completion. [(21)] illustrates:

(21) a. ?Mary walked to school for an hour. (telic)
b. Mary stopped walking to school. (telic)
c. Mary walked in the park for an hour. (atelic)
d. Mary stopped walking in the park. (atelic) (Smith (1997: 43))

Here we notice that *for*-adverbials serves as a reliable diagnostic for atelicity, but both telic and atelic verb phrases appear as the complement of the verb *stop*. Smith states that when a telic verb phrase occurs as the complement of *stop*, it does not entail the completion it encodes. When an atelic verb phrase serves as the complement of *stop*, it does not entail completion because it does not have completion in its meaning. In other words, only when a telic verb phrase serves as the complement of *stop* is not all the lexical information it encodes entailed by the resultant sentence. But this difference in entailment is not as intuitively easy to understand as *for*-adverbials, and therefore we do not use the verb *stop* as a diagnostic for atelicity.

The telic verb phrase *walk to school* is incompatible with *for an hour*, whereas the atelic phrase *walk in the park* occurs with it. This means that *for*-adverbials act as a diagnostic for atelicity and correctly divide the telic phrase *walk to school* from the atelic phrase *walk in the park*.

Thus far we have considered how Smith (1997) analyzes Vendlerian aspectual classes. In particular, we have concentrated on activities, achievements and accomplishments, which are particularly pertinent to the investigation of motion verbs. In the rest of this chapter, we will look at the theory based on event structure templates which is proposed by Beth Levin and Malka Rappaport Hovav.

3.2. Lexical Decomposition in Generative Semantics

In a series of papers, Beth Levin and Malka Rappaport Hovav have proposed a theory of lexical semantics based on event structure templates, or what have been recently renamed "event schemas." Their approach rests on the assumption that verb meaning can be decomposed into more primitive semantic elements. In linguistics, it is known that the idea of lexical decomposition was first propounded and justified by the school of Generative Semantics, which flourished in the late 1960s and the early 1970s and was advocated by George Lakoff, John Robert Ross, Paul Postal, and James D. McCawley. A discussion of McCawley (1968) will provide a useful starting point. Actually, this is a watershed paper which seems to have influenced decompositional analyses of verb meaning ever since, and it is famous for its analysis of the verb *kill*.

McCawley (1968) is famous for its lexical decomposition of the verb *kill* into the four predicates CAUSE, BECOME, NOT and ALIVE. In Generative Semantics, semantic representations are assumed to be directly mapped onto syntactic structure by syntactic rules. This leads to the other premise that verbs in syntactic structure are associated with predicates in semantic representations. McCawley, however, issues the following caveat:

(22) The repertory of predicates will be enormous, although not matching lexical items one-to-one, i.e. some lexical items are semantically complex. (McCawley (1968: 71, 1973: 156))

Here the phrase "some lexical items are semantically complex" is worthy of notice. This suggests that, in some cases, a verb in syntactic structure does not correspond exactly to one predicate but rather to more than one predicate in semantic representations.

McCawley illustrates his point by the following decompositional analysis of the verb *kill*:

(23) *Kill* can be resolved into components as *cause to die*; moreover, [at] least one of those components, namely *die*, is itself semantically complex, meaning 'cease to be alive', i.e. 'become not alive'. However, this is not sufficient to describe the semantic representations of sentences involving *kill*, since a sentence involving it refers to two participants, one of whom causes the event in question and the other of whom dies in that event, i.e. the meaning of *x killed y* would require a representation along the lines of

(24)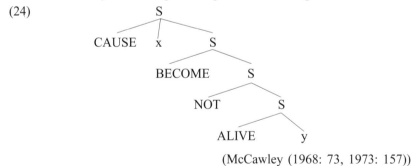

(McCawley (1968: 73, 1973: 157))

What has to be noted here is that McCawley uses four predicates, namely CAUSE, BECOME, NOT and ALIVE, to anatomize the verb *kill*. He capitalizes the predicates to show that they are elements in semantic representations and do not agree entirely with their English lexical counterparts.

Then what are x and y in the tree diagram? McCawley regards them as indices in semantic representations; however, they reasonably correspond to variables in mathematics and logic, since they can take a variety of values, in contrast to constants, whose value remains unchanged. The values they take denote the participants in events.

McCawley (1973) contains a revised version of McCawley (1968) as a chapter, in which he adds the following annotation to the verb *cause*:

(25) The English word *cause* is used in a variety of ways. The 'CAUSE' that appears in [(24)] corresponds to a relationship between a person and an event, as in *John caused Bill to die*. However, *cause* can also be used to express a relationship between an action or event and an event, as in *John's reckless act caused Bill's death*. (McCawley (1973: 164–165))

In accordance with this analysis, he proposes the tree diagram below as another possible form of lexical decomposition of the verb *kill*:

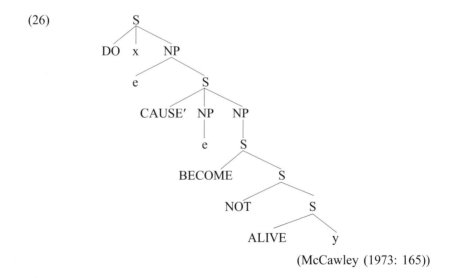

(McCawley (1973: 165))

Here the predicate DO is added in order to make it clear that what causes the event is not a person but an action carried out by a person.

His analysis is fascinating, because a word, which is conventionally considered to be atomic and irreducible, is decomposed to several predicates that denote its semantic elements. Additionally, by doing so, we can find, study and explain the similarities and differences in meaning between words. At a superficial level, verbs appear to be atomic and semantically unrelated, but at a deeper level, we identify some similarities and differences between them by the way they are decomposed. More specifically, when two verbs have the same and different predicates at a deeper level, the same predicates denote their semantic commonality, whereas the different predicates encode their difference. His approach provides a bountiful supply of analytical resources for lexical semantics, and it can be applied to almost every word.

So far his logic has seemed impeccable, but we need to be alert to a potential pitfall: How deeply should we analyze a verb's lexicalized meaning? This leads him and his cohorts inexorably to the problem of infinite decomposition.

The inadequacy of his approach lies in the fact that he does not clarify how many predicates there are in the repertory. As he states in (22), "[t]he repertory of predicates will be enormous", but he does not specify how enormous it is. We could be therefore caught in a predicament over whether to further decompose the meaning or not. For example, the predicate ALIVE can be theoretically decomposed into HAVE LIFE. The noun *life*, which is thought to be the lexical equivalent of the semantic element LIFE, is defined by *Oxford Advanced Learner's Dictionary* (8th edition) as "the ability to breathe, grow, reproduce, etc. which people, animals and plants have before they die and which objects do not have." Then should the verbs *breathe*, *grow* and *reproduce* be decompositional predicates in semantic representations? How about the nouns *people*, *animal* and *plant*? Suppose that we went on decomposing the meaning this way, the logical result would be the sheer ludicrousness and futility of the whole analysis. In order to make our decomposition strategy plausible and viable, we have to curb the excessive decomposition. But how?

The important point to note is a qualitative difference among the predicates in (26). The predicates DO, CAUSE and BECOME have verbal properties, and they are actually inherited by more recent theories of lexical semantics, while the predicates NOT and ALIVE are not. It is evident that the problem stems from the decomposition of the latter predicates. Thus we should restrict the range of the decomposition in semantic structures so as not to anatomize non-verbal predicates such as NOT and ALIVE and devise another method of representing the meaning symbolized by NOT ALIVE.

The distinction between what should and should not be decomposed is significant when we consider the lexical meaning of verbs, and as we will see below, recent semantic theories based on lexical decomposition draw this crucial distinction. In the next section, we will look at how Rappaport Hovav and Levin incorporate the distinction into their system.

3.3. Lexical Decomposition in Recent Studies

Rappaport Hovav and Levin (1998) is a seminal article on the lexical semantics of verbs. They propose a novel and efficient theory of verb meaning by integrating the key findings from studies on "elasticity" (Rappaport Hovav and Levin (1998: 100)), or allowable variations, in verb meaning, including some of their own, such as Levin and Rapoport (1988) and Levin and Rappaport Hovav (1992, 1995).

3.3.1. Two Components of Verb Meaning

As already mentioned at the outset of this chapter, their analysis is based on the possibility of lexical decomposition, and they propose a solution to the problem of infinite decomposition. The solution lies in a clear separation between two components of verb meaning, and, as we will see in detail later, the two parts are represented in quite different ways in their event structures.

For the sake of clarity, let us use a metaphor and liken lexical decomposition to division in mathematics: Verb meaning can be "divided" by a limited set of primitive predicates that denote abstract semantic aspects shared by, or common to, many verbs. The set of predicates supposedly correspond to "common divisors" in mathematics. Rappaport Hovav and Levin call this part of verb meaning "the structural part or component." After this semantic "division," the semantic "remainder" of verb meaning consequently represents the semantic element carried only by and peculiar to each verb. They dub this part "the idiosyncratic part or component," probably following a precedent set by Pinker (1989: 173, 182), as we will see just below.

In their theory, the two parts of verb meaning perform quite different functions when we classify verbs in a grammatically relevant fashion:

(27) The structural part of a verb's meaning is that part which is relevant to determining the semantic classes of verbs that are grammatically relevant, while the idiosyncratic part of a verb's meaning distinguishes that verb from other members of the same class.
(Rappaport Hovav and Levin (1998: 106))

Verbs are divided into semantic classes according to their grammatical behavior. The structural part of verb meaning encodes grammatically relevant semantic characteristics and categorizes verbs into semantic classes, whereas the idiosyncratic part of meaning encodes grammatically irrelevant subtle nuances and differentiates one verb from another within the semantic classes. To put it another way, the verbs in the same semantic class share the same structural part of meaning, while they differ from one another in their idiosyncratic part of meaning.

They further elaborate on each component of verb meaning as follows:

(28) a. It is usually assumed that the structural component of verb meaning is that aspect which is grammatically relevant—for example, relevant to argument realization—and defines the grammatically-relevant semantic classes of verbs—that is, those semantic classes of verbs whose members share syntactically- and morphologically-salient properties.
(Rappaport Hovav and Levin (1998: 106))
b. In contrast, the idiosyncratic aspect of verb meaning serves to differentiate a verb from other verbs sharing the same structural aspects of meaning; the idiosyncratic aspect is not relevant to the verb's grammatical behavior.
(Rappaport Hovav and Levin (1998: 106))

Here they define "grammatically relevant" as pertinent to argument realization, syntax and morphology. As we will see later, the relevance of the structural part of verb meaning to argument realization is absolutely vital to a detailed analysis of manner of motion verbs. Conversely, they argue that the idiosyncratic part of verb meaning is not relevant to the behavior of verbs. But this proves to be not always the case when we see event coidentification in the next chapter.

3.3.2. Similar Distinctions Proposed by Other Authors

Actually, the two semantic facets are treated and represented differently by several authors predating them, such as Pinker (1989), Grimshaw (2005) and Goldberg (1995). Rappaport Hovav and Levin (1998: 106) rightly point out that "[m]uch recent work in lexical semantics either implicitly or explicitly recognizes a distinction between two aspects of verb meaning." We will now look at the three researchers in turn.

3.3.2.1. Pinker (1989)

Let us begin by looking briefly at Steven Pinker's monumental study on the relationship between lexical semantics and language acquisition. Pinker (1989) proposes a theory of the representation of grammatically relevant semantic structures, in order to resolve a paradox in language acquisition. Pinker (1989: 166) states that in order to consider verb meaning in terms of language acquisition, we need to distinguish a small, privileged set of semantic elements from others. It is these elements that determine the grammatical behavior of verbs, and he emphasizes the important role they play as follows:

(29)   Perhaps there is a set of semantic elements and relations that is much smaller than the set of cognitively available and culturally salient distinctions, and verb meanings are organized around them. Linguistic processes, including the productive lexical rules that extend verbs to new argument structures, would be sensitive only to parts of semantic representations whose elements are members of this set.   (Pinker (1989: 166))

He argues that this restricted set of grammatically relevant elements constitute the structural framework or "scaffolding" of verb meaning. The grammatically irrelevant semantic "remainder" is plugged into a compatible slot in the skeletal framework.

(30)   ... the verb definitions sought will be hybrid structures, consisting of a scaffolding of universal, recurring, grammatically relevant meaning elements plus slots for bits of conceptual information ...

(Pinker (1989: 168))

Here Pinker refers to the semantic residues as "bits of conceptual information," but Pinker (1989: 173) paraphrases them as "idiosyncratic cognitive elements."

Moreover, Pinker elucidates the inherent atomicity of idiosyncratic elements by comparing them to "a black box":

(31)   The idiosyncratic information about the topography of rolling is a black box as far as grammar is concerned, and we need not be concerned about decomposing it, ...   (Pinker (1989: 182))

This metaphor is appropriate and striking, aptly describing a defining characteristic of the idiosyncratic part of meaning. A black box literally means a piece of equipment whose internal mechanism is unknown to the user. This metaphorically denotes that the contents of the idiosyncratic component are impenetrable and inaccessible to grammar, and therefore grammatically atomic and indecomposable.

3.3.2.2. Grimshaw (2005)

Next, we take a look at the chapter titled "Semantic Structure and Semantic Content in Lexical Representation" in Grimshaw (2005). In fact, it was first circulated as a manuscript in 1993, and Rappaport Hovav and Levin (1998) refer to it as Grimshaw (1993). Grimshaw defines two facets of verb meaning as follows:

(32)   The argument I will make is that semantic properties of predicates divide into two fundamentally different kinds of information. I suggest that the division corresponds to the distinction between information that is linguistically analyzed and information that, while it may be cognitively analyzed, is linguistically atomic.

(Grimshaw (2005: 75))

The contrast between two types of meaning is described as the opposition between "linguistically analyzed" and "linguistically atomic." Here the adverb "linguistically" is used synonymously with the adverb "grammatically" in (30). The verb "analyze," which is used in the passive form, roughly corresponds to the verb "decompose" in (31). Given this parallelism, we can assume that Grimshaw (2005) refers to the same distinction between two aspects of verb meaning as Pinker (1989).

Grimshaw (2005: 76) then redescribes the characteristics "analyzed" and "atomic" as "active" and "inactive," respectively, and labels the two different facets of lexical meaning as follows:

(33) The aspect of lexical meaning which is linguistically active I will call "semantic structure." The aspect of lexical meaning which is inactive linguistically I will call "semantic content".

(Grimshaw (2005: 76))

Here "semantic structure" refers to the structural or constructional aspect of verb meaning, whereas "semantic content" designates the idiosyncratic aspect of verb meaning.

Moreover, Grimshaw elaborates on the relationship between "semantic structure" and "semantic content" as follows:

(34) Thus *melt* and *freeze* have the same semantic structure, as do *write* and *draw*, *push* and *pull*, *sing* and *dance*. They have different semantic content, ... (Grimshaw (2005: 76))

As we have seen in (27), the two parts of verb meaning serve fundamentally different functions in Rappaport Hovav and Levin (1998). Here Grimshaw demonstrates that her "semantic structure" and "semantic content" play entirely different roles in her theory as do the structural and idiosyncratic parts of meaning in their theory. The verbs that share the same structure, such as *melt* and *freeze*, are grammatically the same, and fall under the same semantic class (in this case, they both fall under the rubric "change-of-state verbs"). But they differ in semantic content, and the difference distinguishes them within the same class.

What is more, Grimshaw stresses that semantic structure and semantic content are also different in the way they influence argument expressions. In particular, the former determines the argument structure of a predicate.

(35) Semantic structure but not semantic content determines the syntactic expression of the arguments of a predicate. For example, change-of-state predicates are unaccusative, i.e. they have no external argument, and no deep structure subject.

(Grimshaw (2005: 76))

The argument structure of a predicate is specified by grammatically relevant information; therefore, given the statements (28) and (35), it follows that Grimshaw's "semantic structure" is equivalent to "the structural part or component" in Rappaport Hovav and Levin (1998).

Indeed, Rappaport Hovav and Levin publicly acknowledge the approximate correspondences between the two kinds of meaning in Grimshaw's theory and the two components of verb meaning in their approach:

(36) For example, Grimshaw (1993) distinguishes between "semantic structure," roughly the structural component of meaning, and "semantic content," roughly the idiosyncratic component of meaning.

(Rappaport Hovav and Levin (1998: 106))

To put it the other way around, Rappaport Hovav and Levin (1998) adapt or recast Grimshaw's semantic distinction for their own theory based on event structure templates.

3.3.2.3. Goldberg (1995)

Finally, we review how Goldberg analyzes the meaning denoted by verbs and constructions. Goldberg (1995) applies a construction grammar approach to several English argument structures. We do not go into the details of her approach, but we focus on her demarcation between verb meaning and construction meaning.

She defines the nature of verb meaning as follows:

(37) Verbs, as well as nouns, involve frame-semantic meanings; that is, their designation must include reference to a background frame

rich with world and cultural knowledge. It is typically difficult to capture frame-semantic knowledge in concise paraphrase, let alone in formal representation or in a static picture. Still, it is indisputable that speakers do have such knowledge ...

(Goldberg (1995: 27))

Under her definition, verb meaning includes rich frame-semantic knowledge that is difficult to state explicitly. This is probably because the knowledge is peculiar to the background frame of each verb and not shared by other verbs. This means that Goldberg's verb meaning roughly corresponds to "the idiosyncratic part or component" in Rappaport Hovav and Levin (1998)'s theory.

Let us turn to the characteristics of her construction meaning. Goldberg (1995: 39) argues that constructions "designate a humanly relevant scene," which is abstract enough to be compatible with verbs that occur in the same construction. She characterizes it by formulating the following hypothesis:

(38) *Scene Encoding Hypothesis:* Constructions which correspond to basic sentence types encode as their central senses event types that are basic to human experience. (Goldberg (1995: 39))

Here the phrase "event types that are basic to human experience" reminds us of the statement "a scaffolding of universal, recurring, grammatically relevant meaning elements" by Pinker (1989: 168), which we have seen in (30). The adjective "basic" is not synonymous but related with the adjectives "universal" and "recurring." This suggests that Pinker and Goldberg grasp the similar concepts of the skeletal outline of verb meaning, and this observation impact on the way Rappaport Hovav and Levin (1998) analyze verb meaning.

3.3.3. Summary

In summary, we have looked at several recent theories of lexical semantics that draw a line between two types of semantic elements. Unlike McCawley (1968), which represents all verb meaning by predicates, Rappaport Hovav and Levin (1998) distinguish two facets of verb meaning, namely the structural and the idiosyncratic parts, as do Pinker (1989),

Grimshaw (2005) and Goldberg (1995). All the authors concur with the view that the structural or constructional facet of meaning determines the grammatical behavior of verbs, whereas the idiosyncratic part of meaning unique to each verb distinguishes synonymous verbs that share the same structural part of meaning. Given this consensus, we will discuss another interesting feature of their theory in detail.

3.4. Representations of the Two Components

Let us now turn to how Rappaport Hovav and Levin (1998: 107) represent lexically decomposed verb meaning. They begin by mentioning that many current theories of lexical semantics have "an articulated lexical semantic representation taking the form of a predicate decomposition." Here the adjective "articulated" means "clearly expressed," hinting that the representation must accurately reflect the crucial distinction between the two components of meaning, in contrast with McCawley (1968, 1973), which lumps them together and represents both as predicates.

As we will see below, their articulate representation system is ultimately founded on four dichotomies, namely (i) primitive predicates vs. constants, (ii) manner vs. result verbs, (iii) structure vs. constant participants, and (iv) simple vs. complex event structures. The four dichotomies are functionally interrelated and interdependent and have significant ramifications for their theory. In this section, we will examine the four dichotomies in turn.

3.4.1. Primitive Predicates vs. Constants

Rappaport Hovav and Levin (1998) explain their own articulate way of lexical decomposition as follows:

(39) A predicate decomposition is made up of two major types of components, primitive predicates and what have been called "constants." Specific combinations of primitive predicates represent the structural aspect of verb meaning, while the constants represent the idiosyncratic element of meaning. The various combinations of primitive predicates constitute the basic stock of lexical semantic

templates of a language....
(Rappaport Hovav and Levin (1998: 107))

The two components of verb meaning are represented by different types of elements in their semantic representations. The structural part is symbolized by combinations of predicates, whereas the idiosyncratic part is encoded by atomic constants that are not subject to further decomposition. By limiting the use of decompositional representation in the form of combinations of predicates to the structural facet of meaning, they adeptly bypass the problem of infinite decomposition that has continued to plague generative semanticists.

Here the expression "specific combinations of primitive predicates" deserves careful attention. In particular the two adjectives "specific" and "primitive" are noteworthy. The adjective "specific" often connotes that the range of something is fixed or restricted. The adjective "primitive" also suggests simplicity with no extra elements. This means that the varieties of combinations and predicates are not expected to be enormous like the repertory of predicates in McCawley (1968). Then how do they cope with the proliferation of predicates?

Rappaport Hovav and Levin (1998) do not definitely state how many kinds of predicates they assume, but they enumerate the possible combinations of predicates. Rappaport Hovav and Levin (1998: 107) posit "an inventory of lexical semantic templates consisting of various combinations of primitive predicates," and dub the templates "event structure templates."

They use the term "event structure" because they presume that the structural facet of verb meaning represented by combinations of predicates defines "types of events, which correspond roughly to [...] Vendler-Dowty aspectual classes of verbs" (Rappaport Hovav and Levin (1998: 106)). In other words, they directly associate or equate event types with aspectual classes proposed by Vendler (1957). But as we will see in sections 3.5–3.7, they are compelled to revise this idea in their later papers.

The inventory of event structure templates they compile is as follows:

(40) a. [x ACT$_{<MANNER>}$] (activity)
 b. [x $<STATE>$] (state)
 c. [BECOME [x $<STATE>$]] (achievement)

d. [[x ACT$_{<MANNER>}$] CAUSE [BECOME [y <*STATE*>]]]
(accomplishment)
e. [x CAUSE [BECOME [y <*STATE*>]]] (accomplishment)
(Rappaport Hovav and Levin (1998: 108))

In the inventory, they attach aspectual labels to the event structure templates, since they assume that the aspectual properties of verb meaning are in most cases fully determined by event structures. Here the capitalized verbs ACT, CAUSE and BECOME are primitive predicates, while the italicized capitals in angle brackets represent constants. The latter are associated with or integrated into the former, and the resultant structures represent the whole meaning of verbs.

Rappaport Hovav and Levin (1998: 108) add that the list of event structure templates is "fixed", or unable to be changed. This implies that the five templates are all and only structures they postulate, and represent all the events that are assumed to occur.[2] Interestingly enough, this dovetails with the fact that Vendler (1957) proposes only four time schemata and Smith (1997) classifies all situations into just five idealized types. That is to say, the variety of event structures and that of aspectual classes are both limited, and are thus assumed to correlate closely. This clearly suggests that the event structure templates introduced by Rappaport Hovav and Levin (1998) are initially grounded in the aspectual classification based on time schemata.

They go on to state that the group of constants, by contrast, is "open-ended," that is, there is no limit on the number of constants. This means that a myriad of constants are associated with the same event structure template and spawn a cornucopia of different verbs. The vocabulary of languages is also open-ended, and thus it can be said that the open-endedness of vocabulary is reflected by that of constants.

Then how are constants related with event structure templates? Rappaport Hovav and Levin (1998: 108) formulate the following rules according to which constants are integrated into event structure templates:

---

[2] One might wonder why there are two accomplishment templates, but Rappaport Hovav and Levin have not given a clear and plausible reason up to now.

(41) a. manner → [x ACT$_{<MANNER>}$] (e.g., *jog, run, creak, whistle,* ...)
 b. instrument → [x ACT$_{<INSTRUMENT>}$]
   (e.g., *brush, hammer, saw, shovel,* ...)
 c. placeable object → [x CAUSE [BECOME [y WITH <*THING*>]]]
   (e.g., *butter, oil, paper, tile, wax,* ...)
 d. place → [x CAUSE [BECOME [y <*PLACE*>]]]
   (e.g., *bag, box, cage, crate, garage, pocket,* ...)
 e. internally caused state → [x <*STATE*>]
   (e.g., *bloom, blossom, decay, flower, rot, rust, sprout,* ...)
 f. externally caused state → [[x ACT] CAUSE [BECOME [y <*STATE*>]]]
   (e.g., *break, dry, harden, melt, open,* ...)
   (Rappaport Hovav and Levin (1998: 109))

They refer to them as the "fundamental canonical realization rules," and the name of the rules does not deny the existence of other rules, since the adjective "fundamental" implies that there exist other less important rules.

Rappaport Hovav and Levin (1998: 108) argue that there are two ways of incorporating constants into event structure templates. One way is to attach constants as (subscript) modifiers to ACT predicates, as shown in (41a) and (41b). This sort of constant denotes a manner of activity in a broad sense. The other is to put constants into the argument positions of predicates in event structure templates, and as a result they "serve as arguments of predicates." This type of constant encodes some kind of resultant state.[3]

3.4.2. Manner vs. Result Verbs

Another intriguing feature of their theory is a sharp distinction between manner and result verbs. As mentioned in chapter 2, this distinc-

---

[3] A close examination of the rules in (41) reveals that some of the proposed templates are not among the enumerated event structure templates in (40). Above all, (41c) is highly problematic because both the predicate WITH and the constant <*THING*> are not mentioned, let alone defined in other parts of Rappaport Hovav and Levin (1998). (41a) and (41d) is less problematic, but in order to reconcile them with the templates in (40), we still have to reinterpret $_{<INSTRUMENT>}$ as a kind of $_{<MANNER>}$, and <*PLACE*> as a variety of <*STATE*>. However, we will not probe deeper into the matter, since the problematic templates are not directly concerned with motion verbs, which we will pursue further.

tion is closely related with satellite-framed and verb-framed lexicalization. Characteristically, motion verbs in satellite-framed languages lexicalize a co-event or a manner, whereas motion verbs in verb-framed languages encode the core schema including a result, and in Rappaport Hovav and Levin (1998: 102), the former are called "manner of motion verbs," while the latter are dubbed "verbs of directed motion."

One of the basic tenets of their theory is manner/result complementarity. Specifically, they assume that manner verbs lexicalize a manner but no result, whereas result verbs encode a result but no manner. They first mention this complementary distribution of lexicalized meaning in Levin and Rappaport Hovav (1991: 147).

(42) [T]here do not seem to be verbs in English that lexicalize both manner/means and result/direction components. Why should these meaning components be in complementary distribution?
(Levin and Rappaport Hovav (1991: 147))

This fundamental principle underpins all their recent studies on event structure, and in Levin and Rappaport Hovav (2013: 50), it is explicitly formulated as follows:

(43) MANNER/RESULT COMPLEMENTARITY: Manner and result meaning components are in complementary distribution: a verb lexicalizes only one.   (Levin and Rappaport Hovav (2013: 50))

This complementarity has significant ramifications for the analysis of verb meaning, and we will look at them below.

Let us first look at manner verbs. Rappaport Hovav and Levin (1998) characterize them as follows:

(44) [The verbs *sweep*, *whistle*, and *run*] all lexically specify or "lexicalize" the manner in which the action denoted by the verb is carried out. [...] We therefore refer to verbs like *sweep* and *run* as "manner verbs" [...].
(Rappaport Hovav and Levin (1998: 100–101))

Among manner verbs, the verb *run* is subclassified as a verb "of manner of motion," and Rappaport Hovav and Levin give the following explanation of this subgroup:

(45) Verbs of manner of motion such as *run*, *skip*, and *jog* are distinguished from each other with respect to the manner of motion each specifies; however, no achieved location (a kind of result) is entailed by such verbs unless an explicit goal phrase is added.

(Rappaport Hovav and Levin (1998: 101))

As with other manner verbs, verbs of manner of motion lexicalize no result. In the motion domain, the result is the arrival at a place, but the verb *run* does not encode the information. They cite the sentence *Pat runs* as an example. According to Rappaport Hovav and Levin (1998: 101), the sentence does not entail that Pat leaves the place where he was before running, unless it takes a goal phrase like *to the station*. Furthermore, they point out that the sentence *Pat ran in place* does not entail "any displacement at all," which provides additional evidence for their claim.

Next we turn to result verbs. Rappaport Hovav and Levin (1998) describe the characteristics of result verbs in the following way:

(46) [R]esult verbs [...] lexicalize a particular result, but more often than not are vague as to how the result is achieved. There are two types of result verbs: one type lexicalizes a resulting state and the other a resulting location.

(Rappaport Hovav and Levin (1998: 101))

The verb *arrive* is subclassified as a verb "of directed motion," and Rappaport Hovav and Levin clarify the nature of this kind of verb as follows:

(47) Verbs which lexicalize an achieved location are the second type of result verbs. These are verbs of directed motion such as *come*, *go*, and *arrive*, which lexicalize an achieved location (and usually also a direction), but not a manner of motion.

(Rappaport Hovav and Levin (1998: 102))

Similar to other result verbs, directed motion verbs lexicalize no manner. Thus, as Rappaport Hovav and Levin (1998: 102) show, "someone could arrive at the station by running, walking, driving, or bicycling."

As we have seen in (41), manner and result verbs differ in the way their constants are integrated into event structure templates. The idiosyncratic component of the meaning of manner verbs is represented by a constant encoding a manner, or in Rappaport Hovav and Levin's terms "a manner constant." As Rappaport Hovav and Levin (1998: 100) states, a manner is a way "in which the action denoted by the verb is carried out," and so it is ontologically dependent on an activity, which is represented by the predicate ACT. Thus a manner constant must be associated with the predicate ACT, and not with other predicates such as CAUSE and BECOME. On the other hand, the idiosyncratic facet of the meaning of directed motion verbs is represented by a constant denoting a result, which we can dub "a result constant." A result arises when something "becomes" a new state; therefore it is ontologically related with "becoming", represented by the predicate BECOME. This is why a result constant must be incorporated into the argument position of the predicate BECOME.

Let us now return to two types of motion verbs. In the case of manner of motion verbs like *run*, a manner constant <*RUN*> is associated with the predicate ACT, in accordance with the canonical realization rule (41a), which is repeated below for ease of reference:

(48) manner → [x ACT$_{<MANNER>}$] (e.g., *jog, run, creak, whistle, …*)

As for directed motion verbs, no canonical realization rule is proposed in (41). However, the verb *arrive*, a directed motion verb, is generally assumed to be an achievement, whose template in the inventory (40) is repeated below for convenience:

(49) [BECOME [x <*STATE*>]] (achievement)

The canonical realization rule applied to directed motion verbs is reasonably assumed to be the following:

(50) directed motion → [BECOME [x <*STATE*>]]

(e.g., *arrive*, *enter*, ...)

Thus far, we have looked at how manner of motion verbs like *run* and verbs of directed motion like *arrive* are analyzed systematically in terms of event structure templates. Given the discussion above, it seems reasonable to conclude that the distinction between the two verb classes reflects the opposition or complementarity between manner and result verbs.

Finally, Let us return for a while to aspectual labels on the templates. Since the templates are aspectually categorized, we can associate them with the temporal schemata put forward by Smith (1997). We can link the templates of activities, accomplishments and achievements to the time schemata in Smith (1997) as follows:

(51) a. [x ACT$_{<MANNER>}$] (activity)
          I............................F$_{Arb}$
     b. [BECOME [x <*STATE*>]] (achievement)
          F$_{Nat}$ R
     c. [[x ACT] CAUSE [BECOME [y <*STATE*>]]] (accomplishment)
          I............   F$_{Nat}$ R

These diagrams tell us that there are some one-to-one correspondences between the elements in the event structure templates and those in the time schemata proposed by Smith (1997). First, in Smith's schemata, the subscript R designates the result state yielded by the change of state, and it constitutes a natural final endpoint and in turn gives telicity to the situation. As we can see from (51b) and (51c), the R matches up with the result constant <*STATE*>. This means that result constants are assumed to encode telicity. On the other hand, the dotted line between I and F denoting the successive stages of events represents durativity in Smith's time schemata. As shown in (51a), the dotted line is associated with the manner constant$_{<MANNER>}$. We can assume from this that manner constants are thought to lexicalize durativity.

In addition, because of the manner/result complementarity in (43), manner constants cannot lexicalize a result that gives rise to telicity. This automatically means that manner constants also entail atelicity.

Rappaport Hovav and Levin do not clearly state but seem to tacitly assume that result constants correspond to telicity or the existence of a natural final endpoint, and that manner constants represent durativity and atelicity. This leads ineluctably to the conclusion that result verbs are achievements or accomplishments, whereas manner verbs are activities. As a matter of fact, Rappaport Hovav and Levin (1998: 104) assume the strong correlation between the two verb classes and aspectual classification.

(52)   [W]e point out that manner verbs and result verbs have different lexical aspectual classifications: manner verbs [like *run*] are activities, whereas result verbs are either achievements (e.g., *arrive*) or accomplishments (e.g., transitive *break*).
(Rappaport Hovav and Levin (1998: 104))

Here they affirm that manner of motion verbs like *run* are activities, while the verb *arrive*, one of the directed motion verbs, is an achievement and the transitive verb *break*, a causative change of state verb, is an accomplishment. This bears out the parallels between the event structure templates and the temporal schemata shown in (51).

Assuming that we limit our discussion to the verbs cited here, their claim is correct. However, as we will see in section 3.6.2, not all result verbs are either achievements or accomplishments, and not all accomplishments are result verbs. This lack of aspectual consistency has impelled Rappaport Hovav and Levin to modify their theory in their later papers.

3.4.3. Structure vs. Constant Participants

We may now proceed to discuss the nature of participants, whose concept is already mentioned in McCawley (1968). In linguistics, participants mean someone or something involved in an event, and the meaning of the verb describing the event needs to contain accurate information concerning the participants. Then how does verb meaning store the information?

What and how many participants are involved varies from verb to verb, and cannot be reduced to a limited number of event structures. The information about participants is thus assumed to be retained in the idiosyncratic part of verb meaning that is represented by constants. Actually, Rappaport

Hovav and Levin (1998: 108) formulate the relationship between constants and participants as follows:

(53) In addition, each constant also determines the basic number of participants in the event it is associated with. For example, although both running and sweeping are activities, an event of running minimally involves the runner, while an event of sweeping minimally includes a sweeper and a surface because of the nature of sweeping itself. (Rappaport Hovav and Levin (1998: 108))

Here the phrase "because of the nature" is worth noting, because it suggests that the minimally involved participants are determined by the irreducible essence of the verb's meaning.

They cite the three verbs *run*, *sweep* and *break* as examples, the first two being manner verbs and the other a result verb. The sentences that contain the three verbs are shown below:

(54) a. Pat ran. (Rappaport Hovav and Levin (1998: 98))
 b. Terry swept the floor. (Rappaport Hovav and Levin (1998: 97))
 c. Tracy broke the dishes.
 (Rappaport Hovav and Levin (1998: 117))

The manner constants <RUN> and <SWEEP> are attached to the predicate ACT in activity templates. In contrast, the transitive result verb *break* has the result constant <BROKEN>, and it is integrated into the argument position of the predicate BECOME.

As explained in (53), each constant determines, or contains information on, associated participants, but the notation used by Rappaport Hovav and Levin does not carry any information on them. We therefore modify the notation and represent the constants as <RUN [runner]>, <SWEEP [sweeper, surface]>, and <BROKEN [breaker, breakee]>. This is nothing more than a stopgap measure to make the discussion transparent, and this strategy is not suggested by Rappaport Hovav and Levin themselves. We now look at how these constants are integrated into event structure templates.

The canonical realization rule for manner verbs, which are aspectually activities, is repeated below for convenience:

(55) manner → [x ACT_{<MANNER>}] (e.g., *jog, run, creak, whistle, ...*)

In the case of the verb *run*, the association is diagrammed as below:

Figure 1

This diagram shows that the manner constant <*RUN* [runner]> is fused with _{<MANNER>} in the activity template [x ACT_{<MANNER>}], and the runner in <*RUN* [runner]> is associated with the variable *x* in [x ACT_{<MANNER>}]. Then why is the runner associated with the variable *x*?

Rappaport Hovav and Levin (1998: 110) elucidate the relationship between the participants in constants and the variables in templates as follows:

(56) When a constant is associated with an event structure template by a canonical realization rule, the participants associated with the constant must be matched up, if possible, with appropriate variables in the event structure template. We assume that, as Goldberg (1995: 50) puts it, "semantically compatible" participants are paired with each other.   (Rappaport Hovav and Levin (1998: 110))

Here the phrase "semantically compatible" is important, but before proceeding, we should note that there is a serious discrepancy in what they say. In particular, we have to reinterpret their sloppy statement that "'semantically compatible' participants are paired with each other." They use the term "participant" to refer to someone or something encoded by constants, and apply the term "variable" to someone or something entailed by event structure templates. Therefore, they should precisely state that "a participant is paired with a semantically compatible variable."

Let us now return to the issue of semantic compatibility. As mentioned by Rappaport Hovav and Levin, the expression "semantically compatible" is utilized by Goldberg (1995, 2006) in order to explicate the relationship between participant and argument roles, which are Goldberg's versions of participants encoded by constants and variables in event structure templates:

(57) Part of a verb's frame semantics includes the delimitation of *participant roles*. Participant roles are to be distinguished from the roles associated with the construction, which will be called *argument roles*. The distinction is intended to capture the fact that verbs are associated with frame-specific roles, whereas constructions are associated with more general roles such as agent, patient, goal, ...
(Goldberg (1995: 43))

The constraint on association is dubbed "The Semantic Coherence Principle," and is explained more clearly in Goldberg (2006) than in Goldberg (1995: 50):

(58) The Semantic Coherence Principle ensures that the participant role of the verb and the argument role of the construction must be semantically compatible. In particular, the more specific participant role of the verb must be construable as an instance of the more general argument role. (Goldberg (2006: 40))

Here the second sentence is noteworthy. Couched in Rappaport Hovav and Levin's terms, this means that when a participant is "matched up with" a variable, the former must be construed or categorized as an example of the latter.

Let us look at how this works by citing the case of the verb *run* as an example. The variable x in [x ACT$_{<MANNER>}$] denotes a person who does the activity, or an agent. The "runner" is conceptually more specific and thus regarded as an instance of an "agent," which is a general concept for a variety of doers. Accordingly, the runner in the manner constant <RUN [runner]> and the variable x in the activity template are judged to be "semantically compatible," and the former is associated with the latter.

The canonical realization rule for verbs of externally caused change of state operates similarly, which is repeated below for ease of reference:

(59) externally caused state → [[x ACT] CAUSE [BECOME [y <*STATE*>]]]
(e.g., *break, dry, harden, melt, open,* ...)

Chapter 3 Event Structure Templates and their Development

As previously stated, the verb *break* is assumed to be lexicalized by the result constant *<BROKEN* [breaker, breakee]>, which is incorporated into the accomplishment template as shown below:

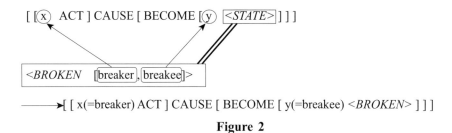

Figure 2

This diagram illustrates that the result constant *<BROKEN* [breaker, breakee]> is amalgamated with *<STATE>* in the accomplishment template [[x ACT] CAUSE [BECOME [y *<STATE>*]]], and the breaker is associated with the variable x, while the breakee is related with the variable y.

As in the case of the activity template, the variable x designates an agent. The breaker is a person or thing that does something that causes breaking, and is therefore considered to be a kind of agent. On the other hand, the variable y represents a person or thing whose state changes by the effect of the activity. This semantic role is commonly known as a theme in linguistics. The breakee changes from the unbroken state to the broken state, and is understood as a kind of theme. Consequently, the breaker and the breakee are judged to be semantically compatible with the variables x and y, respectively, and the association results. So far so good. However, we encounter difficulties when we consider the verb *sweep*.

The verb *sweep* is a manner verb, and as Rappaport Hovav and Levin (1998: 108) argue in (53), its manner constant encodes two participants, namely the sweeper and the surface. Since it is a manner verb, we have to apply the same rule as in the case of the verb *run*, but the procedure goes awry. In this case, the manner constant *<SWEEP* [sweeper, surface]> merges with $_{<MANNER>}$ in the activity template [x ACT$_{<MANNER>}$]. The sweeper is regarded as a kind of agent and matched up with the variable x in the activity template. The surface participant, however, is associated with no variable in the template, because the activity template contains only one variable, and the agent variable has been already matched up with the sweeper participant. In other words, the template has no variable that is semantically compatible with the surface participant. The figure below is indicative of this inconsistency:

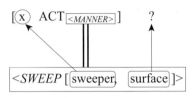

Figure 3

Naturally enough, Rappaport Hovav and Levin recognize the complication, and propose an elaborate mechanism to deal with the ostracized participant. They explain the case where a constant encode more participants than variables in the template as follows:

(60) There is, however, one complication in this process. In certain instances the constant has more associated participants than there are variables in the corresponding event structure template. In such instances, some participants are not paired with variables in the event structure participant. (Rappaport Hovav and Levin (1998: 110))

In brief, the excluded participant is not matched up with variables in the template. Rappaport Hovav and Levin (1998: 111) go on to argue that the surface participant is integrated into the activity template by being "simply licensed by the constant." In other words, the activity template initially has one variable encoding an agent, but when a constant encoding two participants are associated with the template, the constant adds a new variable to the template and associates the extra participant with it. The additional variable y is underlined to show that it is different from the variables that originally exist in the event structure template.

Chapter 3 Event Structure Templates and their Development   101

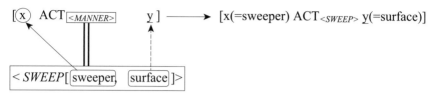

Figure 4

As a result, the surface participant is sanctioned by the constant alone, since the event structure template does not at first contain the corresponding variable. This type of participant is called a constant participant. On the other hand, the sweeper participant is not only encoded by the constant, but also licensed as an agent (that is, the original variable *x*) by the event structure template. This kind of participant is therefore dubbed a structure participant.

Rappaport Hovav and Levin (1998: 111) explain the rationale behind the distinction between two types of participants as follows:

(61) In fact, Grimshaw (1993) argues convincingly for making a dichotomy among arguments along roughly these lines based on differences in the behavior of the two types of arguments; she refers to them as "structure" and "content" arguments, respectively; we will refer to them as "structure" and "constant" participants.

(Rappaport Hovav and Levin (1998: 111))

Here Rappaport Hovav and Levin (1998) acknowledge that they incorporate Grimshaw's dichotomy of arguments into their theory based on event structure templates as the distinction between structure and constant participants.

Let us now look closely at Grimshaw (2005), part of which is a revised version of Grimshaw (1993). She expounds on the dichotomy between structure and content arguments as follows:

(62) Comparing a pair of verbs such as a causative like *melt* and a transitive activity predicate like *study* we find an interesting difference in the status of the object arguments. While it is clear that the object of a verb like transitive *melt* figures in the verb's semantic structure, since it is the argument of a change-of-state predicate, it is much less clear that the object of *study* is an argument by virtue

of the structure of the predicate. Rather it seems plausible that the structure simply involves an activity, and it is the content of the activity that determines that it can involve another argument. Let us then surmise that there is indeed such a distinction, and label arguments that are present by virtue of semantic structure "structure arguments" and arguments that are present by virtue of semantic content "content arguments."   (Grimshaw (2005: 80-81))

Here Grimshaw refers to the transitive verbs *melt* and *study* as examples. As she states, the verb *melt* denotes a change of state, which is considered to be a kind of result, and so it is a result verb in Rappaport Hovav and Levin's theory. The verb *study*, on the other hand, means that someone does the activity of learning or gaining knowledge, and Grimshaw rightly characterizes it as an activity verb, and it is a manner verb in the framework of Rappaport Hovav and Levin.

Grimshaw states that the object of the verb *melt* "figures in the verb's semantic structure," and it corresponds to the variable *y* in the accomplishment template in (40). On the other hand, the status of the object of *study* is much less clear, and she states that "the content of the activity," that is, the idiosyncratic part of the meaning of the verb *study*, "determines that it can involve another argument," namely the studying material. She illustrates the difference between the objects of *melt* and *study* as follows:

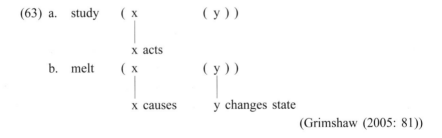

(Grimshaw (2005: 81))

The content of the diagrams can be easily converted into the event structure form and the results are as follows:

Chapter 3 Event Structure Templates and their Development   103

Figure 5

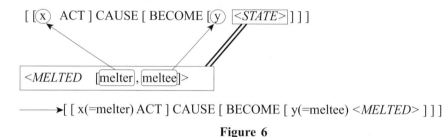

──────► [[x(=melter) ACT] CAUSE [BECOME [y(=meltee) <*MELTED*>]]]

Figure 6

This convertibility indicates that the analysis proposed by Rappaport Hovav and Levin has a lot in common with other theories, and is reasonably thought to reflect the linguistic universality adequately.

3.4.4. Simple vs. Complex Event Structures

Finally, we consider the complexity of event structure templates. Rappaport Hovav and Levin (1998: 104) use the term "complex event" in order to refer to an event "composed of two subevents," and Rappaport Hovav and Levin (1998: 108) apply the term "simple event" to Vendlerian achievements, but they do not delve further into the opposition between simple and complex event structures.

In Levin (1999, 2000) and Levin and Rappaport Hovav (1999), however, the distinction takes on a new significance, and recurs throughout these papers with its ramifications for argument expression. Therefore we will look at these later papers and mull over the implications of the distinction. Let us begin by looking at the following definition of the opposition:

(64)   Simple event structure templates consist of a single subevent; complex event structure templates are themselves constituted of two

subevents, each taking the form of what could independently be a well-formed simple event structure template. (Levin (1999: 229))

Here a complex event structure template is defined as comprising two subevents, each of which constitutes a simple event structure template. This means that a complex event structure template is a synthesized form of two simple event structure templates.

Then we wonder what combines the two templates. The answer lies in the following list of templates:

(65) Simple event structure templates:
  a. [x ACT$_{<MANNER>}$] (activity)
  b. [x <STATE>] (state)
  c. [BECOME [x <STATE>]] (achievement)
(66) Complex event structure template:
  [[x ACT$_{<MANNER>}$] CAUSE [BECOME [y <STATE>]]] (causative)
(Levin (1999: 229-230))

Unlike Rappaport Hovav and Levin (1998), which we have seen in (40), Levin (1999) classifies templates into two groups according to complexity. She gives only one example of a complex event structure template, and it is made up of an activity template and an achievement template, both of which are simple event structure templates, and the predicate CAUSE puts them together. This relation can be diagrammed as below:

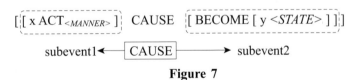

Figure 7

This is the same template as that of (40d), though relabeled "causative."

In the preceding section, we have compared the two transitive verbs *sweep* and *break*, and confirmed that the former is an activity verb and its object expresses a constant participant, whereas the latter is an accomplishment verb and its object syntactically realizes a structure participant. The template representations of their meaning are as follows:

(67) a. [x ACT_{<SWEEP>} y] (activity)
b. [[x ACT] CAUSE [BECOME [y <BROKEN>]]]
(accomplishment)

In fact, the complexity of event structure templates determines whether the direct object of transitive verbs is omissible or not, and this is shown at the beginning of Rappaport Hovav and Levin (1998).

(68) Although *sweep* may occur without an object even in the absence of any context, *break* cannot, and it is even difficult to think of a context that would improve an example such as [(69b)].
(69) a. Leslie swept.
b. *Kelly broke. (Rappaport Hovav and Levin (1998: 102))

In order to explain the difference in omissibility, Rappaport Hovav and Levin (1998: 112-113) propose two well-formedness conditions, namely the Subevent Identification Condition and the Argument Realization Condition. These two conditions, however, constitute a complicated and less explicit system, and so they have been superseded by the Argument-Per-Subevent Condition in Levin and Rappaport Hovav (1999: 202), Levin (2000: 425) and Rappaport Hovav and Levin (2001: 779).

Levin (2000) emphasizes the importance of the distinction between simple and complex event structures and points out that "argument realization patterns […] reflect event complexity." She defines the more explicit condition as follows:

(70) THE ARGUMENT-PER-SUBEVENT CONDITION: There must be at least one argument XP in the syntax per subevent in the event structure. (Levin (2000: 425))

Levin explains how this condition is satisfied as follows:

(71) If correct, the Argument-Per-Subevent Condition requires that event structures with two subevents give rise to sentences with a subject and an object, while simple event structures give rise to sentences which only need a subject. (Levin (2000: 425))

This means that the number of subevents tallies with that of obligatory arguments. We will go into specifics about what this means below.

For example, the verb *sweep* is a transitive verb and its constant encodes two participants. However, it is a manner constant and thus associated with the simple event structure template representing an activity event. The activity template consists of one subevent, as shown below:

$$[\ x\ ACT_{<SWEEP>}\ \underline{y}\ ]\ \text{(activity)}$$

subevent1

Figure 8

As a result, only one argument must occur in syntax, and this is corroborated by the omissibility of the object.

(72) Leslie swept (the floor). (Levin (2000: 425))

It is worthwhile to note that the subject is never omitted. The syntactic obligatoriness of subjects in English is known as a hypothesis named the Extended Projection Principle (EPP) in linguistics. Then this hypothesis might explain the reason why the subject of the verb *sweep* cannot be omitted in English. But there is another way to look at this issue. The underlined variable *y* is not an essential ingredient of the template, but an extrinsic element introduced by the constant. It is therefore assumed that the added variable *y* is irrelevant or "invisible" to the Argument-Per-Subevent Condition. In either case, only the variable *x* associated with a structure participant must be realized in syntax.

In contrast, the verb *break*, which is also a transitive verb, has a result constant associated with the accomplishment or causative template. The template is complex and is composed of two subevents, which are the activity and the achievement templates.

$$[\ [\ x\ ACT\ ]\ \ \ CAUSE\ \ \ [\ BECOME\ [\ y\ <BROKEN>\ ]\ ]\ ]$$

subevent1 subevent2

Figure 9

Chapter 3 Event Structure Templates and their Development   107

In this case, the template contains two subevents and thus two arguments are obligatory; therefore the object of the verb *break* cannot be omitted, even if its content is recoverable from the context.

(73) *Kelly broke again tonight when she did the dishes.
(Levin (2000: 425))

Here we can infer from the context that it is the dishes that Kelly broke, but the sentence *Kelly broke again* is unacceptable.

Finally, we look at the intransitive verb *run*. It has a manner constant, which is associated with the simple activity template containing one subevent.

$$[\text{ x ACT}_{<RUN>}]\text{ (activity)}$$

subevent1

Figure 10

The constant encodes one participant, and the Argument-Per-Subevent Condition requires one argument in syntax. Consequently, the sole variable x in the activity template is realized as the subject in syntax, and this verb is usually intransitive.

What we have seen boils down to the following statement:

(74) Verbs of surface contact and motion have a simple event structure with a single subevent, while, as causatives, change of state verbs have a complex event structure with two subevents. By the Argument-Per-Subevent Condition, change of state verbs are expected to be transitive, while verbs of surface contact and motion need not be, though they describe events with two participants.
(Levin (2000: 425))

Each subevent contains a variable that is associated with a structure participant, and this intrinsic variable must be realized as the subject or the object of a sentence in syntax. Given this, we can reinterpret the Argument-Per-Subevent Condition as stipulating that the number of intrinsic variables, which equals the number of structure participants encoded by constants, has to tally with the number of arguments that must be syntactically realized.

3.5. Revision of Notions of Manner and Result

As we have seen in (40), Rappaport Hovav and Levin (1998) equate manner verbs with activity verbs, and are firmly convinced that result verbs can be either achievements or accomplishments. However, this rash and incorrect conclusion is reexamined in their recent papers. In this section, before proceeding to a discussion of how they revise their theory, we will look at the theoretical rationale behind their departure from aspectual characterizations of manners and results.

3.5.1. Divergence from Aspectual Definition

Levin (1999) reconsiders the identification of event structure templates with aspectual classes, suggesting that except for the stative event structure template, aspectual labeling is sometimes inappropriate.

(75) [Rappaport Hovav and Levin (1998: 108)] provide these types with aspectually-motivated labels since as a first approximation such labels seem appropriate and have been adopted in other work. Although it seems right to posit an aspectually-characterized stative event type, whether the other types of simple events should receive an aspectual characterization is a matter requiring further evaluation. (Levin (1999: 230))

Here she says that the aspectual characterization of the other three templates is "a matter requiring further evaluation." In fact, as we will see below, she and Rappaport Hovav try to reevaluate their event structure templates in their later papers, and abolish the strong correlation between event structure and aspectual classification.

Moreover, Levin (2000) argues definitely that aspect cannot solve all the problems regarding event structure and argument realization.

(76) Yet, despite the enthusiasm for aspectual notions that their proliferation demonstrates, I propose that such notions are not the panacea that their considerable use would suggest. (Levin (2000: 413))

As we have seen in section 3.1, aspectual notions were introduced by Vendler (1957). Since then, they have been widely used in linguistics, and numerous studies have been made. Researchers have been amassing an impressive body of findings on aspectual features, including reliable diagnostic tests for telicity and durativity. In other words, studies on aspect provide well-established methods of analyzing the aspectual meaning of verbs. Accordingly, we are tempted to apply the same methods to analysis of all facets of verb meaning, most notably a detailed analysis of decompositional predicates in semantic representations. Levin (2000) raises this issue and explains as follows:

(77) Since the Vendler classes define a set of event types in terms of their temporal contours, their predicate decompositions would be expected to be temporal in nature. Yet representations such as those in [(40)] are only temporal if the primitives themselves are given such an interpretation, ... (Levin (2000: 414))

Supposing that aspectual notion does not characterize event structure, what does? Rappaport Hovav (2008) and Rappaport Hovav and Levin (2010) argue that the answer should be the concept of scale, and this issue will be discussed in more detail in section 3.7.

3.5.2. Nonaspectuality of Lexical Decomposition

As we have seen in section 3.2, lexical decomposition is launched by generative semanticists. However, it has to be emphasized that though they use predicates to decompose the meaning of verbs, they do not characterize them temporally or aspectually, except for Dowty (1979). This fact has been largely neglected by linguists, and predicates and event structure have been tacitly assumed to represent the flow of time from left to right. This assumption prevails among some lexical semantic studies, and is epitomized by Pinker (1989) and Kageyama (1996: 90), to name but a few.

More recently, Rappaport Hovav (2008) has pointed out that predicate decompositions are initially designed to explain the selectional restrictions and entailments shared between verbs.

(78) However, predicate decompositions of this sort were not originally developed with lexical aspect in mind. They were first introduced by generative semanticists (Lakoff 1968[a], McCawley 1968) to capture systematic morphological relations between classes of verbs and shared selectional restrictions and entailments between them, as in the following triad:

(79) a. The soup is cool.
b. The soup cooled.
c. The chef cooled the soup.   (Rappaport Hovav (2008: 14))

Generative semanticists assumed that there were fewer grammatical categories in deep structure than in surface structure, and not only verbs but also adjectives, adverbs, and prepositions were represented in deep structure by predicates matching or decomposing their surface form. By doing so, they tried to systematically explain every aspect of selectional and co-occurrence restrictions, but we should note that they did not refer to aspectuality.

Evidence corroborating this is readily seen in some statements of then generative semanticists. For example, Lakoff (1968b: 7) argues that the two sentences of (80) "can be analyzed as having essentially the same underlying structure."

(80) a. Seymour sliced the salami with a knife.   [NP_1-V-NP_2-with-NP_3]
b. Seymour used a knife to slice the salami.
[NP_1-use-NP_3-to-V-NP_2]
(Lakoff (1968b: 6, 7))

Lakoff justifies his analysis by stating:

(81) If there exists a level of linguistic analysis at which generalizations about selectional restrictions and co-occurrence are stated, then the constructions of [(80)] must have essentially the same representations at this level.   (Lakoff (1968b: 22))

What is crucial here is that his semantic representations encode selectional and co-occurrence restrictions, and not aspectual classification.

A similar single-minded commitment to semantic selection and co-occurrence is observed in other studies in terms of generative semantics, as epitomized by the following statement:

(82) A theory which claims that verbs and prepositions are essentially different categories at the level of derivation at which selectional restrictions are stated would thus have to allow selectional features to be stated on both verbs and prepositions and would not explain why both categories exhibit such features; on the other hand, claiming that verbs and prepositions belong to the same category at the point at which co-occurrence restrictions are stated allows us to state selectional features on verbs alone. (Geis (1970: 20))

According to Geis, assuming that verbs and prepositions alike are represented by predicates in deep structure, the selectional and co-occurrence restrictions uniformly imposed on both of them can be elucidated systematically.

Up to now, we have looked at their theoretical motivation for dissociating event structure templates from aspectual classes. In the next section, we will examine two pieces of persuasive evidence that have impelled Rappaport Hovav and Levin to discontinue the aspectual characterization of event structure templates.

3.6. Two Pieces of Evidence against Aspectual Characterization

In the previous section, we have looked at why Rappaport Hovav and Levin have determined to reconsider the identification of event structure templates with aspectual classes. In this section, we will consider two pieces of evidence they adduce in order to justify their renunciation of the aspectual characterization of event structure templates.

Let us first consider their statement which denies the direct connection between telicity and a result state.

(83) An obvious move is to equate the notion of result with telicity […]

> Telicity is often said to involve a result state [...], and some result verbs are necessarily telic. There is reason, however, to believe that the two notions should not be equated.
>
> (Rappaport Hovav and Levin (2010: 26))

They provide two pieces of evidence that buttress their argument. The first piece of evidence suggests that the telicity of the whole sentence is determined not simply by the lexical meaning of verbs, but also by that of their direct object. The second piece of evidence demonstrates a lack of equality between aspectual telicity and resultant states encoded by result roots. We will evaluate them in turn.

3.6.1. Evidence #1: Object Determines Telicity

The first evidence comes from recent studies showing that telicity is more often determined by compositional rather than lexical factors. More specifically, as shown by Filip (2004),[4] the boundedness of the direct object determines the telicity of the whole sentence.

(84) a. Ivan ate soup *in ten minutes / for ten minutes.
    b. Ivan ate the soup in ten minutes / for ten minutes.
    c. Ivan ate three pears in ten minutes / *for ten minutes.

(Filip (2004: 92-93))

The three sentences have the same verb *eat*, but they differ in telicity. When the uncountable noun *soup* is used without an article as in (84a), the referent is construed as unbounded, and the unboundedness in turn leads to atelicity in the verbal domain. The whole situation is consequently an atelic activity. On the other hand, as in (84c), when the countable noun *pear* is used in the plural form with the cardinal quantifier *three*, a set of three pears marks a boundary and makes the whole situation telic. Moreover, as in (84b), when the uncountable noun *soup* is used with a definite article, the whole situation has both telic and atelic interpretations, since the boundedness marked by the definite article is not necessarily mapped to telicity in

---

[4] This paper is erroneously cited as Filip (2005) in Rappaport Hovav and Levin (2010).

the verbal domain. In short, the telicity of the situation is not determined conclusively by the verb alone. This means that telicity cannot be encoded by the event structure template that represents the lexical meaning of verbs.

3.6.2. Evidence #2: Telicity does not Equal Result

Secondly, Rappaport Hovav and Levin (2010: 27) suggest that telicity should not be equated with an encoded result.

(85) More importantly, lexical telicity fails to appropriately distinguish manner and result verbs. Although the verbs that these studies reveal to be lexically telic are result verbs (e.g., *arrive*, *reach*, *die*, *crack*, *find*), many result verbs are not lexically telic.

(Rappaport Hovav and Levin (2010: 27))

As we have seen in (52), Rappaport Hovav and Levin (1998: 104) argue that "result verbs are either achievements (e.g., *arrive*) or accomplishments (e.g., transitive *break*)," which conversely implies that accomplishments are result verbs. By separating telicity from the result encoded by result constants, Rappaport Hovav and Levin (2010) debunk their earlier statements.

To support their argument, they present two linguistic facts. The first is that not all result verbs are telic, namely either achievements or accomplishments. The second is that not all accomplishment verbs are result verbs. We will review the two cases in turn.

3.6.2.1. Evidence #2(1): Result Verbs are not Necessarily Telic

Let us first look at the result verbs that are not necessarily telic. Rappaport Hovav and Levin cite the transitive verb *cool* as an example, which is categorized as a degree achievement.

(86) a. The chemist cooled the solution for three minutes.
    b. The chemist cooled the solution in three minutes; it was now at the desired temperature.

(Rappaport Hovav and Levin (2010: 27))

The term "degree achievement" was coined by Dowty (1979: 88) in recognition of the "verbs which would seem to be achievements on some semantic and syntactic grounds but which nevertheless allow durational adverbs." The following are Dowty's own examples:

(87) a. The soup cooled for ten minutes.
  b. The ship sank for an hour (before going under completely).
  c. John aged forty years during that experience.

(Dowty (1979: 88))

Dowty (1979: 88) states that the intransitive verb *cool* has "an inchoative meaning 'come to be cool'," and the predicate "come to be" shows that the verb *cool* is a result verb, and specifically a change of state verb. Intransitive change of state verbs are usually telic achievements because when the change occurs, it marks the temporal boundary and makes the whole event telic. Nevertheless, degree achievements also display atelic behavior, and this is why Dowty deals with this type of verb as an exceptional case.

In its transitive or causative use, the result of the verb *cool* is assumed to be similarly encoded, and its event structure template is generated by the canonical realization rule (41f), repeated below:

(88) externally caused state → [[x ACT] CAUSE [BECOME [y <*STATE*>]]]
      (e.g., *break, dry, harden, melt, open,* ...)

The resultant event structure template of the transitive verb *cool* is as below:

(89) [[x ACT] CAUSE [BECOME [y <*COOL*>]]]

As shown by (86), this type of verb allows both telic and atelic interpretations. This is troublesome for the analysis by Rappaport Hovav and Levin (1998), because they label the event structure template (89) aspectually as "accomplishment," which entails that it is a telic predicate. Nevertheless, the verb *cool* allows an atelic interpretation. This means that the predicate BECOME denotes a change of state, a kind of result, but in this case no telicity is brought about by the result.

3.6.2.2. Evidence #2(2): Telic Verbs do not Necessarily Encode Result

Let us now turn to the second linguistic fact that accomplishment verbs do not necessarily encode a result. The existence of accomplishment verbs without a resultant state reveals that telicity is not always caused by resultant states. Rappaport Hovav (2008) and Rappaport Hovav and Levin (2010) refer to the verb *read* as an example:

(90) Moreover, some instances of telicity cannot be analyzed in terms of a result state since verbs such as *read* and *peruse* have telic uses that do not involve an obvious result state (Levin and Rappaport Hovav 2005; Rappaport Hovav 2008).
(Rappaport Hovav and Levin (2010: 27))

The verb phrase *read a/the book* is generally regarded as an accomplishment predicate. In fact, Rothstein (2004: 6) states that "accomplishments are processes which have a natural endpoint, such as *read the book*," and proves this fact by applying the *in*-adverbial test to the verb phrase *read a book*.

(91) Dafna read a book in twenty minutes. (Rothstein (2004: 26))

Here the predicate *read a book* occurs with *in twenty minutes*, and is therefore diagnosed as having a natural endpoint.

Rothstein (2004) offers a detailed explanation of the semantic representation of accomplishments, and in particular Rothstein (2004: 108) proposes a structure consisting of the activity event and the BECOME event that are connected by the incremental relation INCR.

In addition, she defines the BECOME event as follows:

(92) The BECOME event is constrained to be (i) a change of state, (ii) which happens to the theme participant in the activity event, (iii) while the activity event is going on. (Rothstein (2004: 108-109))

Here the expression "the theme participant in the activity event" is noteworthy, because the participant is assumed to correspond semantically to the added variable in the activity template. Furthermore, she assumes that the argument of the BECOME event has the same reference as the theme participant in the activity event. Given these assumptions, Rothstein (2004: 109) argues that "the BECOME event associated with *read "War and Peace"* will be BECOME-READ(e2) ∧ Arg(e2)=Th(e1)."

Rothstein's semantic representation of "read 'War and Peace'" can be represented in the form of event structure templates as follows:

(93) [[x ACT y] CAUSE [BECOME [y(=y) <*READ*>]]]
$$\text{(y=y="War and Peace")}$$

Rappaport Hovav (2008: 33), however, argues against Rothstein's analysis and asserts that the semantic representation of the verb *read* contains no BECOME event. This means that the event structure template of the verb *read* should be (94) rather than (93).

(94) [x ACT$_{<READ>}$ y]

To buttress her argument, Rappaport Hovav cites two pieces of evidence, which we will look at in turn.

The first piece of evidence is that "the direct object of the verb is not an affected object" (Rappaport Hovav (2008: 33)). To put it differently, the object of the verb *read* does not undergo a change of state. In fact, she refers to this fact in the preceding page of the paper:

(95) [The verb] *read* does not entail a change in the denotee of its direct object, but rather in that of its subject. If you want to know if a road sign was read by someone, you don't check anything about the road sign, but you do check something about the reader.
(Rappaport Hovav (2008: 25))

It is certainly ludicrous to argue that the road sign changes its state from "unread" to "read" by being read, and the same is true for reading a book. It is the reader that undergoes a change of state, that is, the change from the state of having no knowledge to that of having some knowledge.

Let us turn to the second piece of evidence, which is based on two semantic tests:

(96) The second, more important, argument is that verbs like *read*, even on their telic reading, are not associated with a result state, which all predicates assumed to involve a BECOME event should have. Verbs such as *read* and other information ingestion verbs, such as *study* and *peruse*, do not pass any of the tests which have been offered to probe the existence of a state predicate.

(Rappaport Hovav (2008: 33))

Here Rappaport Hovav states that no lexically encoded resultant state arises as a result of reading, and her argument is based on two semantic tests for the presence of resultant states.

The first test is based on ambiguity in the interpretation of *again*. This test has been in use since the Generative Semantics period. Dowty (1979: 252) describes the two interpretations of (98) as (97):

(97) [W]e can describe the two readings of [(98)] as the *external* reading (John has performed the action of closing the door at least once before) and the *internal* reading (John has brought it about that the door is again in a closed state, though he need not have closed it on any earlier occasion):

(98) John closed the door again.   (Dowty (1979: 252))

Here Dowty's terms "internal" and "external" are highly informative. The external reading of the adverb *again* denotes that the whole event occurs again, whereas the internal reading describes that the object again gets into the resultant state caused by the event. The resultant state is entailed by the event, that is, semantically part of the event, and Dowty's terminology properly reflects the part-whole relationship between them.

More recently, the internal and external readings have been renamed restitutive and repetitive readings, respectively. Schäfer (2009: 652) represents the difference between the two interpretations by associating the adverb *again* with the two different positions in template representations.

(99) Under the *restitutive* reading, the subject causes the door to return to its previous state of being open; no further opening event is presupposed [cf. [(100b)]]. Under the *repetitive* reading, the subject

opens the door and it is presupposed that he had done this before [cf. [(100c)]]. (Schäfer (2009: 652))

(100) a. He opens the door again
b. [he CAUSE [BECOME (*again* [the door <OPEN>])]]
c. (*again* [he CAUSE [BECOME [the door <OPEN>]]])
(Schäfer (2009: 652))

We can convert Schäfer's representations into Rappaport Hovav and Levin's version of event structure templates as follows:

(101) a. [[x ACT] CAUSE [BECOME (*again* [y <*OPEN/CLOSE*>])]]
(internal/restitutive reading)
b. [(*again* [x ACT] CAUSE [BECOME [y <*OPEN/CLOSE*>]])]
(external/repetitive reading)

As suggested by Dowty (1979: 252) and Schäfer (2009: 652), ambiguity does not arise when verbs do not have a complex event structure, that is, when they are activities, achievements or statives.

Let us now return to Rappaport Hovav (2008). She applies this ambiguity test to the verbs *read*, *scan* and *peruse*, which she states are accomplishments but not result verbs. She applies the same test for comparison to the activity manner verb *tickle*, and the verbs *open*, *close*, *fill*, which are all typical cases of accomplishment result verbs. Her explanation and the results of the test are as follows:

(102) In [(103)] below, for example, there is a reading in which the door had been open and I caused the door to be in this state once more (though we do not know if it had been opened by anyone before). The other reading is of course one in which there were two events of door-opening. Transitive verbs which do not lexicalize a state do not show this ambiguity. *I tickled my daughter again* can only mean that there were two events of my daughter having been tickled. The verbs in [(103)] all clearly involve a lexicalized result state. In contrast, the verbs in [(104)] are traditional incremental theme verbs, and they do not show this ambiguity.

(103) a. I opened the door again. (ambiguous)
 b. I closed the window again. (ambiguous)
 c. I filled the jar again. (ambiguous)
(104) a. I read the book again. (not ambiguous)
 b. I scanned the book again. (not ambiguous)
 c. I perused the article again. (not ambiguous)

(Rappaport Hovav (2008: 33))

Here it is shown that the verbs *open, close, fill* are ambiguous between the restitutive and repetitive readings of *again*, whereas the verbs *read, scan* and *peruse*, as well as the manner verb *tickle*, have only the repetitive reading. This illustrates that the verbs *read, scan* and *peruse* do not encode a resultant state. These linguistic facts are represented by event structure templates as follows:

(105) a. (*again* [x ACT$_{<TICKLE /READ/SCAN/PERUSE>}$ y])
(external/repetitive reading)
 b. *[[x ACT] CAUSE [BECOME (*again* [y <*TICKLED/READ* ...>])]]
(internal/restitutive reading)

The results of the test indicate that the verbs *read, scan* and *peruse* do not have a complex event structure, and that Rothstein (2004) distorts the truth in order to reconcile the interpretation of the verb *read* with her theory. The verb *read* has no BECOME predicate in its event structure template. This means that the verb *read* is not a result verb but a manner verb in spite of its telicity.

The second diagnostic test for a resultant state is based on the "repair" or coerced interpretation of *for*-adverbials. As we have seen in section 3.1.3, *for*-adverbials essentially act as a diagnostic for atelicity and specify how long the atelic events continue. This straightforward interpretation of *for*-adverbials, in which an atelic event continues for the period of time, can be represented in terms of event structure templates as follows:

(106) Sam walked for an hour: (*for an hour* [x ACT$_{<WALK>}$])

However, as Tenny (1994: 6) points out, *for*-adverbials can have the interpretation in which "a final state, achieved at the end of the event, continues" for a certain time. In this interpretation, *for*-adverbials do not denote the duration of an atelic event, but specify the length of the interval of the resultant state denoted by a telic event. Tenny exemplifies this by the following sentence:

(107) John broke the window for a day.
(c.f. He broke it on Tuesday and it was fixed on Wednesday.)
(Tenny (1994: 6))

In this case, the resultant state "y is broken" is modified by the *for*-adverbial, and this interpretation can be represented as below:

(108) [[x ACT] CAUSE [BECOME (*for a day* [y <BROKEN>])]]

Here it is explicitly shown that the adverbial *for a day* specifies the duration of the resultant state represented by [y <BROKEN>].

This type of interpretation is introduced, or more precisely coerced, in order to reconcile the aspectual incompatibility between events and adverbials and is dubbed a "repair" reading by Kearns (2000: 205), who states as its rationale that "repair readings really demonstrate a hearer's strategy for trying to reconcile incompatible expressions." In the case of the verb *break*, the verb has a complex event structure and denotes a telic event, whereas the *for*-adverbial requires that the modified element be atelic. As a result, the *for*-adverbial seeks an atelic semantic element in the telic event structure and identifies the resultant state as such, specifying its temporal duration.

Rappaport Hovav (2008: 33–34) carries out this diagnostic test on the manner verb *tickle*, the result verbs *open*, *put* and *inflate*, and the verbs *read*, *peruse* and *deliver*.

(109) Sentences with verbs which lexicalize a reversible result state, have […] a reading in which it modifies the amount of time the result state has held. Sentences with verbs which do not lexicalize a result state do not have this interpretation. *I tickled my daughter for three minutes* only means that *I spent three minutes tickling my*

Chapter 3   Event Structure Templates and their Development   121

daughter. Crucially, verbs like *read* pattern with verbs like *tickle*.

(Rappaport Hovav (2008: 33-34))

Here Rappaport Hovav states that the verbs *read*, *peruse* and *deliver* exhibit the same behavior as that of the verb *tickle*, suggesting that *I read the book for two minutes* only means *I spent two minutes reading the book*. The results of this diagnostic are shown below:

(110) a. I opened the door for two minutes. (state reading available)
 b. I put the book on the shelf for two minutes.
(state reading available)
 c. I inflated the tube for two minutes. (state reading available)
(111) a. I read the book for two minutes. (no state reading)
 b. I perused the document for two minutes. (no state reading)
 c. I delivered the sermon for two minutes. (no state reading)

(Rappaport Hovav (2008: 34))

The results clearly demonstrate that the three verbs do not encode a resultant state, similarly to the verb *tickle*. The possible interpretations of the verbs can be represented as below:

(112) a. [[x ACT] CAUSE [BECOME (*for two minutes* [y <*OPEN/CLOSE*>])]]
 b. (*for two minutes* [x ACT$_{<TICKLE/READ/SCAN/PERUSE>}$ y])

Supposing that Rothstein were correct and the verb *read* lexicalized a result, the interpretation in which the book goes into a "read" state and remain in the state for two minutes would be possible, but Rappaport Hovav suggests that it is not the case. This means that the template below and Rothstein's theory are erroneous.

(113) *[[x ACT] CAUSE [BECOME (*for two minutes* [y <*READ/SCANNED/PERUSED*>])]]

Since they are manner verbs that do not encode a resultant state, their template should be (114).

(114) [x ACT_{<READ/SCAN/PERUSE>} y]

Up to this point we have considered Rappaport Hovav's arguments in favor of her analysis of the verb *read* as a manner verb. Her arguments are based on several reliable diagnostic procedures to identify a resultant state, and so more compelling than Rothstein's analysis of the verb *read* as an accomplishment result verb.

3.7. Alternatives to Aspectual Definition

In this section, we will look at how Rappaport Hovav (2008) and Rappaport Hovav and Levin (2010) revise their theory, departing from the original aspectual characterization. More specifically, based on the observations in section 3.6, Rappaport Hovav (2008) and Rappaport Hovav and Levin (2010) discontinue the axiomatic equation of results with telicity. As mentioned in section 3.4.1, Rappaport Hovav and Levin (1998) seem to tacitly assume that result constants encode telicity as well as resultant states, and that manner constants lexicalize atelicity as well as durativity. However, given the two piece of evidence to the contrary, it is obvious that both assumptions cannot survive intact.

3.7.1. Scalar vs. Non-Scalar Changes

In Rappaport Hovav (2008) and Rappaport Hovav and Levin (2010), they renounce the use of aspectual characterization of event structures. Instead, they introduce the concepts of scalar and non-scalar changes in order to characterize manners and results.

(115) Manner and result verbs are dynamic, and all dynamic verbs involve change (Dowty 1979). There is a fundamental distinction, however, between two types of change which are lexicalized by verbs: scalar and non-scalar changes.
(Rappaport Hovav and Levin (2010: 28))

Consequently, they reinterpret result constants as lexicalizing a scalar change, while manner constants are associated with a non-scalar change. In addition, they abandon the term "constant" and rename the idiosyncratic element "root," because the latter term is more widely accepted among linguists. Thereby, scalar and non-scalar changes are encoded by result and manner roots, respectively.

(116) We suggest that all result roots specify scalar changes, while all manner roots specify non-scalar changes. These two types of change are in complementary distribution: a root may only lexicalize one type. (Rappaport Hovav and Levin (2010: 28))

Concomitantly, the notion of result is dissociated from telicity and instead associated with scalar changes.

The expression "scalar change" literally means a change that can be represented by the points on a scale, and Rappaport Hovav (2008) defines this kind of change as follows:

(117) A scalar change is one which involves an ordered set of changes in a particular direction of the values of a single attribute and so can be characterized as movement in a particular direction along the scale. (Rappaport Hovav (2008: 17))

A scale itself is defined as comprising an ordered set of the values or degrees that are located with respect to a particular measurement. Rappaport Hovav and Levin's own definitions are as follows:

(118) a. A scale is an ordered set of values for a particular attribute.
(Rappaport Hovav (2008: 17))
b. [A] scale is a set of degrees—points or intervals indicating measurement values—on a particular dimension.
(Rappaport Hovav and Levin (2010: 28))

Then what can be regarded as scales? Rappaport Hovav (2008) delves deeply into this issue, and so we will thoroughly examine her argumentation.

3.7.2. Three Types of Scalar Changes

Rappaport Hovav (2008: 17) identifies three types of scales, namely "property scales, path scales (scales of position along a path) and volume/extent scales." Though Rappaport Hovav does not explicitly states, all the three scales are similar in that their attribute or dimension is associated with a participant playing the theta-role of theme. But there is also an essential difference between property and path scales on one hand, and volume/extent scales on the other. Given this, we will look more closely at the three scales in turn.

The first two sorts of scales are lexically specified by the idiosyncratic aspect of verb meaning and thus are encoded by result roots. Rappaport Hovav (2008) exemplifies them as follows:

(119) Property scales are associated with change of state verbs such as *lengthen*, *shorten*, *dim*, *open*, *close*, *widen* etc. Path scales, which indicate the position of a theme along a path, are associated with verbs of directed motion, such as *ascend*, *descend*, *enter*, *exit*, *come* and *go*. (Rappaport Hovav (2008: 17))

The attribute of property scales is specified by result roots lexicalizing a change of state and is given to an entity which undergoes it. Similarly, the attribute of path scales encoded by result roots specifying a directed motion is applied to an object which moves, or the figure in Talmy's terms. Here we will pay more attention to path scales, since they are embodied by motion verbs.

Rappaport Hovav argues that a path scale indicates "the position of a theme along a path." This reminds us that Talmy (1985: 61) says that a path "is the course followed or site occupied by the Figure object with respect to the Ground object," and that Talmy (2000) subsumes it under association functions. The use of the terms "scale" and "function" suggests that the values are determined with respect to another thing, and in this case it is the direction of motion or the Ground object. This will pave the way for further integration of the theory by Levin and Rappaport Hovav with Talmy's typology, which we will discuss in the next chapter.

The third type of scale is elucidated as follows:

(120) Extent scales are associated with what are often called incremental theme verbs such as *read*, *eat* and *build*. [...] [I]n most cases, the scale associated with incremental themes have a different status from the other two kinds of scales, since the scale is not directly encoded in the verb, but rather provided by the entity in the denotation of the object of the verb. (Rappaport Hovav (2008: 17))

Interestingly, a volume/extent scale is not specified only by the verb, but is also attributed to the meaning, or more precisely the boundedness, of the direct object. We have already observed in (84) that the telicity of the verb *eat* depends on the boundedness of the direct object. What is more, as we have discussed in section 3.6.2.2, the verb *read* is not a result but a manner verb. Since verbs such as *read*, *eat* and *build* form a distinct class called incremental theme verbs, they are all safely assumed to be manner verbs. This clearly shows that extent scales cannot be intrinsic to roots, since manner roots encode a non-scalar change. Rather, they are produced by the association of certain kinds of manner roots with the denotation of direct objects that provides a particular attribute or dimension.

Up to now we have considered three types of scales posited by Rappaport Hovav (2008) and qualitative differences between them. In fact, one of the noticeable differences between extent scales and the other two scales shows up dramatically in the different ways their roots and participants are combined to form a scale in event structure templates. Below we will first examine property and path scales, and then turn to extent scales.

As explained earlier, property and path scales are encoded by result roots. In addition, the themes associated with these roots are structure participants that are matched up with the variables of event structure templates. As we have seen in section 3.4.3, the theta-role of theme encoded by these types of verbs is represented by the variable y of [BECOME [y <*STATE*>]]. The event structure templates of change of state verbs and verbs of directed motion should be as follows:

(121) a. [[x ACT] CAUSE [BECOME [y <*OPEN/CLOSE*>]]]

(change of state verbs)

b. [BECOME [y <*ARRIVED/ENTERED*>]][5]

(verbs of directed motion)

In both cases, the attribute of scales is encoded by the result roots <*OPEN* [opener, openee]> and <*ARRIVED* [arriver]>, which are paired with the causative and achievement templates, respectively. Then the attribute of scales is imparted to the theme participant by the roots, and consequently the scale is made up of the degrees of the change of the theme in the former case, and the position of the theme along the path in the latter. These can be diagrammed as follows:

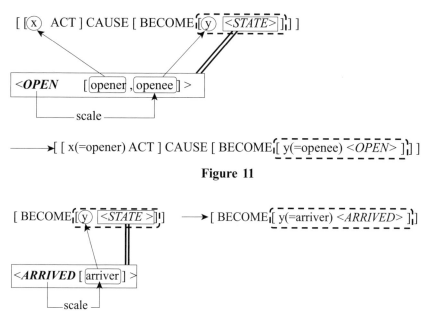

Figure 11

Figure 12

Here the boldface parts of the roots encode a scale, and the parts enclosed

---

[5] Here the sole variable in the template representing verbs of directed motion has been changed from *x* to *y* in order to standardize the notation of the BECOME subevent.

in dashed-line boxes in the templates are associated with the whole scalar changes. The point to be emphasized is that, although both the roots and the theme participants are involved in the formation of scales, it is the roots that give rise to it.

Let us now turn to extent scales, which are associated with incremental theme verbs like *read*, *eat* and *build*. As already observed, these verbs lexicalize not a result but a manner, and so their roots cannot encode a scalar change. The template representation of these verbs is as follows:

(122) [x ACT$_{<READ/EAT/BUILD>}$ y]

The roots, therefore, initially do not have a scale. Contrary to the case of property and path scales, the attribute of extent scales is encoded by direct objects which are incremental themes. More specifically, as Rappaport Hovav (2008: 26) states, "the scale is provided by the physical extent associated with [the] object denoted by the direct object." The scale is then given to or superimposed on the manner root lexicalizing the verb. The procedure is represented below:

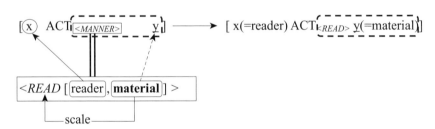

Figure 13

Unlike the roots encoding property and path scales, the boldface part encoding an extent scale is not the root itself but its constant or root participant. On the other hand, similar to the cases of the other two scales, the part enclosed in a dashed-line box in the template contains the root and one of its participants. But in this case, the participant is a constant or root participant, which does not initially exist in the template and is introduced by the root. This demonstrates that extent scales are not provided by the verb itself but are given extrinsically by the incremental theme.

3.7.3. Non-Scalar Changes

Let us now turn to non-scalar changes. Rappaport Hovav and Levin (2010: 32) start by stating that "[a] non-scalar change is any change that cannot be characterized in terms of an ordered set of values of a single attribute." Here we should note that they give a negative definition of non-scalar changes. That is to say, they characterize non-scalar changes as something other than scalar changes. This provokes the impression that the category of non-scalar changes is just a miscellaneous assortment of changes that are not scalar. In order to clarify what initially appears to be a motley collection, Rappaport Hovav and Levin add a more important and interesting feature of non-scalar changes:

(123) The vast majority of nonscalar changes deviate from scalar changes in another, more significant respect: they involve complex changes—that is, a combination of multiple changes—and this complexity means that there is no single, privileged scale of change.

(Rappaport Hovav and Levin (2010: 32))

They illustrate this point by elaborating on the verb *jog*:

(124) For example, the verb *jog* involves a specific pattern of movements of the legs, one that is different, for example, from the pattern associated with *walk*. Furthermore, even though there is a sequence of changes specified by *jog*, collectively these changes do not represent a change in the values of a single attribute [...].

(Rappaport Hovav and Levin (2010: 32))

Rappaport Hovav (2008: 18) also cites some "typical activity verbs, such as *run*, *jog*, *grimace*, and *scribble*", and provides a similar explanation for them. In short, manner of motion verbs such as *walk* and *run* lexicalize a non-scalar change, since they encode a complex combination of changes that do not constitute a change in the values of a single attribute. They present a stark contrast to verbs of directed motion, which encode path scales.

Interestingly enough, this means that non-scalar changes can contain much more detailed information than scalar ones. What is more, since non-scalar changes are made up of complex changes, one of the changes might be a change that has no scale but can be associated with a scale. If so, then is it not possible to choose one of the complex changes comprising a non-scalar change and associate it with another scalar change? Though Rappaport Hovav and Levin do not explore this possibility, we firmly believe that this gives us a reasonable explanation of how and why manner of motion verbs in English take a prepositional phrase denoting a goal and change into accomplishments. We will go into detail about the issue in the next chapter.

Finally, we look at their intriguing remark on the verb *exercise*:

(125)   Furthermore, verbs of non-scalar change need not always be so specific about the precise changes they involve. The verb *exercise*, for example, requires an unspecified set of movements, whose only defining characteristic is that they involve some sort of activity, typically physical, but on occasion mental.

(Rappaport Hovav and Levin (2010: 33))

Here we can see that the verb *exercise*, as well as the verb *study*, which is cited by Grimshaw (2005) in (62) as a semantically less clear verb, just encodes an unspecified or a schematic manner.

This in turn reveals that manner roots lexicalize non-scalar changes at different levels of schematicity. Some manner verbs, such as *walk*, *run*, *jog*, *grimace*, and *scribble*, and incremental theme verbs like *read*, *peruse*, *scan* and *deliver* are specific about a combination of changes, while others like *exercise* and *study* are highly schematic and do not specify details of the non-scalar change, except for its purpose.[6] In other words, the latter lexicalize nothing but a human activity with a particular purpose and have very little, or hardly any, specific lexical content. On the other hand, the former contain a wealth of frame-semantic knowledge, and manner of motion verbs, which fall into this category, include motion as one of the complex changes

---

[6] In Fellbaum (2013), the verb *exercise*, together with *control, help* and *treat*, is classified not as a manner verb, but as a purpose verb. We leave it for future research to determine how to reconcile the existence of purpose verbs with the manner/result complementarity.

they encode.

In brief, there are at least two cases of non-scalar changes. In the first case, they specify a conglomeration of changes that are too heterogeneous to form a single meaningful scale. The second case concerns vague changes that are too unspecified to constitute a single scale of change. In either case, they are encoded by manner roots, which are associated with simple activity templates. But are there other cases of non-scalar changes? Or is it possible to give any non-negative definition to non-scalar changes? These conundrums need to be addressed in future research.

3.7.4. Revision of Event Structure Templates

Based on the observations above, we can propose a number of refinements of event structure templates. As we have seen in 3.7.1, Rappaport Hovav and Levin (2010) suggest that result roots specify scalar changes and manner roots specify non-scalar changes. This means that the notations of manner and result roots, namely $<MANNER>$ and $<STATE>$, should be superseded by those which reflect the qualitative differences of change. In addition, in place of aspectual labels, we should attach other non-aspectual labels to the template except for the stative one. The revised templates should be as follows:

(126) Simple event structure templates:
    a. [x ACT$_{<NON\text{-}SCALAR\ CHANGE>}$]
                                              (complex changes or unspecified change)
    b. [x $<STATE>$] (state)
    c. [BECOME [x $<SCALAR\ CHANGE>$]] (single change)
    Complex event structure template:
    d. [[x ACT] CAUSE [BECOME [y $<SCALAR\ CHANGE>$]]]
                                                           (causative single change)

This modification of event structure templates paves the way for further investigation into the relationship between manner and result verbs, since both manner and result roots are shown to share the common feature: a change.

There remains, however, one vexing problem, which lies in the tautologous nature of the new labels on the event structure templates. We have replaced the notations of the roots $<$*MANNER*$>$ and $<STATE>$ with those of $<$*NON-SCALAR CHANGE*$>$ and $<SCALAR\ CHANGE>$ and concomitantly relabeled all the templates except the stative one. As a result, both roots and templates are characterized in terms of the attributes possessed by changes, and other concepts are not introduced here. This is tautological in that a template represents a certain kind of change because the root encodes the kind of change. The labels give no additional information which can be used to consider templates from a different angle. Now it is obvious that we have to find a legitimate way out of this predicament. This issue will be discussed in more detail in the next chapter.

3.8. Summary and Implications

We have begun this chapter with a brief look at aspectual classification introduced by Vendler (1957), noting that this is a quadripartite system in which verb phrases are categorized according to their time schemata into four types, namely activities, accomplishments, achievements and states. We have then examined three temporal features proposed by Smith (1997) in order to systematically explain the commonalities and differences between Vendlerian classes. We have also looked at her visual representation of temporal schemata and have presented some diagnostic tests for telicity. In section 3.2, we have looked at the lexical decomposition of the verb *kill* proposed by McCawley (1968) and its potential problem. In section 3.3, we have turned to the clear separation between two components of verb meaning espoused by Rappaport Hovav and Levin (1998) and compared it with similar distinctions proposed by other researchers. In section 3.4, we have examined how Rappaport Hovav and Levin (1998) represent the two parts of verb meaning. Their ingenious representation is made up of four dichotomies, that is, (i) primitive predicates vs. constants, (ii) manner vs. result verbs, (iii) structure vs. constant participants, and (iv) simple vs. complex event structures. We have looked at them in turn with their ramifications. In sections 3.5 and 3.6, we have considered why Rappaport Hovav and Levin (1998) reconsider their aspectual labeling of event structure templates. In section 3.7, we have reviewed the revisions Rappaport Hovav (2008) and Rappaport Hovav and Levin (2010) make to their former theory, notably all the refinements of the notions of manners and results. Finally, we have put forward the event structure templates modified to suit the conceptual refinements.

Let us now consider what the implications of the modification of their theory. As explained in section 3.4, the event structure templates were founded on aspectual classes when they were put forward by Rappaport Hovav and Levin (1998). At this point, the concept of results was directly linked to telicity. As we have seen in section 3.6, however, ample evidence has been found that disproves the simple equation of results with telicity. They have consequently refined the concepts of manners and results, identifying results with scalar changes and manners with non-scalar changes.

This remarkable turnaround in their theory has resulted in a reconsideration of the aspectual characterization of the manner/result complementarity. Rappaport Hovav and Levin (1998: 104) argue that "manner verbs are activities, whereas result verbs are either achievements or accomplishments," but the idea is no longer tenable. If we follow the suggestion that "all result roots specify scalar changes, while all manner roots specify non-scalar changes" (Rappaport Hovav and Levin (2010: 28)), then we can conclude that result verbs lexicalize a scalar change and are therefore scalar verbs, while manner verbs lexicalize a non-scalar change and thus non-scalar verbs. In fact, Rappaport Hovav (2008) radically replaces the dichotomy of manner vs. result verbs with that of scalar vs. non-scalar verbs. But Rappaport Hovav's renaming of verbs seems tautological in that the new names of the verb types do not contain much information on qualitative differences between the two types of verbs, and cloud their relationship with Talmy's terms. We therefore do not adopt her new names and continue using the terms "manner verbs" and "result verbs."

Let us return to the implications of the revision for the complementarity. Here we will look at three of the implications, only the first of which is explicitly mentioned by Rappaport Hovav and Levin.

First, by conceptually separating results from telicity, we can automatically explain why result verbs are not always telic. As we have seen in section 3.6.2.1, causative degree achievements have both telic and atelic interpretations. If we were wedded to preserving the equation of result and telicity, we would be obliged to formulate convoluted rules that associate the two interpretations with different templates or that derive one template from the other.

Second, by associating both manners and results with changes, we can automatically explain why "all dynamic verbs involve change" (Rappaport Hovav and Levin (2010: 28)). In Rappaport Hovav and Levin (1998), manner and result constants are regarded as atoms that defy further decomposition. A manner and a result are assumed to be ontologically dissimilar from each other and therefore linked with different predicates. This inevitably leads to the further assumption that they have no commonality and so cannot be associated with each other. However, as stated just above, a manner and a result, both of which are lexicalized by dynamic verbs, have the semantic element of a change in common. Their refining of the notions of manners and results makes it clear why all dynamic verbs involve a change.

Finally and most importantly, by identifying a manner with a non-scalar change consisting of complex changes, we automatically predict that a manner can be informationally much richer than a result, which denotes a simple scalar change in the values of an attribute. In other words, their refining of the definitions of manners and results throws into sharp relief the possible difference in the amount of contained information between manners and results. This suggests that a less informative result can be incorporated or integrated into a more informative manner, but not vice versa. In addition, when prepositional phrases denoting a goal occur with manner of motion verbs in English, they can be assumed to embody this incorporation.

Manner of motion verbs, which lexicalize a non-scalar change, lexicalize a complex combination of movements, including how to move legs, how to move arms, how to change positions and so on. In satellite-framed languages like English, one of the movements, in particular the last one, can be reinterpreted as moving along a path and thus associated with a path scale denoted by a prepositional phrase. In contrast, this reinterpretation process is not available in verb-framed languages. In other words, the availability of the process is concluded to be the add-on satellite-framedness discussed in the end of chapter 2.

The process is termed "event coidentification" in Levin and Rappaport Hovav (1999) and Rappaport Hovav and Levin (2001), but they, regrettably, do not associate it with event structure templates and the dichotomy between scalar vs. non-scalar changes. In the next chapter, we will concentrate two types of motion verbs and look at how they work.

Chapter 4

Event Structure Templates, Event Coidentification, and Macro-event

In the previous chapter, we have looked at how Levin and Rappaport Hovav's theory based on event structure templates has developed. In this chapter, we will relate their theory to the Unaccusative Hypothesis put forward in the framework of relational grammar, on the one hand, and to the motion macro-events depicted by Talmy (2000), on the other.

This chapter is structured as follows. Section 4.1 sketches the basic ideas of the Unaccusative Hypothesis. In section 4.2, we will scrutinize Levin and Rappaport Hovav (1992), one of their earlier studies, and point out two problems with lexical subordination. In section 4.3, we will introduce the process of event coidentification as an alternative to lexical subordination. This mechanism is proposed by Levin and Rappaport Hovav (1999) and Rappaport Hovav and Levin (2001), and so in section 4.4, we will incorporate the later advancements of their theory, notably the concept of scalarity, into event coidentification and propose the event structure template representing coidentified events. By doing so, we will elucidate the mechanism of semantic amalgamation between manner of motion verbs and goal prepositional phrases. Then in section 4.5, we will explore the possibility of relating event coidentification to the configuration of the motion macro-events proposed by Talmy (2000). Finally, in section 4.6, we will compare the event structure template of coidentified events with the template representation of lexical subordination, and clarify the advantages of event coidentification over lexical subordination. Section 4.7 is the recapitulation.

4.1. Unergative vs. Unaccusative Verbs

The distinction between unergative and unaccusative verbs is first made in the framework of relational grammar, typified by Perlmutter (1978), Perlmutter and Postal (1984) and Rosen (1984). This school assumes that grammatical relations are primitives of syntactic theory and obtain at a number of levels called strata. More specifically, the first or initial stratum roughly corresponds to the level of deep structure in Generative Semantics, and is analogous to the structural facet of meaning in semantic representations used by lexical semantics. The final stratum, on the other hand, is the nearest equivalent to surface syntactic structure. Relational grammar also posits the rules called 'advancements', by which an argument bearing one grammatical relation is promoted to a higher grammatical relation in the same clause. Within the relational hierarchy, subjects are represented as 1(-arcs) and higher than direct objects, which are expressed as 2(-arcs). This means that objects in the initial stratum are promoted to subjects under certain circumstances. With these assumptions in mind, let us look at the Unaccusative Hypothesis, which marks the differences between unergative and unaccusative verbs.

Perlmutter (1978: 160) presents the basic claim of the Unaccusative Hypothesis as follows:

(1) Certain intransitive clauses have an initial 2 but no initial 1.
(Perlmutter (1978: 160))

As we have seen in section 3.4.4, subjects are syntactically obligatory in English. Couched in the language of relational grammar, this means that there must exist a 1-arc in the final stratum. The Unaccusative Hypothesis claims that the 1-arc in the final stratum is not always the 1-arc in the initial stratum, but in some cases it has its origin in the 2-arc. Based on this assumption, initial strata are classified into the following three types:

Chapter 4   Event Structure Templates, Event Coidentification, and Macro-event   137

(2) a. A transitive stratum contains a 1-arc and a 2-arc.
   b. An unaccusative stratum contains a 2-arc but no 1-arc.
   c. An unergative stratum contains a 1-arc but no 2-arc.

(Perlmutter (1978: 160))

In the language of lexical semantics, these generalizations can be paraphrased as follows:

(3) In syntactic structure,
   a. a transitive clause contains both a subject and a direct object.
   b. an unaccusative type of intransitive clause contains only a direct object.
   c. an unergative type of intransitive clause contains only a subject.

Then we will turn to how this distinction is rendered in event structure templates below.

A transitive clause is assumed to have two arguments or variables, and so it is associated with the event structure template containing the corresponding two variables, that is, the complex causative event structure template.[1]

An unergative type contains the sole argument that plays the same thematic role as that of the first argument in transitive clauses. The argument is, therefore, associated with the variable x in the [x ACT$_{<NON\text{-}SCALAR\ CHANGE>}$] and the whole clause is expressed by the event structure template previously characterized as "activity." A close affinity between unergative and activity clauses is pointed out by Perlmutter himself as follows:

---

[1] Actually, as explicated by Levin (1999), not all transitive verbs are causative. More specifically, only transitive verbs that Levin (1999) calls 'core transitive verbs' (CTVs) are causative and therefore associated with the complex causative template. In contrast, other non-core transitive verbs (NCTVs) are assumed to have a simple event structure and thus be represented by unergative or unaccusative templates containing a root participant. Among motion verbs, transitive verbs of directed motion such as *enter* and *cross* are assumed to be represented by an unaccusative template containing a root participant.

(4) The class of initial unergative clauses seems to correspond closely to the traditional notion of <u>active</u> or <u>activity</u> (intransitive) clauses.[2]
(Perlmutter (1978: 162))

Perlmutter states that unergative clauses "can be broken down into (at least) two subcategories," as follows:

(5) <u>Predicates determining initially unergative clauses</u>
    a. <u>Predicates describing willed or volitional acts</u>
       work, play, speak, talk, smile, grin, frown, grimace, think, meditate, cogitate, daydream, skate, ski, swim, hunt, bicycle, walk, skip (voluntary), jog, quarrel, fight, wrestle, box, agree, disagree, knock, bang, hammer, pray, weep, cry, kneel, bow, curtsey, genuflect, cheat, lie (tell a falsehood), study, whistle (voluntary), laugh, dance, crawl, walk, etc.
       This category includes <u>manner-of-speaking verbs</u> such as whisper, shout, mumble, grumble, growl, bellow, blurt out, etc. and <u>predicates describing sounds made by animals</u> such as bark, neigh, whinny, quack, roar (voluntary), chirp, oink, meow, etc.
    b. <u>Certain involuntary bodily processes</u>
       cough, sneeze, hiccough, belch, burp, vomit, defecate, urinate, sleep, cry, weep, etc.   (Perlmutter (1978: 162))

Here we notice that Perlmutter cites some manner of motion verbs like *swim*, *walk*, *skip* and *jog* as examples of unergative clauses. In addition, the verb *study*, which we have examined in sections 3.4.3 and 3.7.3 as a highly schematic verb, is included in this list. We can reasonably assume from these facts that manner or non-scalar verbs, which are represented by the event structure template of "complex changes or unspecified change," are unergatives.

On the other hand, an unaccusative type has the one and only argument whose thematic role is equivalent to that of the second argument in transitive clauses. The argument in turn corresponds to the variable y in the [y <SCALAR CHANGE>], which is the state event structure template

---

[2] In the citations from Perlmutter (1978), all the underlining is in the original.

Chapter 4   Event Structure Templates, Event Coidentification, and Macro-event   139

and is also part of the event structure template formerly labeled "achievement," which now represents a non-causative scalar change. Certainly the two event structure templates are similar in that they encode a state, but they differ in several respects. In particular, the former denotes a static condition, whereas the latter encodes a scalar change without referring to the non-scalar change that gives rise to it. It is therefore difficult to provide a uniform semantic characterization of unaccusativity. Actually, Perlmutter abandons his attempt to identify unaccusative clauses semantically and instead provides a negative definition of them, stating that they are clauses that are intransitive and not unergative.

(6)   [A]n approach that seems promising is to characterize precisely the class of meanings that determine initial unergative strata, assigning initial unaccusativity to all other initially intransitive clauses.

(Perlmutter (1978: 163))

Perlmutter merely enumerates a long list of verbs, with the caveat that "[n]othing hinges on the particular subcategories given here; alternative classifications are possible":

(7)   Predicates determining initially unaccusative clauses
   a.   Predicates expressed by adjectives in English
       This is a very large class, including predicates describing sizes, shapes, weights, colors, smells, states of mind, etc.
   b.   Predicates whose initial nuclear term is semantically a Patient
       burn, fall, drop, sink, float, slide, slip, glide, soar, flow, ooze, seep, trickle, drip, gush, hang dangle, sway, wave, tremble, shake, languish, flourish, thrive, drown, stumble, trip, roll, succumb, dry, blow away, boil, seethe, lie (involuntary), sit (involuntary), bend (involuntary), etc. This includes the class of inchoatives, including melt, freeze, evaporate, vaporize, solidify, crystallize, dim, brighten, redden, darken, yellow, rot, decompose, germinate, sprout, bud, wilt, wither, increase, decrease, reduce, grow, collapse, dissolve, disintegrate, die, perish, choke, suffocate, blush, open, close, break, shatter, crumble, crack, split, burst, explode, burn up, burn down, dry up, dry out, scat-

ter, disperse, fill, vanish, disappear, etc.
c. Predicates of existing and happening
exist, happen, transpire, occur, take place, and various inchoatives such as arise, ensue, result, show up, end up, turn up, pop up, vanish, disappear, etc.
d. Non-voluntary emission of stimuli that impinge on the senses (light, noise, smell, etc.)
shine, sparkle, glitter, glisten, glow, jingle, clink, clang, snap (involuntary), crackle, pop, smell, stink, etc.
e. Aspectual predicates
begin, start, stop, cease, continue, end, etc.
f. Duratives
last, remain, stay, survive, etc. [Perhaps these should be considered a subclass of group (c) above.] (Perlmutter (1978: 162))

Here state verbs are categorized into (7a), (7d) and part of (7c), namely "predicates of existing." This shows that the state event structure templates are identified as unaccusatives.

With respect to non-stative verbs in the list, there are two important points to note. First, Perlmutter points out in (7b) that the sole participant, or the "initial nuclear term" in his terms, is "semantically a Patient." But judging from the listed verbs, notably *fall*, *drop*, *soar*, *dry*, *boil* and many inchoatives, "a theme" is a better term to describe it. Furthermore, the above enumeration of verbs proves inadequate in that it does not account for verbs of directed motion such as *arrive* and *enter*. The verb *fall*, however, is cited as an example of this class in Rappaport Hovav (2008: 17) and Levin and Rappaport Hovav (2013: 52). This suggests that verbs of directed motion should be subsumed under the category (7b). Semantically, all the verbs in (7b) encode a scalar change of state in the theme participant and are represented by the event structure template of a single change, and so the classification of verbs of directed motion into (7b) seems to be reasonable. Given these observations, we can conclude that the verbs represented by the event structure template of a single change are also unaccusatives.

Up to this point, all the three types of clauses in (3) are associated with the event structure templates in the inventory. The following list of event structure templates shows how they are classified under the Unaccusative

Hypothesis.

(8) Simple event structure templates:
 a. [x ACT_{<NON-SCALAR CHANGE>}] (unergative)
 b. [y <SCALAR CHANGE>] (unaccusative)
 c. [BECOME [y <SCALAR CHANGE>]] (unaccusative)
 Complex event structure template:
 d. [[x ACT] CAUSE [BECOME [y <SCALAR CHANGE>]]]
 (transitive, causative)

From this, we can see the following: if the template contains the predicate CAUSE, it is transitive. If the template only contains the predicate ACT, it is unergative. In all other cases, it is unaccusative. Of course, further research is needed to judge whether there is a strong one-to-one correspondence between the types of initial strata and those of event structure templates, but we adopt the assumption as a working hypothesis and continue the discussion.

4.2. The Origin of Research into Motion Verbs

In this section, we will carefully examine Levin and Rappaport Hovav (1992), one of their earlier studies. In it, they divide motion verbs into three classes according to the Unaccusative Hypothesis, which we have discussed in section 4.1. They point out that, among the three classes, the *run* verbs, or manner of motion verbs, are basically unergative but they show unaccusative behavior when they take a goal prepositional phrase. In order to explain this intriguing behavior of the *run* verbs, they introduce the mechanism of lexical subordination. But when we integrate this process into their current theory based on event structure templates, two thorny problems arise. The first is its incompatibility with the Argument-Per-Subevent Condition, and the second is that lexical subordination does not satisfactorily explain the facts about temporal adverbial modification. A viable alternative to lexical subordination will be presented in section 4.3.

4.2.1. Three Types of Motion Verbs

The distinction between "verbs of manner of motion" and "verbs of directed motion" has its origins in Rosen (1984), where she describes it as "special complications" arising with regard to motion verbs:

(9) The class of motion verbs presents special complications, such as the fact that some express manner of motion and others essentially only directionality or result of motion. (Rosen (1984: 66))

Levin and Rappaport Hovav (1992: 252) adapt this contrast to classify motion verbs into the following three classes:

(10) a. *arrive* class: arrive, come, go, depart, fall, return, descend ...
b. *roll* class: roll, slide, move, swing, spin, rotate ...
c. *run* class: run, walk, gallop, jump, hop, skip, swim ...
(Levin and Rappaport Hovav (1992: 252))

Here the *arrive* class refers to verbs expressing only directionality or a result of motion. Manner of motion verbs are subdivided into two types, namely the *roll* class and the *run* class.

Levin and Rappaport Hovav (1992) first shed some light on the *arrive* class. After indicating that the classification has its roots in Rosen (1984), they describe what the verb *arrive* means:

(11) The members of this class have sometimes been called verbs of inherently directed motion (Rosen (1984)) since their meaning includes an inherently specified direction of motion: the verb *arrive* denotes achievement of motion to a specific point [...].
(Levin and Rappaport Hovav (1992: 252))

Here we should note that Levin and Rappaport Hovav interpolate the phrase "inherently specified" into the definition. The word "inherent" means that the qualities of something cannot be separated from it, and so this suggests that the directionality is unique or idiosyncratic to each verb in the class. Though they do not use the term "idiosyncratic" in this paper, this can be regarded as an early sign of their later dichotomy between the structural and idiosyncratic components of verb meaning.

Levin and Rappaport Hovav (1992) go on to describe verbs encoding a manner of motion. As we have seen in section 3.4.2, they first mentioned the manner/result complementarity in Levin and Rappaport Hovav (1991: 147). In this paper, they apply it to motion verbs and argue that the *arrive* class is complementary to the *roll* and *run* classes.

(12) A component of meaning which appears to be in complementary distribution with direction is manner of motion. This component is present in the meanings of the *roll* and *run* verbs, and we refer to these two classes jointly as manner of motion verbs.

(Levin and Rappaport Hovav (1992: 252))

Moreover, they introduce the notion of direct external cause in order to subclassify the manner of motion verbs into two subtypes:

(13) Direct external cause subdivides the manner of motion verbs into the *run* and *roll* verbs. Running generally involves protagonist control; rolling does not necessarily, since it can be attributed to an external force, such as a push or gravity.

(Levin and Rappaport Hovav (1992: 253))

A lack of direct external cause signifies the spontaneity of the mover, and it is here described as "protagonist control," which roughly corresponds to agentivity, a semantic factor familiar to linguistics. In other words, the *run* verbs are always but the *roll* verbs are not necessarily agentive.

4.2.2. Motion Verbs and Unaccusativity

Let us now look at how the three classes of motion verbs have been analyzed in terms of unaccusativity.

As we have seen in section 4.1, the *arrive* verbs, or verbs of directed motion, are semantically assumed to be unaccusatives, and in fact, Levin and Rappaport Hovav (1992) argue that they are unaccusative.

(14) All *arrive* verbs display unaccusative behavior independent of whether or not they are used agentively.

(Levin and Rappaport Hovav (1992: 253))

Levin and Rappaport Hovav base their judgment on the possibility of locative inversion, which has been argued to be possible only with unaccusative verbs. Levin and Rappaport Hovav illustrate this point by the following examples of the verbs *come* and *go*:

(15) a. ... out of the house came a tiny old lady and three or four enormous people ...
b. And when it's over, off will go Clay, smugly smirking all the way to the box office ...

(Levin and Rappaport Hovav (1992: 254))

In these locative inversion structures, the locative expressions *out of the house* and *off* have moved from their default postverbal position to a position preceding the verbs, and concomitantly their subject and finite verb are inverted. Locative inversion is assumed to be found only with unaccusative intransitives, and therefore the examples (15) show that the *arrive* verbs are unaccusative.

What we have to consider next is manner of motion verbs. Levin and Rappaport Hovav (1992) subclassify them into the *roll* verbs and the *run* verbs, and the former class is not necessarily agentive and therefore the mover is considered to be a theme, whereas the latter is always agentive, describing a willed or volitional act, and so the mover is an agent. This difference is noticeable in the lists of unergative and unaccusative verbs compiled by Perlmutter (1978). More specifically, the verb *roll* is included in (7b), which is the second subclass of unaccusatives, while agentive manner of motion verbs like *swim*, *walk*, *skip* and *jog* are subsumed in (5a), which is the first subgroup of unergatives. In other words, it is reasonably assumed that the *roll* verbs are unaccusative and the *run* verbs are unergative. Indeed, Levin and Rappaport Hovav characterize them as follows:

(16) [T]he *roll* verbs are basically unaccusative, while the *run* verbs are basically unergative.   (Levin and Rappaport Hovav (1992: 254))

Chapter 4   Event Structure Templates, Event Coidentification, and Macro-event   145

In order to support these claims, they use locative inversion as a diagnostic for unaccusativity.

They begin by examining the verb *roll*, which is assumed to be unaccusative and actually occurs in the locative inversion construction as shown below:

(17)   She was about to tell him when in again rolled the trolley, now with afternoon tea on it.   (Levin and Rappaport Hovav (1992: 254))

Here the locative expression *in* precedes the finite verb *rolled*, which is inverted and comes before the subject. This exemplifies locative inversion, and the verb *roll* in this example is judged to be unaccusative.

Furthermore, they investigate the intriguing behavior of the verb *run*. It is well known that the verb *run*, which basically denotes an activity and is thus atelic, can be converted into a telic verb by adding a goal prepositional phrase. Levin and Rappaport Hovav (1992) explain this fact as follows:

(18)   The effect of goal phrases on the aspectual classification of the verb *run* has been widely discussed: this verb is an activity verb when it occurs without a goal phrase, but an accomplishment verb when it takes a goal phrase (e.g., Dowty 1979).
(Levin and Rappaport Hovav (1992: 258))

The relationship between goal prepositional phrases and telicity is pointed out by Dowty (1979: 60-61) and has been extensively investigated in semantics. As for the verb *run*, this phenomenon is exemplified as follows:

(19) a.   Maria ran for an hour/*in an hour.
     b.   Maria ran to the next town *for an hour/in an hour.
(Tenny (1994: 77))

Most intriguingly, it is known that goal prepositional phrases also have an effect on the unaccusativity of the *run* verbs. The connection between goal prepositional phrases and unaccusativity is first pointed out by Hoekstra (1984: 177, 242-252) and Rosen (1984: 66-67), which are concerned with Dutch and Italian examples, respectively. Here we will look briefly at Rosen

(1984).

Rosen (1984: 66) examines the behavior of the Italian counterpart of the verb *run*. Italian has a composite past tense that consists of an auxiliary and a past participle. In this sort of past tense, unergative verbs select *avere* "to have" as their auxiliary, while unaccusative verbs take *essere* "to be." Rosen applies this simple diagnostic test based on auxiliary selection to the Italian verb *correre* "to run":

(20) a. Ugo ha corso meglio ieri.
'Ugo ran better yesterday.'
b. Ugo è corso a casa.
'Ugo ran home.' (Rosen 1984: 66-67))

Here the verb *correre* takes *avere* when it occurs without a goal phrase and selects *essere* when it takes the goal phrase *a casa* "home." Given this evidence, Rosen concludes that the verb *correre* is unergative when denoting an activity, whereas it is unaccusative when it appears with a goal phrase and describes the arrival at the destination.

Let us now return to the verb *run* in English. Levin and Rappaport Hovav (1992) argue that the same effect of goal prepositional phrases on the verb *run* is observed and exemplify this as follows:

(21) The contrast in [(22)] provides evidence for the unaccusativity of *run* verbs with goal phrases, as locative inversion is only possible when the inverted PP is interpreted as defining the endpoint rather than the location of motion.
(Levin and Rappaport Hovav (1992: 259))

(22) a. *In the room ran a shrieking child.
b. Into the room ran a shrieking child.
(Levin and Rappaport Hovav (1992: 259))

Here the verb *run* has the locative inversion structure only when it takes a goal prepositional phrase as in (22b), that is, only when it is made into an unaccusative. In (22a), the prepositional phrase *in the room* does not denote a goal but the location in which the child ran around, and no conversion from unergatives to unaccusatives occurs. This is why locative inversion is impossible in (22a). This clearly demonstrates that the *run* verbs are basically unergative, but they become unaccusative when followed by a goal prepositional phrase.

4.2.3. Lexical Subordination and *Run* Verbs

Moreover, Levin and Rappaport Hovav (1992) analyze this interesting behavior of the *run* verbs in terms of lexical conceptual structures (henceforth abbreviated as LCSs), which are presumably the predecessors of event structure templates. They suppose that the LCS of the verb *run*, in its basic use as a simple activity, takes the following form:

(23)   *run* (manner of motion): [x MOVE in-a-running-manner]
(Levin and Rappaport Hovav (1992: 260))

Here the predicate MOVE corresponds to the predicate ACT in event structure templates, but the latter formulates a broader concept that also includes what is represented by the predicate DO(-SOMETHING).

For the moment let us look closely at what the predicate MOVE encodes. Levin and Rappaport Hovav (1992: 260) posit that the predicate "MOVE represents movement without any necessary displacement." Here the phrase "without any necessary displacement" means that the movers need not leave the place where they are. The dictionary definitions of the noun *treadmill* elucidate what this really means.

(24) a. a piece of exercise equipment that has a large belt around a set of wheels, that you can walk or run on while staying in the same place
(*Longman Dictionary of Contemporary English*, 5th Edition)
   b. an exercise machine that consists of a moving strip or two step-like parts on which you walk without moving forward
(*Cambridge Advanced Learner's Dictionary*, 4th Edition)

Here the expressions "walk or run on while staying in the same place" and "walk without moving forward" reveal that the denotation of the *run* verbs does not involve leaving the place or going elsewhere, which is encoded by verbs of directed motion and represented by [x GO TO y] in LCSs, as we will see below.

As we have seen in section 4.2.2, the verb *run* is assumed to be unaccusative when it occurs with a goal prepositional phrase. In order to reconcile the LCS representations with variable unaccusativity, Levin and Rappaport Hovav (1992) invoke the mechanism called "lexical subordination," which is elaborated in Levin and Rapoport (1988) and Rappaport and Levin (1988). The motive for assuming this process is to discern "when many existing English verbs can productively take on new meanings and what these new meanings may be" (Levin and Rapoport (1988: 275)), or, to put it differently, "the elasticity of verb meaning" (Rappaport Hovav and Levin (1998: 100)).

The process of lexical subordination is schematized in terms of LCSs as follows:

(25) LCS: manner/instr → LCS: [result BY manner/instr]
(BY is used to represent 'by means of' or 'in the manner of')[3]

(Levin and Rapoport (1988: 282))

The LCS written on the left side of the arrow is the input to the rule. Here it is notated as manner/instr, and this means that the input is restricted to LCSs containing information about a manner or an instrument.

Let us turn to the output or result of the process of lexical subordination. In the new LCS presented on the right side, the input LCS is subordinated and, in consequence, embedded under the LCS of result, which is further fleshed out by the predicate BECOME or GO. The predicate BY serves a crucial role in subordinating the original LCS of manner/instr to the LCS of result. Since the verb *run* contains information on a manner, its LCS can be input to lexical subordination. Levin and Rapoport therefore apply the operation to the LCS of the verb *run* in (23) and derive the following augmented structure:

---

[3] The underlining of BY is in the original.

(26) *run* (directional): [x GO TO y BY [x MOVE in-a-running-manner]]
(Levin and Rappaport Hovav (1992: 260))

Here the predicate GO represents a change of location and can be subsumed by the predicate BECOME in event structure templates, and the latter denotes a broader concept that also includes a change of state. The original LCS of the verb *run* is subordinated to the result LCS, namely [x GO TO y]. As Rappaport and Levin (1988: 27) argue, they "assume that, as a general convention, the main clause of the decomposition determines the basic class membership of the verb," that is, whether the verb is unergative or unaccusative. Based on this assumption, Levin and Rappaport Hovav (1992: 260) argue that "directional *run* is unaccusative since the meaning specified in the main clause of [(26)] is that of a verb of inherently specified direction." Though they do not present the LCS of the *arrive* verbs, we can assume that it is the same as the main clause of the extended LCS of the verb *run*. Semantically, the *arrive* verbs denote a change of location, and so this is a reasonable assumption to make. The basic and derived LCSs of the verb *run* is presented below, along with the LCS of the verb *arrive*:

(27) a. *run* (manner of motion): [x MOVE in-a-running-manner] (=(23))
     b. *run* (directional): [x GO TO y BY [x MOVE in-a-running-manner]]
(=(26))
     c. *arrive* (directed motion): [x GO TO y]

From this enumeration of LCSs, we can see that unergativity is represented by the predicate MOVE, whereas unaccusativity is encoded by the predicate GO, and that whether a verb is unergative or unaccusative is determined by which of the two predicates is in the main clause of the LCS.

Let us now look at how the LCSs in (27) are rendered in event structure templates we have examined up to section 4.1. As already explained, the predicates MOVE and GO in LCSs are subsumed or superseded by the predicates ACT and BECOME in event structure templates, respectively. The predicate BY is tentatively left as it is, and the agent variable x and the theme variable y must be interpreted as coreferential since the runner is the mover. The resultant event structure templates are as follows:

(28) a. *run* (manner of motion): [x ACT$_{<RUN>}$]   (unergative)
   b. *run* (directional): [BECOME [y <*ARRIVED*>] BY [x ACT$_{<RUN>}$]]
       (x=y)   (unaccusative)
   c. *arrive* (directed motion): [BECOME [y <*ARRIVED*>]]
                                                         (unaccusative)

These templates correctly encode unergativity and unaccusativity by their combinations of predicates. This is consistent with our earlier characterization of event structure templates at the end of section 4.1. More specifically, the event structure template (28a) does not contain the predicate CAUSE and contains the predicate ACT, and so it is unergative, while the event structure templates (28b) and (28c) contain neither the predicate CAUSE nor ACT in their main clause, and they are therefore unaccusative.

But here the question arises as to why Levin and Rappaport Hovav apply the process of lexical subordination to the verb *run*. Apart from its independent motivation in lexical semantics and its mere applicability to the verb *run*, do they have any strong grounds for analyzing the verb *run* in terms of lexical subordination? In fact, Levin and Rappaport Hovav (1992) make their decisions on the basis of Talmy's detailed analysis of motion events, which we have scrutinized in chapter 2.

(29) Following Talmy (1975; 1985), we assume that when a manner of motion verb such as *run* takes a goal phrase, its meaning is roughly "go to some location by manner of motion run".
                                        (Levin and Rappaport Hovav (1992: 259-260))

As we have seen in section 2.1.1, Talmy (1985: 61) assumes that a motion event "is analyzed as having four components: besides 'Figure' and 'Ground', there are 'Path' and 'Motion'," and that it "can have a 'Manner' or a 'Cause', which [constitutes] a distinct external event." This means that a manner of motion is conceptually not included in the motion event itself and thus treated as a kind of modifier subordinate to it. The expression "go to some location by manner of motion run" is understood to reflect this relationship between the whole motion event and its manner of motion.

Chapter 4   Event Structure Templates, Event Coidentification, and Macro-event   151

4.2.4. Arguments against Lexical Subordination Analysis

It is true that the structure or configuration (27b) or (28b) dovetails nicely with that of the macro-events proposed by Talmy (1991, 2000), which we have examined in section 2.2.4. But it does not jibe with the surface syntactic structure of the verb *run* followed by a goal prepositional phrase. More specifically, the manner of running is extrinsic and subordinate to the motion in event or semantic representations but mapped onto the main verb in syntax, whereas the motion is denoted by the subordinate prepositional phrase. In brief, the relationship between the main and subordinate clauses is reversed in syntax. Then should we match the semantic configuration to the syntactic structure?

Actually, the semantic representation that reflects syntax is also possible, and Pinker (1989) argues that such a representation is semantically plausible and theoretically preferable. Pinker first states that there are two possible paraphrases of the sentence *John ran into the room*:

(30)   For *run*, as with many other verbs, it is not clear on conceptual grounds whether we should represent the event [i.e. *John ran into the room*] as "to run, with the effect of motion along a path" or "to move along a path, by means of a running action" (Talmy, 1985).   (Pinker (1989: 197))

The first paraphrase conforms to syntax, and the second agrees with Talmy's analysis of motion events and is reflected by the structure of the LCS proposed by Levin and Rappaport Hovav (1992).

Furthermore, Pinker adds that the second paraphrase in (30) is undesirable on theoretical grounds and offers the following semantic representation of the verb *run* followed by a goal prepositional phrase:[4]

---

[4] A similar causative analysis of the *run* verbs followed by a goal prepositional phrase is also proposed by Geis (1970:171–210) in the framework of Generative Semantics.

(31) John ran into the room.

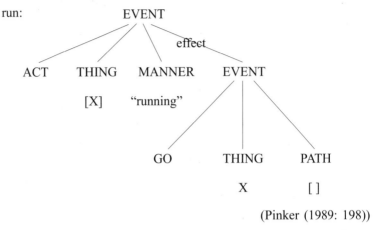

(Pinker (1989: 198))

This practically constitutes a refutation of the analysis by Levin and Rappaport Hovav (1992) of the directional usage of the verb *run*. Here "with the effect of" in the first paraphrase in (30) is represented as a causal relationship between the two subevents, and so it roughly corresponds to the predicate CAUSE in event structure templates. We can therefore convert this representation into the following event structure template:

(32) [[x ACT$_{<RUN>}$] CAUSE [BECOME [y $<ARRIVED>$]] (x=y)

In the same way as (28b), the agent variable *x* and the theme variable *y* are interpreted as coreferential.

By way of summary, let us compare the template versions of the two different semantic representations of the *run* verbs accompanied by a goal prepositional phrase.

(33) a. [[x ACT$_{<RUN>}$] CAUSE [BECOME [y $<ARRIVED>$]] (x=y)
         (= to run, with the effect of motion along a path)
     b. [BECOME [y $<ARRIVED>$] BY [x ACT$_{<RUN>}$]] (x=y)
         (= to move along a path, by means of a running action)

The first event structure template is the rendition of the representation adopted by Pinker (1989), and it has the advantage of being close to the syntactic configuration. The second is the template version of the LCS proposed by Levin and Rappaport (1992) and it also has the merit of being consistent with the composition of motion described by Talmy. At first sight, it might seem as if both event structure templates would provide a natural way of representing the relevant meaning and therefore it would be difficult to judge which is better.

However, both semantic representations are undesirable on grounds of the relationship, or more precisely consistency, between event structures and argument realization. As we have seen in section 3.4.4, the Argument-Per-Subevent Condition is imposed on event structures and it prohibits semantic representations from having two subevents when they are realized as intransitive sentences. The condition is repeated below for ease of reference.

(34) THE ARGUMENT-PER-SUBEVENT CONDITION: There must be at least one argument XP in the syntax per subevent in the event structure. (Levin (2000: 425))

As corollaries, this requires that "event structures with two subevents give rise to sentences with a subject and an object, while simple event structures give rise to sentences which only need a subject" (Levin (2000: 425)).

When the *run* verbs take a goal prepositional phrase, the resultant sentences are usually intransitives, such as *Maria ran to the next town* and *John ran into the room*. This means that the event structure of these sentences is more likely to be a simple event structure consisting of only one subevent. However, the semantic representations proposed above both constitute a complex event structure made up of two subevents. This can be diagrammed as follows:

(35) a. $[\,[\,x\ ACT_{<RUN>}\,]\,CAUSE\,[\,BECOME\,[\,y\ <ARRIVED>\,]\,]\,]\,(x=y)$
    subevent1   subevent2

 b. $[\,[\,BECOME\,[\,y\ <ARRIVED>\,]\,]\,BY\,[\,x\ ACT_{<RUN>}\,]\,]\,(x=y)$
    subevent1   subevent2

If the Argument-Per-Subevent Condition is correct, these complex event structure templates should generate a transitive sentence, but the actual sentence is intransitive. Therefore, it makes no difference which of these event structure templates we adopt. The problem is the same, and the solution no easier to find. Then how should we remove the inconsistency between the event structure of the directional *run* verbs and the Argument-Per-Subevent Condition? There are only two ways out of this predicament, and we will examine the two in turn.

4.2.5. First Alternative and its Problems

Probably the simplest way for us to handle this would be to reformulate the Argument-Per-Subevent Condition in order to account for the exceptional intransitivity of the *run* verbs and to leave the event structure templates unchanged. But it is a poor choice as an alternative. Since its introduction to their theory, Levin and Rappaport Hovav have applied the Argument-Per-Subevent Condition to several linguistic phenomena concerning transitivity, explaining the behavior of diverse verbs. In particular, it spells out what verbs allow for the omission of the direct object and can occur with "non-subcategorized" objects. The modification of the condition can therefore have repercussions for the whole theory, causing untoward effects elsewhere. This is the first reason why we should not choose this option.

There is also an empirical reason against this strategy. We have seen in section 3.6.2.2 that when verbs have a complex event structure, *for*-adverbials should have a "repair" reading in which the resultant state continues for a certain time. As shown in Rappaport Hovav (2008: 33–34), the verb *open* can have the interpretation in which the *for*-adverbial specifies how long the state of being open has continued, and we have represented this by the following event structure template:

(36) a. I opened the door for two minutes.
    b. [[x ACT] CAUSE [BECOME (*for two minutes* [y <OPEN>])]]

Here the adverbial *for two minutes* modifies the resultant state [y <OPEN>].

If the *run* verbs followed by a goal prepositional phrase had the event structure template (33a) or (33b), they should have a "repair" reading parallel to that of the verb *open*. More specifically, the sentence *Sam walked to school for an hour*, which is cited as an odd example in Smith (1997: 45), should have a coerced interpretation in which the *for*-adverbial indicates how long Sam has stayed at the school. But this reading is impossible. A possible alternative reading is that the *for*-adverbial specifies how long the walker has walked towards school, as explained by Smith (1997):

(37) Sentences like [?*Sam walked to school for an hour*] can be interpreted as derived Activities, in which there is no intention of reaching the goal. (Smith (1997: 45))

This demonstrates that the following event structure templates, in which the modification by the *for*-adverbial is represented in a similar manner to (36b), are incorrect:

(38) a. [[x ACT$_{<WALK>}$] CAUSE [BECOME (*for an hour* [y <*ARRIVED*>])]
     b. [BECOME (*for an hour* [y <*ARRIVED*>]) BY [x ACT$_{<WALK>}$]]

In short, the *run* verbs accompanied by a goal prepositional phrase do not contain the resultant state [y <*ARRIVED*>] in their event structure template.

In order to confirm the above observations, let us consider the possible coerced interpretations of the following sentences:

(39) a. John opened the gate for an hour.
     b. John walked to the station for an hour.   (Demizu (2001: 133))

As we have seen in section 3.1.3, *for*-adverbials essentially act as a diagnostic for atelicity and do not usually occur with telic verb phrases, and these sentences are therefore not so natural. But when native speakers are asked to give a plausible interpretation to the sentences, they try to reconcile aspectually incompatible expressions. Demizu (2001) examines this by eliciting judgments from native speaker informants of English about the possible paraphrases of each sentence.

The verb in (39a) is the causative change of state verb *open*, and so we can fully expect that it has a repair reading in which the *for*-adverbial indicates how long the state of being open has continued, since its event structure template contains a resultant state [y <*OPEN*>]. This prediction is indeed borne out. According to the informants, if the sentence (39a) is interpretable, it means (40b), and not (40a).

(40) a. John *tried to open* the gate for an hour.
(the interpretation in which the *for*-adverbial specifies how long the activity of trying to open has continued)
b. John opened the gate and *it was open* for an hour.
(the interpretation in which the *for*-adverbial specifies how long the resultant state of being open has continued)
(Demizu (2001: 133))

On the other hand, the sentence (39b) contains the verb *walk* and the goal prepositional phrase *to the station*. Given the claim by Smith (1997), it should have a coerced interpretation in which the *for*-adverbial modifies the duration of walking. This expectation is also fulfilled. The informants state that the sentence (39b) can be interpreted only as (41a).

(41) a. John *walked towards the station* for an hour.
(the interpretation in which the *for*-adverbial specifies how long the activity of walking has continued)
b. John walked to the station and *stayed there* for an hour.
(the interpretation in which the *for*-adverbial specifies how long the resultant state of being at the station has continued)
(Demizu (2001: 133))

To put it briefly, we have confirmed that the phrase *walk to the station* does not have a resultant state in its event structure template as the verb *open* has. This difference clearly demonstrates that both event structure templates (33) do not faithfully represent the meaning of the *run* verbs followed by a goal prepositional phrase, and therefore should be superseded by a more accurate one. This in turn leads to the conclusion that what should be corrected is not the Argument-Per-Subevent Condition but the proposed event structure templates of the *run* verbs accompanied by a goal prepositional phrase.

All in all, it is clear that the first avenue, that is, the reformulation of the Argument-Per-Subevent Condition is undesirable for both theoretical and empirical reasons. We have to therefore employ the other tactic to circumvent the violation of the Argument-Per-Subevent Condition.

4.3. Event Coidentification as Second Alternative

In the previous section, we have discussed the possibility of leaving the event structure templates essentially unchanged by tampering with the Argument-Per-Subevent Condition, and have dismissed the idea for two reasons. Given this, the purpose of this section is to explore the other possibility, namely the possibility of recasting event structure templates instead of the Argument-Per-Subevent Condition. In order to avoid violating the the condition, it is also theoretically possible to modify the semantic representations so as to comply with the limitation on them. Actually, Levin and Rappaport Hovav (1999: 213) and Rappaport Hovav and Levin (2001: 782) pursue this strategy, proposing an "event coidentification" analysis. This operation takes two subevents as input and outputs a single event by identifying them as a conceptual unit, and we discuss it in greater detail below.

4.3.1. What is Event Coidentification?

First of all, we have to make sure what the operation named "event coidentification" is. Levin and Rappaport Hovav (1999) begin their discussion by stating as follows:

(42) English allows XPs denoting nonlexically entailed results to be added to verbs, giving rise to what is usually referred to as the resultative construction.   (Levin and Rappaport Hovav (1999: 200))

The resultative construction is a very broad concept that embraces several different sentence patterns, and Levin and Rappaport Hovav (1999: 205) and Rappaport Hovav and Levin (2001: 782) argue that sentences such as *Kim ran into the room* fall into one of its subclasses dubbed "Bare XP resultatives." In this example, the XP refers to the prepositional phrase denoting a goal, namely *into the room*, and the adjective "bare" means that "result XPs are predicated directly of their subjects without the mediation of reflexives" (Levin and Rappaport Hovav (1999: 204)). In other words, bare XP resultatives are intransitive sentences that have an XP immediately after the verb.

As explained in section 4.2.4, this type of sentence should not be analyzed as having a complex event structure if we adhere strictly to the Argument-Per-Subevent Condition. However, as the analyses by Pinker (1989) and Levin and Rappaport Hovav (1992) reveal, its denotation does seem to conceptually consist of two subevents. In order to bridge the gap between the seemingly binary semantic configuration and the theoretically simple event structure, Levin and Rappaport Hovav (1999) and Rappaport Hovav and Levin (2001) introduce the operation named "event coidentification." Through this mechanism, two closely related subevents are reinterpreted as a non-causative single event.

Take *Kim ran into the room* for example. The situation described by this sentence can also be expressed by the two sentences *Kim ran* and *Kim entered the room*. Therefore, it is conceptually plausible to regard the situation as made up of two subevents.

(43) We suggest that bare XP resultatives are compositionally derived in that the happening in the world that they describe involves two temporally anchored sets of properties which can each be lexicalized by a separate predicate; thus, this happening can potentially be conceptualized as involving two distinct events.
(Levin and Rappaport Hovav (1999: 212–213))

However, Levin and Rappaport Hovav go on to argue that the two subevents, namely the running subevent and the entering subevent, are related so strongly that it is also possible to conceptualize the whole situation as a single event. In the latter case, the two subevents are "coidentified" in their terms.

(44) [W]e argue that the relation between the constituent events—i.e. the two temporally anchored sets of properties—is tight enough that the two sets of properties can be conceptualized as being properties of a single event […]. We say that bare XP resultatives are represented as simple events in event structure terms as a result of the COIDENTIFICATION of the constituent subevents.
(Levin and Rappaport Hovav (1999: 213))

Based on some previous studies of event structures, they argue that the fol-

Chapter 4 Event Structure Templates, Event Coidentification, and Macro-event   159

lowing conditions are imposed on event coidentification:

(45) a. The subevents must have the same location and must necessarily be temporally dependent.
 b. One subevent must have a property that serves to measure out that subevent in time; this property is predicated of an entity that is necessarily a participant in both subevents.
(Levin and Rappaport Hovav (1999: 213))

The first condition stipulates that the two coidentified subevents have the same spatial properties and unfold at the same rate. Here the phrase "temporally dependent" not only means that they have the same duration, but also suggests that, as elaborated more fully in the second condition, one of the subevents possesses a property that measures it out, or marks its temporal sequence. This property is virtually identical to the concept of a scale we have examined in section 3.7.1 and in fact Rappaport Hovav and Levin (2001: 781-782) refer to the same property as "a scale that can be used to measure out a change in a participant in the event."

This in turn means that one of the subevents must denote a scalar change we have seen in section 3.7 in order for them to undergo the process of event coidentification. In the case of motion events, one of the subevents that constitute a motion event must possess a path scale explicated in section 3.7.2. Additionally, as the second condition of (45) specifies, the entity of which the scalar property is predicated must be shared by both subevents. This further entails that the scale which one of the subevents initially possesses is duplicated onto the other subevent through the predication of the shared entity. Consequently, the scale measures out both subevents, or to put it more accurately, the coidentified single event.

In the sentence *Kim ran into the room*, the subevent of entering the room has a property, or more specifically a path scale, that measures out the whole event temporally. In addition, "an entity that is necessarily a participant in both subevents" is unequivocally identified as the participant *Kim*, which is the agent in the running subevent and the theme in the entering subevent at the same time. The path scale of the entering subevent is composed of Kim's positions along the path into the room. Consequently, both conditions governing event coidentification are satisfied, and so the running and entering subevents are successfully coidentified.

4.3.2. Event Coidentification and Semantic Representation

Let us now turn to how Levin and Rappaport Hovav represent a single event comprising two coidentified subevents. Rappaport Hovav and Levin (2001: 782) take the sentence *Kim ran into the room* as an example and clarify the status of coidentified events as follows:

(46) Formally, coidentified events could be seen as predicated of the same event variable, as in the neo-Davidsonian representation for *Kim ran into the room* in [(47)]; we use the label RUN-INTO to suggest the two event descriptions become one and the label AGENT-THEME to indicate that one participant has two roles.

(47) ∃e [RUN-INTO (e) & AGENT-THEME (e, Kim) & GOAL (e, room)]   (Rappaport Hovav and Levin (2001: 782))

Here the predicates RUN and INTO are predicated of the same event variable *e*, and they are hyphenated in order to accentuate the state of being coidentified. Moreover, the participant *Kim* is also predicated of the variable *e*. As we have seen just above, the participant is both the agent in the running subevent and the theme in the entering subevent, and this is represented by the hyphenation of the two labels AGENT and THEME. At first glance, this representation seems adequate to show the result of event coidentification, but if we examine it minutely, the semantic representation (47) proves to be faced with three problems.

First, the representation (47) does not give all the information pertinent to the relationship between the coidentified subevents. Here the two subevents and their participants are both coidentified, or interpreted as coreferential, and are represented by the hyphenated labels RUN-INTO and AGENT-THEME, respectively. However, one question remains unanswered. If event coidentification just means that the two subevents are "represented as one event" (Rappaport Hovav and Levin (2001: 782)) and no more than that, why do they use the labels RUN-INTO and AGENT-THEME? Theoretically, it should be equally possible that the resultant event is represented by the label INTO-RUN, and the shared participant is a THEME-AGENT as well. Since event coidentification does not stipulate the relationship between the two subevents in the merged structure, it is difficult to discern which subevent is more salient. However, their notation seems to suggest that they tacitly assume the first predicate or theta role in each label to be primary. Then what is the rationale behind their labels?

Next, their explanation by way of event coidentification is inadequate in that neither Levin and Rappaport Hovav (1999) nor Rappaport Hovav and Levin (2001) associate the representation of event coidentification with event structure templates they have developed. More specifically, the representation (47) does not contain predicates such as ACT, BECOME and CAUSE, which have been used in their event structure templates. Instead it contains the predicates RUN and INTO, but they are just the capitalized versions of the verb *run* and the preposition *into*, and do not reveal their relationship with the predicates ACT, BECOME and CAUSE and, in turn, with event structure templates. In a sense, we can say that the predicates RUN and INTO are arbitrarily introduced and are represented as atomic and irreducible. Of course, it is intuitively apparent that the predicates RUN and INTO are subsumed by the more general predicates ACT and BECOME, respectively, but Levin and Rappaport Hovav do not make it explicit. As a result, (47) appears to be an ad hoc representation, in that it comprises the unforeseen predicates RUN and INTO and is not connected with their previous studies.

The third drawback is that it does not incorporate all the recent advancements in their theory, notably the supersession of aspectual notions with scalar and non-scalar changes. In retrospect, when they wrote their 1999 and 2001 papers, they had not introduced the concept of scalarity into their theory of event structure templates, and the dichotomy between scalar and non-scalar changes began to be explicitly stated in Rappaport Hovav (2008) and Rappaport Hovav and Levin (2010). It is therefore perfectly natural that Levin and Rappaport Hovav (1999) and Rappaport Hovav and Levin (2001) do not use the notion of scalarity in order to characterize event coidentification. But we are now familiar with the notions of scalar and non-scalar changes through the above discussion, and so it is time for us to apply them to event coidentification. In the next section, therefore, we will consider how to link the scale-based event structure templates to event coidentification, together with how we should represent the relationship between the two coidentified events.

4.4. Event Coidentification and Event Structure Templates

In this section, we will contemplate how event coidentification is represented by event structure templates based on scalar and non-scalar changes. In other words, we will consider how to solve the three problems posed at the end of section 4.3.2. Given the discussion up to section 4.1.2, the event structure templates of the *run* verbs and the *arrive* verbs and their canonical realization rules are revised so as to incorporate the concept of scalarity. The relabeled templates of the *run* verbs and the *arrive* verbs are presented below, along with the amended versions of the canonical realization rules.

(48) a. [x ACT$_{<RUN>}$] (complex changes, unergative)
    b. [BECOME [y <ARRIVED>]] (single change, unaccusative)
(49) a. manner → [x ACT$_{<NON\text{-}SCALAR\ CHANGE>}$]
                                                (e.g., *jog, run, creak, whistle, ...*)
    b. directed motion → [BECOME [y <SCALAR CHANGE>]]
                                                              (e.g., *arrive, enter, ...*)

In accordance with (49), the root of the *run* verbs, which encodes a combination of multiple changes that constitutes a non-scalar change, is incorporated into the unergative event structure template, whereas that of the *arrive* verbs, which lexicalizes a single change along a path scale, is fused into the unaccusative change of state event structure template. Considering the event structure template (48a) and the canonical realization rule (49a), we can reasonably assume that the predicate RUN in (47) is replaced with the predicate ACT modified by the root $_{<RUN>}$, and the role AGENT is matched up with the semantically compatible variable *x* in the template [x ACT$_{<RUN>}$].

4.4.1. Event Structure Template of Goal Prepositional Phrases

Before proceeding further, we need to consider what event structure template goal prepositional phrases following the *run* verbs are associated with. In the representation (47), Rappaport Hovav and Levin (2001: 782) represent the goal prepositional phrase *into the room* by the predicates INTO and GOAL, and the predicate INTO is just hyphenated to the predicate RUN without further elaboration. Since the predicate INTO denotes a change of state in which some entity moves from the outside to the inside of something, it seems reasonable to assume that the predicate INTO is subsumed into the more general predicate BECOME, but Rappaport Hovav and Levin are not explicit about the relationship between the predicates INTO and BECOME. This is probably because Rappaport Hovav and Levin concentrate their efforts more on providing empirical evidence for event coidentification than on the refinement of event structure representations. But we have to provide a specific event structure template for the subevent denoted by the goal prepositional phrase *into the room* in order to represent event coidentification by event structure templates.

Let us now turn to the fact that the subevent denoted by the goal prepositional phrase *into the room* can also be expressed by the sentence *Kim entered the room*, which includes the verb *enter*, one of the *arrive* verbs. This means that the semantic contribution of goal prepositional phrases is also lexicalized into the *arrive* verbs, and in turn that goal prepositional phrases and the *arrive* verbs, or verbs of directed motion, are assumed to be semantically equivalent and should be represented by the same event structure template.

At first sight, it might seem quite absurd to indiscriminately represent prepositions and verbs alike by the same event structure template. However, in Generative Semantics, several verbs of directed motion and prepositions were assumed to have the same semantic deep structures. For example, Binnick (1968) supposes that the preposition *across* and the transitive verb of directed motion *cross* have the same semantic representation, or the same underlying structure in his terms.

(50)　The structure underlying
　　　　John went across the river in a punt.
　　also underlies
　　　　John punted across the river.
　　and
　　　　John crossed the river in a punt.　　　　　(Binnick (1968: 7-8))

Binnick (1968: 3) further suggests that similar relationships also exist between other morphologically related prepositions and verbs, such as *around* and *surround*, and *in* and *enter*. Likewise, Becker and Arms (1969) point out an interesting fact about the verb phrase *run to the river*.

(51)   For instance, the English sentence,
       He ran to the river.
   can be expressed in Bahasa Indonesia as
       Dia berlari sampai sungai.
       'He ran arrived river'
   What is in English a sequence of verb plus preposition is in Indonesian a sequence of two verbs.   (Becker and Arms (1969: 7))

Here the goal prepositional phrase *to the river* in English is translated as "arrived river" in Bahasa Indonesia. This demonstrates that the meaning of goal prepositional phrases corresponds closely to that of the *arrive* verbs. Becker and Arms go on to state that there is a similar semantic parallelism between goal prepositional phrases and the *arrive* verbs within English.

(52)   We went across the river.
       We crossed the river.
   In the first sentence, the features motion and location are expressed in two words, a verb and a preposition (Go + across), while in the second, both features are expressed in a single word closely related to the preposition (cross). We would assume that the underlying structure of both sentences was the same [...].
                                                (Becker and Arms (1969: 7))

Here they state that the two features of motion and location, which can be separately lexicalized as the verb *go* and the preposition *across*, are unified and as a result expressed by the single verb *cross*. The verb *go* is one of the *arrive* verbs, and so their analysis does not accord fully with ours, in which the event coidentification of the *run* verbs and goal prepositional phrases is at issue. However, from a broader perspective, both seem to point in one direction.

   Of course we have to keep in mind that these generative semanticists did not assume absolute uniformity between prepositions and directed motion verbs, as is evident from the following statement:

(53) Please note that we are not saying that prepositions are verbs: our contention is only that verbs and prepositions may be surface realizations of the same abstract semantic categories.

(Becker and Arms (1969: 1))

Certainly prepositions cannot appear as finite verbs, and in this respect, goal prepositions and the *arrive* verbs are markedly dissimilar. But the paraphrastic relationships shown above are at least suggestive of certain semantic similarities, and seem to validate the semantic representation of goal prepositional phrases by the event structure template of the *arrive* verbs.

By pursuing this line of reasoning, we might feel as if we just reverted to the old-fashioned view, espoused by generative semanticists over 40 years ago, that adjectives, adverbs and prepositions, as well as verbs, are all predicates in deep semantic structure, irrespective of their different syntactic properties. But not only generative semanticists but also some lexical semanticists today seem to equate prepositions with verbs. For example, Randall (2010) assumes that the goal prepositional phrase following the verb *put* has the same semantic structure as that of the verb *go*.

(54) The C[onceptual] S[tructure]s of causative verbs, such as *put* in (63), are more complex. Their highest CS function, CAUSE, takes a THING as its first argument. But its second argument is not a PLACE; it is an entire CS clause. This clause, like our CS for *go*, is headed by BECOME, and it can be paraphrased as "cause something to come to be at a new location."

(55) a. [NP Sue] put [NP the books] [PP into crates]
b. *put:* [EVENT CAUSE ([THING], [EVENT BECOME ([THING], [PLACE AT ([PLACE])])])] (Randall (2010: 27))

Here we do not go into detail about her elaborate theory and focus on the relevant aspects. Randall argues that the verb *put* takes two arguments. The first argument is a THING and is realized as the subject in the sentence, that is, *Sue*. It appears that the verb *put* takes a THING and a PLACE as the other arguments, but she states that this is the wrong analysis. Randall instead proposes that the verb *put* takes as the second argument an entire CS clause, or another event structure template in Rappaport Hovav and Levin's terms. Furthermore, Randall argues that the CS clause is the same as that of the verb *go*, which she represents as follows:

(56) a. The books went to Boston. (Randall (2010: 25))
 b. *go:* [EVENT BECOME ([THING], [PLACE AT ([ ])])]
 (Randall (2010: 26))

This means that the goal prepositional phrase *into crates* and the verb *go*, one of the verbs of directed motion, have the same semantic representation. This proves that our analysis of goal prepositional phrases and the analysis by Randall (2010) point in the same and right direction.

Based on these considerations, we can safely assume that goal prepositional phrases such as *to the station* and *into the room* are represented by the non-causative change of state, that is, unaccusative event structure template, and their denotation can be alternatively lexicalized into verbs of directed motion such as *arrive* and *enter*. The result root encoding goal prepositions should be <TO/INTO [mover, goal]>, and it merges with <SCALAR CHANGE> in the unaccusative event structure template [BECOME [y <SCALAR CHANGE>]]. We tentatively propose the following canonical realization rule and event structure template for goal prepositions such as *to* and *into*.[5]

(57) a. goal preposition → [BECOME [y <SCALAR CHANGE> $\underline{z}$]]
 b. [BECOME [y <TO/INTO> $\underline{z}$]]

Here the underlined variable z does not exist in the original unaccusative event structure template and is added by the root of the prepositions *to* and *into*. Then what function does the variable z serve? At this point, let us remember what we have learned in sections 3.4.3 and 3.7.2.

In section 3.4.3, we have looked at the differences between structure

---

[5] In fact, there are intriguing semantic differences between the prepositions *to* and *into*. For further details, see Beavers (2002: 15–16).

Chapter 4 Event Structure Templates, Event Coidentification, and Macro-event   167

and root or constant participants. We now apply this to the event structure template of goal prepositions. It is reasonably assumed that the root of goal prepositions encodes two participants, namely the moving entity and the goal, or Figure and Ground in Talmy's terms, as we have seen in sections 2.1.1 and 2.2.1. The mover participant is matched up with the variable y in the non-causative change of state template, since it can be subsumed under the category of theme represented by the variable y. It is therefore the structure participant of the preposition *into*. On the other hand, there is no variable in the template with which the goal participant can be associated, and so the underlined variable z is added by the root to rescue the ostracized goal participant. As a result, the goal participant is only licensed by the root and regarded as a root participant.

Let us turn to the path scale encoded by goal prepositions. As Talmy (1985: 61) states and we have seen in section 2.1.1, the position of the mover or Figure is characterized with respect to that of the goal or Ground. This means that not only the former but also the latter are involved in the formation of the path scale. More specifically, the root of goal prepositions <*TO/INTO* [mover (=Figure), goal (=Ground)]> encodes the scale determined by the position of the theme or Figure along the path defined with respect to the goal or Ground. In other words, the root forms a scale together with the goal and imparts it to the theme. Similar to the verb *arrive*, which we have considered in section 3.7.2, the scale formation of the preposition *into* is diagrammed as below:

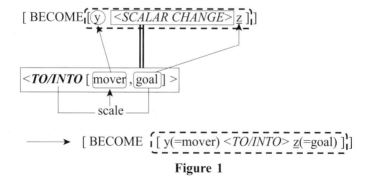

Figure 1

Here, in a similar vein, the boldface part of the root encodes a scale, and the part enclosed in the dashed-line box in the template is associated with the whole scalar change.

At first glance, the addition of the variable *z* might seem ad hoc, but it is independently motivated by other transitive verbs of directed motion like *enter*. As shown above, the goal prepositional phrase *into the room* can also be expressed by the sentence *Kim entered the room*. The result root that lexicalizes the verb *enter* is <*ENTERED* [mover, goal]>, and it is fused with <*SCALAR CHANGE*> in the unaccusative template [BECOME [y <*SCALAR CHANGE*>]]. The verb *enter*, whether transitive or intransitive, is a verb of directed motion and associated with the following template:

(58) [BECOME [y <*ENTERED*>]] (single change, unaccusative)

When it is transitive, the goal participant expressed by the direct object has no variable to be matched up with in the event structure template, and it is therefore necessary for the root of the verb *enter* to introduce into the template the variable *z* to associate the extra participant with. This can be diagrammed below in a similar manner to the prepositions *to* and *into*:

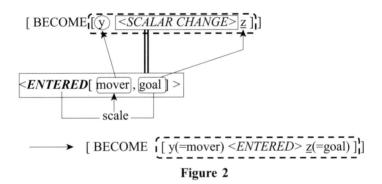

Figure 2

This also suggests a semantic parallelism between goal prepositions and verbs of directed motion, confirming our analysis of goal prepositions.

Given the above observations, it is reasonable to assume that the predicate INTO in the representation (47) should be replaced by the predicate BECOME and its argument root <*INTO*>. In addition, the predicates THEME and GOAL are paired with the variables *y* and *z* in the template [BECOME [y <*TO/INTO*> z]], respectively, because of their semantic compatibility.

4.4.2. Event Coidentification and Scalarity

Let us now consider the semantic characteristics of the coidentified event in terms of scalarity. Since goal prepositional phrases are semantically equivalent to the *arrive* verbs in spite of their syntactic differences, they are assumed to denote a scalar change. In contrast, the *run* verbs, one of the subcategory of manner verbs, encode a non-scalar change. This points to the conclusion that the unified event initially includes two qualitatively different changes, namely a non-scalar change denoted by the *run* verbs and a scalar change denoted by goal prepositional phrases. This composite of two types of changes and the semantic elements encoding them can be schematically represented as follows:

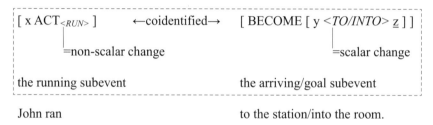

Figure 3

However, it remains unclear how the two kinds of changes, namely scalar and non-scalar changes, are coidentified, or coalesce into a single change.

As we have examined in section 4.3.1, the process of event coidentification uses a scale encoded by the goal subevent to measure out a change in the participant in both subevents, and in turn in the whole event. This means that the scalar change denoted by goal prepositional phrases is superimposed onto, and gives a scale to, the non-scalar change encoded by the running subevent. To put it differently, event coidentification is a mechanism for reconciling the two qualitatively different changes and turning them into a unified change that possesses a scale. Thus, by applying the concept of scalarity to the subevents coidentified in the process of event coidentification, we can systematically associate the semantic interpretation of goal prepositional phrases with that of the *run* verbs. So far so good.

Nevertheless, the conundrum remains of how the scalar change denoted by the goal subevent gives a scale to the non-scalar change encoded by the running subevent. Let us here remember how the two types of changes differ in quantity, or in the amount of contained information. As we have seen at the end of section 3.8, a non-scalar change consists of complex changes or a combination of multiple changes, while a scalar change constitutes a simple change in the values of a scale. This line of thought suggests that, when the two types of changes are combined, the scalar change is associated with one of the multiple changes comprising the non-scalar change. Let us apply this idea to the coidentification of the *run* verbs and goal prepositional phrases. The *run* verbs denote a non-scalar change, that is, a combination of multiple changes including leg movements, arm movements, springing steps, position changes, and so on. Among them, position changes are the most crucial, because only the positions of the runner are conceptually compatible with the path scale introduced by another event, for example, the directed motion denoted by goal prepositional phrases. The changing positions of the runner can therefore be reinterpreted as the values of the scale. The diagram below illustrates this point.

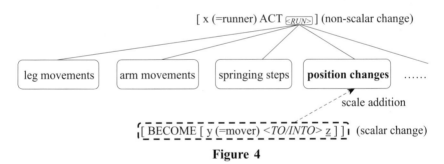

Figure 4

This process relates the scalar change encoded by goal prepositional phrases to the non-scalar change lexicalized by the *run* verbs. Thus one of the manifold changes that form the non-scalar change takes on a scalar meaning while the others are left completely untouched. As a result, the coidentified event described by the sentence *John ran to the station/into the room* denotes an amalgam of scalar and non-scalar changes, namely a combination of many changes one of which possesses a path scale property.

Given these observations, we further assume that event coidentification or, to put it more accurately, scale addition is a one-way process. As the term "scale addition" suggests, the scale is copied from scalar onto non-scalar changes in this process; on the other hand, the process of scale deletion is thought to be impossible: we cannot remove the scale from scalar changes, since they lexically entail the scale and its cancellation leads inevitably to a semantic contradiction. This means that the process of event coidentification, or to put it another way, the reconciliation of the two different types of changes, must be unidirectional, namely from scalar to non-scalar changes.

In conclusion, it is clear that the denotation of the *run* verbs, which is by its very nature non-scalar, can be associated with a path scale. This seems to square with what Rappaport Hovav (2008) states about the general semantic properties of dynamic verbs:

(59) [W]hile all dynamic verbs are potentially associated with a scale, (at least in English) with some verbs this is a lexical property and with other verbs this is not. (Rappaport Hovav (2008: 18))

Here the adverb "potentially" means "not always," and when the *run* verbs take no goal prepositional phrase, event coidentification is not made and no path scale is added to the meaning of the *run* verbs. As we have seen just above, when the *run* verbs take a goal prepositional phrase, event coidentification associates the path scale encoded by the goal prepositional phrase with their denotation, and as a result the movement of the runner assumes a scalar character.

Given the discussion above, the process of event coidentification applied to the sentence *John ran to the station/ into the room* is diagrammed as follows:

172   *Lexicalization Typology and Event Structure Templates*

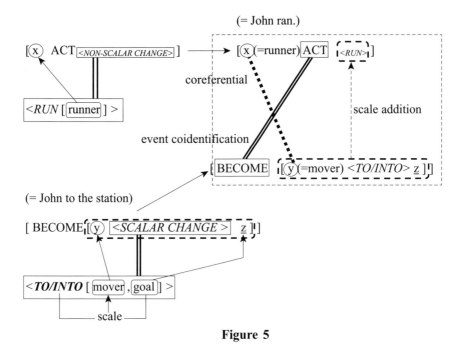

Figure 5

As shown in the upper left of the figure, the manner root <*RUN* [runner]> is associated with _{*<NON-SCALAR CHANGE>*} in the unergative template [x ACT_{*<NON-SCALAR CHANGE>*}]. As we have seen at the end of section 4.4.1, the result root <*TO/INTO* [mover, goal]> is matched up with <*SCALAR CHANGE*> in the unaccusative template [BECOME [y <*SCALAR CHANGE*>]] and inserts a root participant designating a goal or Ground into the template. As we will see just below, the two resultant event structure templates, that is, [x ACT_{*<RUN>*}] and [BECOME [y <*TO/INTO*> z]], are coidentified and amalgamated into a single event structure template. But then how should we represent the coidentified event structure template? Below we will provide a definitive answer to the question.

4.4.3. Coidentified Event Structure Template

By the process of event coidentification, the running subevent and the goal subevent are coidentified, or reinterpreted as coreferential. In section 4.3.2, this coreferentiality is shown by the hyphenation between RUN and

INTO in the representation (47). But these two predicates are merely the capitalized versions of the verb *run* and the preposition *into*, and therefore not independently motivated. In addition, the other three predicates in (47), namely AGENT-THEME and GOAL, represent the participants in the coidentified event, but they should be represented by variables in event structure templates.

Accordingly, up to the end of section 4.4.1, we have replaced all the above predicates with the two event structure templates [x ACT$_{<RUN>}$] and [BECOME [y <*INTO*> z̲]]. More specifically, the predicates RUN and INTO have been superseded by the combinations of a predicate and a root, that is, ACT$_{<RUN>}$ and BECOME [<*INTO*>]. On the other hand, the predicates AGENT-THEME and GOAL have been supplanted by the variables *x*, *y* and *z*, respectively. As a result, the predicates RUN and INTO are divided into the predicates and their roots, and so both the predicates and the roots should be hyphenated. Furthermore, the hyphenated predicates AGENT-THEME is replaced by the two variables *x* and *y*. Thus these variables also need to be joined by a hyphen.

One significant complicating factor remains. What status should we give the amalgamated and hyphenated root? The two coidentified roots have a different status in event structure templates. In particular, the manner root $_{<RUN>}$ is a modifier of the predicate ACT, whereas the result root <*INTO*> serves as the argument of the predicate BECOME. Here lies a fundamental difference between manner and result roots, as Rappaport Hovav and Levin (1998: 108, 2010: 24) describe. Then what function does the hyphenated root fulfill in the resultant event structure template?

Let us return again to the difference in the amount of encoded information between the two types of changes. As we have argued in section 3.8, a manner, which is compounded of multiple changes that make up a non-scalar change, is assumed to be informationally much richer than a result, which encodes a simple scalar change. In the case of motion events, the running subevent described by the *run* verbs is informationally richer, and as a result semantically more salient, than the goal subevent denoted by prepositional phrases. From this, it is reasonable to assume that when the two subevents are coidentified, the goal subevent, which contains only schematic information, is not only superimposed onto but also absorbed into the running subevent, which encodes substantial information. Or to put it differently, the skeletal semantic content of the goal subevent is overshadowed by the substantial amount of information denoted by the root of the *run* verbs, and is integrated into one of the changes, that is, the change in position of the runner. Accordingly, the goal subevent is assimilated into the running subevent and loses its status as an independent semantic entity. The resultant coidentified event is therefore a running event incorporating the path scale denoted by a goal subevent.

Furthermore, this is assumed to be the underlying reason why Rappaport Hovav and Levin (2001) use the labels RUN-INTO and AGENT-THEME rather than the labels INTO-RUN and THEME-AGENT. The event generated by event coidentification is a running event augmented with a path scale, and not a goal event to which a running manner is added. This means that the resultant event is semantically identified not with the goal subevent but with the running subevent. In other words, the goal subevent is semantically embedded in the running subevent, and so the goal subevent and its participant THEME are appended afterward with a hyphen to the running subevent and its participant AGENT, respectively, in the representation (47). Therefore, also in the revised event structure template, we should mete out this irreverent treatment to the subjugated predicate, root and variable, namely BECOME, <*INTO*> and *y*.

The event structure template revised along these lines that represents the coidentified event should be as follows:

(60) [x-y ACT-BECOME$_{<RUN-INTO>}$ z].

Here the amalgamated root serves as the modifier of the synthesized predicate ACT-BECOME and is represented by the subscript $_{<RUN-INTO>}$. This event structure template clearly shows that the result of event coidentification is a semantic amalgamation of manner and result verbs that denotes complex changes one of which has become scalar.

4.5. Event Coidentification and Macro-events

In the previous section, we have struggled successfully to represent event coidentification by scale-based event structure templates in an ingenious way. The argument has revolved around how to express the meaning of goal prepositional phrases by using event structure templates and how to associate it with the meaning of the *run* verbs. In this section, we reexamine the components of the motion macro-events described by Talmy (2000). At first sight, it might seem pointless to look back on what we have already pondered in chapter 2. But there are two compelling reasons for this.

First, as we have mentioned at the end of section 2.3.6, the very mechanism necessary for satellite-framed mapping is event coidentification, and so we should ultimately integrate event coidentification with Talmy's theory. In order to achieve this aim, we have scrutinized the process of event coidentification from section 4.3 onward and managed to represent it by event structure templates in section 4.4.3. Given all this, what we have to do next is to connect the template representation with the components of Talmy's macro-events.

Second, we can justify the analysis we have developed up to now by pointing out analogies between the semantic elements involved in event coidentification and the components of Talmy's macro-events. In fact, the idea of relating event coidentification to Talmy's theory is less farfetched than it seems, because they have a lot in common. As we will see below, the theoretical differences between Talmy's macro-event analysis and Levin and Rappaport Hovav's event coidentification analysis are not too difficult to reconcile.

4.5.1. Parallelism between Talmy's and Levin & Rappaport Hovav's Analyses

Given the above discussion, we now clarify the parallelism between Talmy's and Levin and Rappaport Hovav's analyses. More specifically, we will point out three similarities between the running subevent and the subordinate event in macro-events. Concomitantly, we will refer to commonalities between the goal subevent and the framing event.

First of all, in terms of semantic content, the subordinate event and the framing event in Talmy's macro-events roughly correspond to the running subevent and the goal subevent in the process of event coidentification, respectively. To be more specific, the running subevent and the subordinate event denote a manner of motion, whereas the goal subevent and the framing event encode a path scale.

Next, as we have argued in sections 3.8 and 4.4.3, the running subevent is informationally richer and therefore semantically more salient than the goal subevent. This is in accord with Talmy's semantic characterization of the subordinate and the framing events. In particular, as we have seen in section 2.2.3, Talmy (2000: 219) states that "the semantic character of the framing event is more that of an abstract schema, while that of the subordinate event tends to be more substantive or perceptually palpable," and that the subordinate event might "seem semantically more primary than the framing event." Since it is reasonable to assume that the more schematic and the less substantive a semantic element is, the less information it contains, we arrive at the conclusion that the subordinate event is informationally much richer than the framing event. This demonstrates that the subordinate and the framing events correlate beautifully with the running and the goal subevents also in terms of the amount of contained information.

Finally, as we have seen at the outset of section 2.2.4, Talmy (2000: 220) argues that the subordinate event is frequently and prototypically an aspectually unbounded activity. On the other hand, as we have seen at the end of section 3.4.2, Rappaport Hovav and Levin (1998: 104) state that manner verbs like *run* are activities. This aspectual characterization has later been superseded by the concept of a non-scalar change, but having no scale also automatically leads to unboundedness. This means that the running subevent denoted by the *run* verbs is aspectually identical to the subordinate event in motion macro-events.

Given these considerations, we can now associate the event structure templates of the goal and running subevents with the hierarchical representation of the components of motion events depicted by Talmy (2000). The diagram below shows how the two coidentified subevents represented as event structure templates are related with the components of Talmy's motion macro-events:

Chapter 4   Event Structure Templates, Event Coidentification, and Macro-event   177

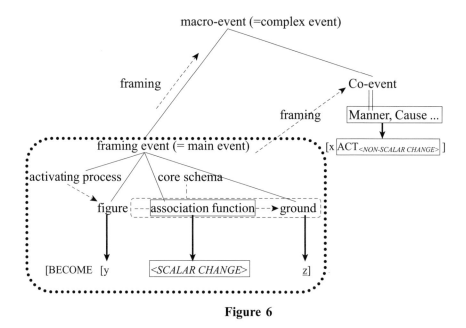

Figure 6

Here the event structure templates representing the two subevents are shown below the corresponding events within the macro-event, and the one-to-one correspondences between the elements are designated by the arrows connecting them.

Moreover, the scale addition we have discussed in section 4.4.2 can be regarded as an instantiation of the structuring function the framing event exercises over the subordinate event. More specifically, as we have seen in section 2.2.3, Talmy (2000: 219) argues that "the framing event can act as an abstract structure conceptually imposed on the subordinate event." Given the fact that the goal and running subevents are analogous with the framing and subordinate events, respectively, and the goal subevent gives a scale to the running subevent, it is reasonable to assume that the framing event gives a scalar property to the subordinate event. This addition of scalarity can be interpreted as a clear manifestation of the role of the framing event as a "structurer" (Talmy (2000: 219)). We can show this correspondence between the scale addition and the structuring function by the following diagram:

178 *Lexicalization Typology and Event Structure Templates*

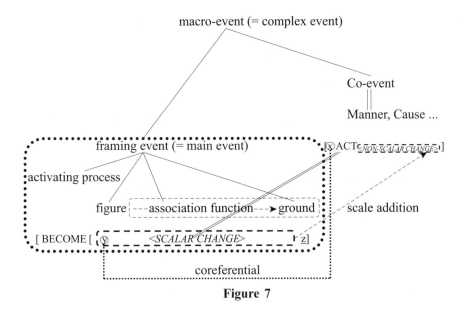

Figure 7

Adding everything up, we have confirmed that the process of event coidentification proposed by Levin and Rappaport Hovav (1999) and Rappaport Hovav and Levin (2001) is ultimately equivalent to the relation of "structurer" the framing event bears to the subordinate event (Talmy (2000: 219)). In particular, when the framing event "structures" the subordinate event, the abstract structure of the framing event is imposed on the subordinate event. Here the abstract structure equals the path scale copied from the framing event onto the subordinate event. When this process occurs, the subordinate event, which initially denotes an aspectually unbounded activity with no path scale, takes on a new scale introduced by the framing event.

But this is not the whole story. Concomitantly, the process of scale addition is expected to affect the status of the framing event. The framing event initially occupies an important place in macro-events by its nature. But, as we have seen in section 4.4.3, it is assumed that the informationally weaker goal subevent is not only superimposed onto but also absorbed into the informationally richer running subevent, and consequently loses its status as a discrete semantic entity. This suggests that their counterparts in Talmy's theory are expected to behave similarly. Specifically, when event coidentification is applied to motion macro-events, the framing event should be overwhelmed by the subordinate event and lose its privileged position in macro-events. However, as we have looked at in section 2.2.2, Talmy (2000: 219) states that notwithstanding their paucity of information, framing events always play a dominant role in macro-events. Then how should we reconcile the two theories?

This would lead us to the conclusion that we should characterize the framing and subordinate events in terms of two separate facets, that is, the dominance in macro-events and the amount of semantic information. In more concrete terms, this amounts to saying that, in macro-events, the framing event is more influential, on the one hand, and less informative, on the other, than the subordinate event. Or to put it another way, the framing event is influentially stronger and informationally weaker, whereas the subordinate event is influentially weaker and informationally stronger. This contrast between influential and informational strengths takes on a further significance in the consideration of mapping patterns. In brief, the problem is which facet takes precedence in mapping. This will be discussed in more detail below.

4.5.2. How to Solve Problems with Mapping?

Let us now move on to the problems with mapping we have mentioned at the end of section 2.2.6. As we have observed, in the case of verb-framed expressions, the configuration of macro-events is isomorphic to the syntactic structure. On the other hand, in the satellite-framed pattern, the components of macro-events are related but not isomorphic to the syntactic constituents. Given these, we have suggested the possibility that satellite-framed languages have a special conceptual apparatus that allows the deviations of syntax from the semantic configuration, and now we know that the apparatus is event coidentification. Therefore, what we have to do now is to elucidate the mechanism that makes possible the non-isomorphic mapping.

Let us first examine the case where motion macro-events do not undergo the process of event coidentification. The influentially stronger framing event in the configuration is not coidentified and as a result retains its privileged status in macro-events. Befitting its special status, it is mapped onto the main verb position and lexicalized into a verb of directed motion, or one of the *arrive* verbs. The manner subordinate event, which is influentially weaker, is described by the gerundive clause *walking*, if necessary, which reflects its subordinate status in macro-events. In brief, macro-events are mapped isomorphically onto syntactic structure. This type of mapping is supposed to be characteristic of verb-framed languages, but in fact it is also possible in satellite-framed languages like English, as shown by the example *John entered the room*. Consequently, satellite-framed languages like English also have a small but appreciable number of verb-framed motion verbs. On the other hand, in verb-framed languages, this is the only way in which motion macro-events are mapped onto syntactic structure, since they have no mechanism of event coidentification. This mapping pattern is represented in the diagram below:

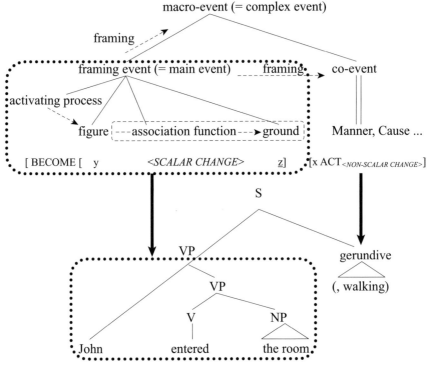

Figure 8 (= revised from Figure 10 in chapter 2)

This is therefore a straightforward mapping, in that it reflects the original configuration of Talmy's macro-events and therefore requires no extra burden. In other words, when the influential aspect of the strength of events has priority over the informational aspect, the structure of Talmy's macro-events remains intact. This is hardly surprising because his characterization of events in macro-events is based on their influential aspect. This type of mapping generates the *arrive* verbs or verb-framed motion verbs in Talmy's terms in both verb-framed and satellite-framed languages, since no special conceptual apparatus is necessary.

Let us now turn to the case when event coidentification is applied to motion macro-events. In this case, the informationally stronger subordinate event in the macro-event, that is, the running subevent, is mapped onto the main verb. In section 2.2.6, we have diagramed this pattern of mapping as below:

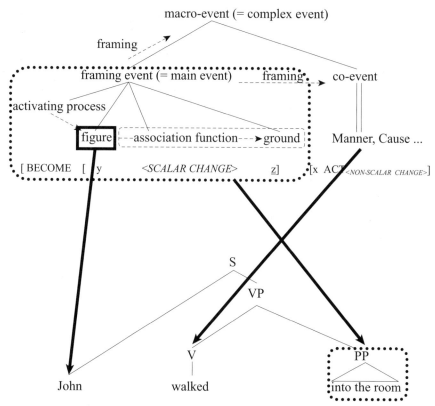

Figure 9 (= revised from Figure 11 in chapter 2)

But as we have observed there, if this mapping mechanism is right, then the framing event is divided into two parts, which in turn are mapped onto different parts of the sentence. To put it simply, this mapping pattern appears too complicated to be usable. Clearly something should be done. In order for it to be viable, a special conceptual apparatus is needed that can simplify the structure of macro-events so as to make possible a more straightforward mapping, and the apparatus is the process of event coidentification, which alters the hierarchical structure of macro-events by embedding the framing event in the subordinate event as a path scale.

As we have argued in section 4.4.3, in the process of event coidentification, the goal subevent is absorbed into the running subevent, and so their equivalents in Talmy's macro-events should behave in the same way. Therefore, we argue, counter to Talmy (2000), that the influentially stronger framing event is overshadowed by and integrated into the informationally stronger subordinate event when event coidentification occurs. As a result, the framing event loses its status as a discrete semantic entity.

In this type of mapping, the informational aspect of the strength of events is given precedence, and the structure of Talmy's macro-events is changed so as to reflect semantic saliency, and as a result it conforms to the syntactic configuration. More specifically, the framing event is assimilated into the subordinate event and the two events coalesce into a new event that has both substantive semantic content and an abstract scalar property. And the new event is represented by the event structure template of the coidentified event we have proposed at the end of section 4.4.3. The mapping from the amended version of macro-events onto syntactic structure is schematically represented below:

Chapter 4   Event Structure Templates, Event Coidentification, and Macro-event

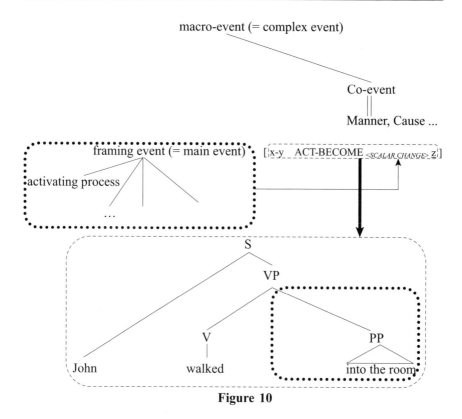

Figure 10

Here the altered configuration of the macro-event is mapped isomorphically onto syntactic structure. To put it differently, the process of event identification removes irregularities in mapping and brings about isomorphism between the configuration of macro-events and syntactic structure. This pattern of mapping is purported to be characteristic of satellite-framed languages, but more accurately, it is restricted to satellite-framed languages. This is because this type of complicated mapping is only made possible by the process of event coidentification, and only satellite-framed languages have the mechanism in their system. This pattern of mapping generates constructions in which the *run* verbs or manner of motion verbs are accompanied by a goal prepositional phrase, and such constructions are generally possible only in satellite-framed languages.

4.6. Advantages of our Approach

So far, we have examined how event coidentification is represented by scale-based event structure templates and associated with the components of motion macro-events postulated by Talmy (2000). In this section, we will discuss the advantages of the revised event structure template representing the *run* verbs accompanied by a goal prepositional phrase over the previous ones.

At the end of section 4.4.3, we have proposed the following event structure template in order to represent the coidentified running and goal subevents:

(61) [x-y ACT-BECOME$_{<RUN\text{-}INTO>}$ z]. (=(60))

Let us now compare this with the rejected event structure templates presented in section 4.2.4. They are repeated below as (62) for convenience:

(62) a. [[x ACT$_{<RUN>}$] CAUSE [BECOME [y <ARRIVED>]] (x=y)
    (=(33a))   (= to run, with the effect of motion along a path)
 b. [BECOME [y <ARRIVED>] BY [x ACT$_{<RUN>}$]] (x=y) (=(33b))
          (= to move along a path, by means of a running action)

As we have seen in section 4.2.5, both of these templates have two problems. First, they constitute a violation of the Argument-Per-Subevent Condition. Second, they do not explain why the resultant state [y <ARRIVED>], which they contain as a discrete element, cannot be modified by *for*-adverbials. In this section, we concentrate on the second problem and consider how our revised event structure template resolves it.

In section 4.2.5, we have taken the following sentence for example:

(63) John walked to the station for an hour. (=(39b))

If the sentence had the semantic structure represented by either of the templates (62), the *for*-adverbial could modify the resultant state and specify how long John stays at the station. This hypothesized interpretation is represented by event structure templates as follows:

(64) a. [[x ACT$_{<WALK>}$] CAUSE [BECOME (*for an hour* [y <*ARRIVED*>])]
b. [BECOME (*for an hour* [y <*ARRIVED*>]) BY [x ACT$_{<WALK>}$]]

But this prediction is not borne out. As we have discussed in section 4.2.5, Demizu (2001: 133) argues that this sentence can have a coerced interpretation in which the *for*-adverbial specifies how long the activity of walking has continued, but cannot be interpreted as stating that John walked to the station and stayed there for an hour. This means that both event structure templates (62) do not accurately represent the meaning of the phrase *walk to the station*.

On the other hand, if we assume that the meaning of the phrase *walk to the station* is represented by the following template, which is analogous to (61), the problem is satisfactorily solved.

(65) [x-y ACT-BECOME $_{<WALK-TO>}$ z]

It is obvious that this template does not contain an independent and discrete state template [y <*SCALAR CHANGE*>], which denotes a resultant state that can be the target of modification by *for*-adverbials. Here the event structure template representing the resultant state denoted by the goal preposition *to the station*, that is, [y <*TO*> z], is amalgamated into and subordinated to the manner root $_{<WALK>}$, and as a result it is assumed to lose its status as a discrete semantic entity. Therefore, it can no longer be the target of modification by *for*-adverbials. In this case, *for*-adverbials are coerced into modifying the whole amalgamated event. This interpretation is represented as follows:

(66) (*for an hour* [x-y ACT-BECOME$_{<WALK-TO>}$ z])

Interestingly, this interpretation is parallel to the interpretation of (106) in chapter 3, which are repeated as (67) for convenience:

(67) Sam walked for an hour: (*for an hour* [x ACT$_{<WALK>}$])

This aspectual resemblance between (63) and (67) is aptly represented by the templates (66) and (67), both of which do not contain an independent and discrete state event structure template representing a resultant state.

Furthermore, the event structure template (61) automatically account for why the *run* verbs with no goal prepositional phrase are unergative, while the *run* verbs accompanied by a goal prepositional phrase is unaccusative. Here let us remember the systematic correlations between the predicates in event structure templates and the unaccusativity of event structure templates. We have seen at the end of section 4.1 that if the template contains the predicate CAUSE, it is transitive, and that if the template contains the predicate ACT and no other predicates, it is unergative. Otherwise it is unaccusative.

The inventory of event structure templates we have presented as (8) at the end of section 4.1 is repeated below for ease of reference:

(68) Simple event structure templates:
    a. [x ACT$_{<NON\text{-}SCALAR\ CHANGE>}$] (unergative)
    b. [y <*SCALAR CHANGE*>] (unaccusative)
    c. [BECOME [y <*SCALAR CHANGE*>]] (unaccusative)
    Complex event structure template:
    d. [[x ACT] CAUSE [BECOME [y <*SCALAR CHANGE*>]]]
                                                                       (transitive, causative)

The *run* verbs taking no goal prepositional phrase is represented by the following event structure template.

(69) [x ACT$_{<RUN>}$]

By comparing this with the event structure templates (68), we can easily see that it is an instantiation of the unergative event structure template (68a). This squares with the fact that "the *run* verbs are basically unergative" (Levin and Rappaport Hovav (1992: 254)).

On the other hand, the *run* verbs followed by a goal prepositional phrase display unaccusative behavior, and their meaning is represented by the event structure template (61). This event structure template seems to be a variant of the unergative event structure template (68a), since they contain the predicate ACT and the modifier root$_{<RUN>}$. But it contains the additional hyphenated predicate BECOME. As we have seen just above, the unergative event structure template contains the predicate ACT and no other predicates, and so the template (61) cannot be unergative. In addition, the template (61) does not contain the predicate CAUSE. Therefore, it is diagnosed as unaccusative. This automatically accounts for the fact the *run* verbs exhibit unaccusative behavior when they appear with a goal prepositional phrase.

Given these considerations, the tabulation of event structure templates we have provided at the end of section 4.1 should be revised as below:

(70)   Simple event structure templates:
   a.   [x ACT$_{<NON\text{-}SCALAR\ CHANGE>}$]   (unergative)
   a'.   [x-y ACT-BECOME$_{<SCALAR\ CHANGE>}$ z]   (unaccusative)
   b.   [y <*SCALAR CHANGE*>]   (unaccusative)
   c.   [BECOME [y <*SCALAR CHANGE*>]]   (unaccusative)
   Complex event structure template:
   d.   [[x ACT] CAUSE [BECOME [y <*SCALAR CHANGE*>]]]
                                                                     (transitive, causative)

Here the event structure template (61) is added as a variant of (70a), namely (70a'), and is categorized into simple event structure templates, since it does not contain the predicate CAUSE, which encodes a causative relationship between two subevents.

4.7.   Conclusion

We have begun this chapter by outlining the Unaccusative Hypothesis put forward by Perlmutter (1978). In section 4.2, we have examined in detail how Levin and Rappaport Hovav (1992), one of their earlier articles, deal with the differences between manner of motion verbs and verbs of directed motion verbs, in particular between the *run* verbs and the *arrive* verbs. Then we have exposed the imperfections in the mechanism of lexical subordination, which they have devised in order to explain the vagaries of the *run* verbs in terms of unaccusativity. In section 4.3, we have introduced the process of event coidentification, which is proposed by Levin and

Rappaport Hovav (1999) and Rappaport Hovav and Levin (2001), as an alternative to lexical subordination. Event coidentification is an elaborate and sophisticated mechanism that plausibly explains how the *run* verbs and goal prepositional phrases such as *to the station* and *into the room* are semantically conflated. But regrettably, as we have argued in section 4.3.2, the semantic representation of event coidentification presented by Rappaport Hovav and Levin (2001) is beset with three problems. In section 4.4, therefore, attempts have been made to rectify these problems. After creating the event structure representation of goal prepositional phrases, we have integrated the concept of scalarity into the process of event coidentification. Based on this, we have produced the event structure template representing the resultant coidentified event. Then in section 4.5, we have investigated the possibility of relating event coidentification to the configuration of Talmy's motion macro-events, and have proved that event coidentification is analogous to the structuring function carried out by framing events. Finally, in section 4.6, we have compared the event structure template of coidentified events with the template representation of lexical subordination, and have shown that event coidentification is more favorable than lexical subordination in terms of event structure templates.

In trying to relate event coidentification to Talmy's macro-events, we have felt that most of the pieces of the jigsaw are there and what we have to do next is to put them together and find the one big piece that is still elusive, which has later proved to be the concept of scalarity. It is evident and important that the very concept of scalarity, which is introduced by Rappaport Hovav (2008) and Rappaport Hovav and Levin (2010) and which we have discussed in chapter 3, has opened up the possibility of developing a more systematic analysis of motion events.

Chapter 5

English Examples and Translations

The earlier chapters of this book have dealt with two semantic theories and the significant correlations between them. In particular, in chapter 2, we have reconsidered Talmy's well-known dichotomy between satellite-framed and verb-framed languages, and have concluded that it is more reasonable to assume that satellite-framedness is an "add-on module" to verb-framedness. In order to explain encoding possibilities in satellite-framed languages, which sometimes exhibit verb-framed characteristics, this strategy is more practical than accepting the conventional theory based on binary opposition. The viewpoint on lexicalization of motion events can be encapsulated as follows:

(1) a. Verb-framed languages like Japanese and French do not allow liberal use of satellite-framed expressions, even though they have lexical resources such as manner verbs and adpositional phrases denoting the path to a goal. That is to say, a lack of satellite-framed lexicalization in verb-framed languages is generally attributed to the constraints that the grammatical system imposes.

b. In satellite-framed languages, such as English, German and Chinese, verb-framed encoding options are possible whenever lexical resources are available. To put it differently, a lack of verb-framed expressions in satellite-framed languages results from lexical gaps, and verb-framed lexicalization itself is not totally prohibited by the grammatical system of satellite-framed languages.

As we have already seen in section 2.3.6, what emerges from these considerations overall is the following unsurprising conclusion:

(2) (i) Verb-framed expressions are linguistically more basic than satellite-framed ones.
 (ii) More basic verb-framed lexicalization options are available and observed in almost all languages.
 (iii) Satellite-framed conflation is an add-on to basic verb-framed lexicalization ubiquitous in the language system, and is therefore limited to the languages traditionally classified as satellite-framed.

What we have to do now is to support it by citing reliable raw data collected from sources that are independent of linguistic research.

In order to achieve this purpose, we use examples of the verb *walk* which have been culled from a variety of novels written in English. In addition, we compare them with their Japanese, French, German and Chinese translations. In the following extracts from novels, the (a)-examples are the English originals. The (b)-examples are the Japanese translations given in alphabetical form. The (c)- and (d)-examples are the French and German versions, respectively. Finally, the (e)-examples are the Chinese translation and their romanized notation under the Pinyin system. In each translation, the number in parentheses refers to the number of the page on which the example is found.

This chapter is organized as follows. In section 5.1, we will look at examples in which *walk* occurs alone, that is, takes no prepositional phrase, and we will confirm that *walk* can be literally translated as a semantically equivalent manner of motion verb in all the four languages. In section 5.2, we will turn to cases in which *walk* takes a goal prepositional phrase headed by the preposition *into* or *to*. We will observe that the manner of motion is lost in translation into verb-framed languages as expected, but intriguingly, it is sometimes dropped from the translations into satellite-framed languages like German and Chinese. In section 5.3, we will consider examples where *walk* takes a directional prepositional phrase headed by the preposition *toward*. Since satellite-framed encoding is characterized by path conflation that involves a goal or Ground entity, it is reasonable to expect that directional prepositional phrases are not sensitive to whether or not satellite-framed lexicalization is possible. This further predicts that the phrase *walk toward* will be faithfully translated into verb-framed languages. Indeed, the theoretical prediction is borne out by Japanese data. However, in most French translations, the typical collocation *se diriger vers* "to head for" is used to express the motion, instead of the exactly corresponding phrase *marcher vers* "to walk toward." This shows that translators tend to follow general usage rather than to translate word for word. Finally, in section 5.4, we will look at how the phrase *walk away* is translated. Most intriguingly, in the examples we will consider, the manner of motion denoted by *walk* can be lost in translation into all the four languages. To put it differently, all the four languages of translation can use a verb-framed expression to describe the motion expressed in a satellite-framed manner in English. This proves conclusively that verb-framed encoding is possible even in satellite-framed languages as long as they have a verb to express it. To further bolster up our argument, we will take a look at how the directed motion verb *leave* is translated. Section 5.5 is the recapitulation.

5.1. When Verb *walk* Takes no Prepositional Phrase

We begin by looking at the *verb* walk that is not accompanied by any prepositional phrase in the original English text, as in the following examples:

(3) a. They *walked* quickly, ...
　　　　　　　(J. le Carré, *The Spy Who Came in from the Cold*: 238)
　　b. Futari-wa　isogi　ashi-ni　*susun*-da. (328)
　　　　they-Top　quick　pace-at　advance-Past
　　　'They *advanced* at a quick pace.'

c. Ils   *marchaient*   à   grandes   enjambées (325)
   they were-walking at great   strides
   'They *walked* with big strides.'
d. Sie   *gingen*   schnell. (254)
   they walked   quickly
   'They *walked* quickly'
e. 他们   走   得   很   快， … (258)
   tāmen zǒu   de   hěn   kuài
   they   walk way-is very quick
   'Their way of *walking* is very quick.'

Here the English verb *walk* is literally translated as the verb *marcher* in French, the verb *gehen* in German and the verb 走 *zǒu* in Chinese, and all these lexicalize a walking manner of motion.[1] The Japanese translation is exceptional in that it describes the motion as *susumu* "to advance," which is a verb of directed motion and does not encode any manner. But we can also depict the same situation as follows:

(4) Futari-wa   isogi   ashi-de   *arui*-ta.
     they-Top   quick   pace-at   walk-Past
     'They *walked* at a quick pace.'

All these translations make it clear that *walk* can be rendered into the other four languages by using manner of motion verbs when it does not appear with prepositional phrases.

In the following examples, the writer gives more attention to Dalgliesh's ability to walk than to the action of walking.

(5) a. When he was able to *walk*, Dalgliesh removed himself to Seal
        Cottage.   (P. D. James, *The Lighthouse*: 456)
    b. Darugurisshu-wa   *aruk*-eru   youni   naru   to
        Dalgliesh-Top   walk-can   like   become   when

---

[1] Here the German verb *gehen* is glossed as "to walk," since it does not mean going or traveling somewhere in general, but it specifies its manner of motion as walking (see also note 2.)

    Shiiru-sou-ni   modot-ta. (393)
    Seal-Cottage-to return-Past.
    'When he came to be able to *walk*, Dalgliesh returned to Seal Cottage.'
 c. Quand il   put   *marcher*, Dalgliesh regagna
    when   he   could walk   Dalgliesh got-back-to
    Seal Cottage. (494)
    Seal Cottage.
    'When he was able to *walk*, Dalgliesh got back to Seal Cottage.'
 d. Als   Dalgliesh wieder *gehen* konnte, zog   er   sich
    When   Dalgliesh again   walk   could   drew he   himself
    ins   Seal Cottage zurück. (451)
    into-the   Seal Cottage back.
    'When Dalgliesh was able to *walk* again, he moved back into Seal Cottage.'
 e. 达格利什   能   *走动*   之后   就   搬   回   了
    dágélìshí néng   zǒudòng   zhīhòu   jiù   bān   huí   le
    Dalgliesh can   walk (around) after   just   move   back Perf
    海狮   别墅。(271)
    hǎishī   biéshù
    sea-lion   villa
    'After Dalgliesh can *walk around*, he has just moved back to Sea-Lion Villa.'

Here the English verb *walk* is translated as the verb *aruku* in Japanese, the verb *marcher* in French, and the verb *gehen* in German. The three verbs are roughly equivalent in meaning to *walk*. In Chinese, the translator is presumed to choose the phrase 走动 *zǒudòng* "to walk around" instead of 走 *zǒu* "to walk" in order to make it clearer that the ability matters more than the action itself.

The examples below also depict the situation in which the ambulatory ability is regarded as more important than the action itself.

(6) a. "... he will never be able to *walk* or speak again."

(S. Sheldon, *A Stranger in the Mirror*: 253)

b. "Goshujin-wa   futatabi *aruku*-koto ya   hanasu-koto wa
your husband-Top again   walk-to   or   speak-to   Top
deki-nai deshou." (220)
cannot   will

'"Your husband will never be able to *walk* or speak again."'

c. ... il   ne sera jamais   capable   de   recommencer   à *marcher*
he   never will be   capable   of   start-again   to walk
ou   à parler. (273)
or   to speak.

'"He will never be capable of starting to *walk* or speak again."'

d. ... wird er   nie   wieder *gehen* oder sprechen
will he   never   again   walk   or   speak
können. (215)
can

'"He will never be able to *walk* or speak again."'

e. 他   不   可能   再   行动   或   说话   了。(224)
tā   bù   kěnéng   zài   xíngdòng   huò   shuōhuà   le
he   not   can   again   move   or   speak   Perf

'"He will not be able to *move* or speak again."'

Similar to (5), the verbs *aruku*, *marcher* and *gehen* are used in Japanese, French and German, respectively, and all the three semantically correspond to the English manner of motion verb *walk*. Interestingly, the verb 行动 *xíngdòng* "to move" is used in Chinese, which is the superordinate of the verb 走 *zǒu* "to walk." More specifically, the denotation of 走 *zǒu* "to walk" is a subset of that of 行动 *xíngdòng* "to move." This means that the Chinese translator chooses a verb with a broader meaning to depict the situation.

Sometimes, the verb *walk* with no prepositional phrase is translated in a verb-framed way by inferring the direction of the motion from the context. In addition, it is striking that this type of translation is observed in all the four languages, as shown by the following examples:

(7) a. '… why don't we *walk*?'

                        (J. Archer, *Shall We Tell the President?*: 125)

   b. "*Arui*-te   *ik*-anai." (140)
      walk   go-not
     '"Why not go walking?"'

   c. Pourquoi ne pas y   aller   à pied … (119)
      why   not   there go   on foot
     '"Why not go there *on foot*?"'

   d. … warum *gehen* wir nicht *zu Fuß* hin? (125)
       why   go   we   not   on foot away-from-the-speaker
     '"Why not go *on foot* from here?"'

   e. 干脆   咱们   走着   去   吧? (95)
      gān cuì   zánmen   zǒuzhe   qù   ba
      might as well we   walk-Manner go Aux.
     '"We might as well go *walking*."'

Here the manner of motion encoded by the main verb *walk* in English is described by the subordinate phrases *arui-te* "(by) walking," *à pied* "on foot," *zu Fuß* "on foot," and 走着 *zǒuzhe* "(by) walking" in Japanese, French, German, and Chinese, respectively. But even more strikingly, the deictic information that the movement is away from the speaker's location, which is unexpressed in the original English text, is gleaned from the context and is described by the main verb in the translations.

In Japanese, the verb of directed motion *iku* "to go," which encodes the deictic information, occurs as the main verb, and as a result, the manner of motion is verbalized in the gerundive position as a *-te* construction. In French, the main verb *aller* "to go" lexicalizes the deictic information, and the prepositional phrase *à pied* "on foot" expresses the manner of motion. In German, the prepositional phrase *zu Fuß* "on foot" portrays the manner of motion, while the main verb *gehen*, which in this case means "to go," encodes the deictic information.[2] Interestingly, the separable verb prefix

---

[2] Here the German verb *gehen*, which cooccurs with the prepositional phrase *zu Fuß*, is glossed as "to go." This is because, in this case, the prepositional phrase *zu Fuß* "on foot" expresses the walking manner, and the verb *gehen* just encodes a directed motion of "away-from-the-speaker," corresponding to the English verb *go* (cf. note 1 above); indeed,

hin also shows that the motion is away from the speaker's position, lexicalizing the deictic information. In a word, the German translation conveys the deictic information in two positions. Lastly, in the Chinese version, the main verb is 去 *qù* "to go." The phrase 走着 *zǒuzhe* functions as a modifier of the main verb, specifying the manner of the "going" action as "walking." In Chinese, when two verbs are connected by 着 *zhe*, the compound made up of the first verb and 着 *zhe* serves as a modifier of the second verb, and it elaborates on the manner of the action denoted by the second verb.³

These translations deserve more than a passing notice, since they are not faithful renditions of the original English text. In particular, the position of the main verb is usurped by a newly introduced verb of directed motion, and the element describing the manner of motion, which is in the main verb position in the original text, is relegated to a subordinate position. But how is this irregular mapping motivated?

This can be explained quite naturally as the ubiquity of verb-framedness in the language system, which we have so far demonstrated. In the examples concerned, the main verbs *iku*, *aller*, *gehen*, 去 *qù* are all verbs of directed motion that are roughly equivalent in meaning to the English verb *go*. It expresses the framing event in Talmy's theory and therefore fits a verb-framed lexicalization pattern. This means that translators sometimes use verb-framed encoding options by interpreting the depicted situation more restrictively; specifically, in some translations, the direction of motion not described in the original text is understood from the context, and consequently expressed by the main verb in a verb-framed manner, even when satellite-framed encoding is possible. This empirically demonstrates that even in satellite-framed languages, verb-framed encoding options are allowed whenever lexical resources are available.

Let us now turn to another set of examples, which show that idiomatic

---

the whole phrase *zu Fuß gehen* is translated as "go on foot" in *Oxford German Dictionary (Third Edition)*.

³ *Shogakukan Chinese Japanese Dictionary* (second edition) defines the meaning of this construction as follows:

    verb¹+着 *zhe* expresses in what way or under what circumstances the action denoted by verb² is carried out.
    (*Shogakukan Chinese Japanese Dictionary* (second edition), s.v. 着 *zhe*, English translation by TD)

expressions are sometimes chosen irrespective of, or sometimes defying, typological classification.

(8) a. They parked the car and *walked*.
        (G. Greene, *Our Man in Havana*: 35)
   b. Futari-wa kuruma-o tome-te *arui*-ta. (41)
      they-Top car-Acc   park   walk-Past
      'They parked the car and *walked*.'
   c. Ils rangèrent la voiture et *continuèrent à pied*. (60)
      they parked the car and continued on foot
      'They parked the car and *continued on foot*.'
   d. Sie parkten das Auto und *gingen zu Fuß*. (41)
      they parked the car und went   on foot
      'They parked the car and *went on foot*.'
   e. 他们 停   了   车, 下   来   走路。(36)
      tāmen tíng le   chē xià   lai   zǒulù
      they park Perf car get out come walk (along the road)
      'They parked the car, got out, and *walked (along the road)*.'

Here the Japanese version is a literal translation from English. In French and German, the phrases *à pied* "on foot" and *zu Fuß* "on foot" are juxtaposed to the main verbs *continuer* "to continue" and *gehen* "to go," in order to express the manner of motion. Similar to (7c) and (7d), the manner of motion is depicted by the adverbial phrases *à pied* "on foot" and *zu Fuß* "on foot," and the main verb position is occupied by the aspectual verb *continuer* "to continue" and the directed motion verb *gehen* "to go." The verb *continuer* "to continue" is chosen here because the translator focuses more on the maintenance of the motion, than on the direction of the motion.[4] Furthermore, in Chinese, the phrase 走路 *zǒulù*, which literally means "to walk along the road," is used to denote the motion. This is because the scene described by the sentence unfolds on the road, and the Chinese

---

[4] In this French translation, the main verb *continuer* "to continue" does not lexicalize a directed motion nor a manner of motion and, as a consequence, it cannot be explained by Talmy's typology nor its revised version proposed by this book. We have no specific proposal on this matter, and we must leave it as a topic for future investigation.

translator incorporates the information into the verb phrase. The French and Chinese translations show that translators do not translate verbatim when they have better words or phrases to describe the situation.

The verb *walk* has another meaning that refers to a stroll for pleasure or exercise. In this case, it is variously translated in order to clearly indicate that the purpose of walking is not to get somewhere but to get exercise or pleasure. The examples below illustrate this point:

(9) a. We *walked* ...   (P. D. James, *The Lighthouse*: 278)
    b. Isshou-ni *sampo*-o   shi-te ... (241)
       together   stroll-Acc   do
       'We took *a stroll* together.'
    c. Nous *nous promenions* ... (304)
       we   strolled
       'We *strolled*.'
    d. Wir sind *spazieren gegangen*, ... (279)
       we are   gone for a stroll
       'We *went for a stroll*.'
    e. 我们   一起   散步… (167)
       wǒmen yīqǐ   sànbù
       we   together stroll
       'We *strolled*.'

In Japanese, the verb *walk* is translated as the accusative noun phrase *sampo-o* "stroll," followed by the verb *suru* "to do." The whole phrase *sampo-o suru* "take a stroll" is roughly equivalent in structure to English light verb constructions. The word *sampo* means an idle and leisurely walk, implying that the purpose of walking is not to arrive at a certain destination, but to relax or get exercise. A similar observation applies to the Chinese case, in which the verb 散步 sànbù carries much the same meaning as the Japanese word *sampo*. Therefore, the Chinese version also states that the purpose of walking is not to reach a destination. Moreover, in German, the compound verb *spazieren gehen* "go for a stroll" is idiomatically used to denote the same thing.

Finally, let us turn to the French translation. The verb *walk* is translated as the verb *se promener*, which is tentatively glossed in (9c) as "to stroll." Intriguingly, however, *se promener* does not limit the manner of motion to "walking," but just specifies the purpose of going out as not getting somewhere, as shown by the excerpts from dictionaries.

(10) IIv. pron. (1485) SE PROMENER
1 Aller d'un lieu à un autre pour se détendre, prendre l'air, etc.
'to go from one place to another, in order to relax, to get some fresh air, etc.'
(*Le Nouveau Petit Robert de la langue française, 2008 nouvelle édition* S.V. SE PROMENER; English translation by TD)

(11) **se promener** *vpr* (pour se distraire) (à pied) to go for a walk; (en voiture) to go for a drive; (en bateau) to go out in a boat; (à bicyclette, à cheval) to go for a ride
'**se promener** *vpr* (to amuse or enjoy oneself) (on foot) to go for a walk; (by car) to go for a drive; (by boat) to go out in a boat; (by bicycle, on horseback) to go for a ride'
(*Oxford-Hachette French Dictionary* (Fourth Edition) French-English S.V. SE PROMENER; English translation by TD)

Unlike the English verb *walk* and the German verb *spazieren gehen*, the French verb *se promener* might be a purpose verb (the category newly proposed by Fellbaum (2013)) rather than a manner of motion verb. Consequently, the French translator describes the scene more vaguely, leaving out the information that the manner of motion is "walking," because there is no semantically equivalent verb in French.

Let us look at the next group of examples, in which the verb *walk* occurs as a gerundive form, fleshing out the purpose of the going out denoted by the main verb *go*.

(12) In the afternoon they went *walking* again.
(J. le Carré, *The Spy Who Came in from the Cold*: 149)
b. Sono gogo futari-wa mata *sampo-ni*
that afternoon two persons-Top again stroll-for
dekake-ta. (197)
go out-Past
'That afternoon, the two persons *went for a stroll* again.'

c. Cet après-midi-là, ils   *allèrent* à nouveau *faire un tour*. (196)
   That afternoon   they went   anew   go around
   'That afternoon, they *went around* again.'
d. Nachmittags   *gingen*   sie   noch einmal *spazieren*. (155)
   in the afternoon   walked   they more once   stroll
   'In the afternoon, they *went for a stroll* again.'
e. 那   天   下午,   他们   又   出   去   散步。 (163)
   nà   tiān xiàwǔ   tāmen   yòu   chū   qù   sànbù
   that day   afternoon they   again   out   go   *stroll*
   'That afternoon, they *went for a stroll* again.'

Here the gerundive verb *walking* follows the main verb *go*, serving the function of modifying it. Additionally, the modification relationship is maintained in all the four translations. Note that this is the dominant lexicalization pattern in verb-framed languages.

In Japanese, the gerundive verb *walking* is translated as the adverbial phrase *sampo-ni* "for a stroll," which modifies the main verb *dekakeru* "to go out." In German, in a similar way to (9d), the idiomatic expression *spazieren gehen* "to go for a stroll" is used, but in this case it is the translation equivalent of the whole phrase *go walking*. From a different perspective, it is possible to assume that its individual components, namely *spazieren* and *gehen*, each correspond to the English verbs *walking* and *go*, respectively. Furthermore, in French and Chinese, the strolling manner is expressed by the subordinate phrases *faire un tour* "to go around" and 散步 *sànbù* "to stroll."[5] Similar to the Japanese version, the phrases serve to elaborate on the purpose of the action denoted by the main verbs *aller* "to go" and 出去 *chūqù* "to go out," respectively.

All these things make it clear that, in all the five languages, the main verb can describe not a manner of motion, but a movement away from the speaker's location. In addition, the phrase preceding or following the

---

[5] Strictly speaking, the phrase *faire un tour* does not specifies any manner of motion, but just means "going around without a destination in mind," as illustrated by the following definition:
  faire le tour de qch
    «gén» to go around sth; (en voiture) to drive around something
      (Oxford-Hachette French Dictionary (Fourth Edition) French-English S.V. TOUR)

main verb elaborates on the purpose of the going out denoted by the main verb. This lexicalization pattern is typically observed in verb-framed languages rather than in satellite-framed languages. Therefore, similar to the examples (7), this justifies the omnipresence of verb-framedness in the language system.

5.2. When Verb *walk* Takes Goal Prepositional Phrase

In English, the verb *walk* is often followed by a goal prepositional phrase headed by the preposition *to* or *into*. In verb-framed languages such as Japanese and French, the walking manner is often lost in translation and the motion is expressed by a verb of directed motion. Let us first look at four groups of examples in which *walk* takes a prepositional phrase headed by the preposition *into*.

In the examples below, the verb *walk* is translated as a semantically equivalent manner of motion verb in German and Chinese (satellite-framed languages). On the other hand, the motion is depicted by a verb of directed motion in Japanese and French (verb-framed languages), without specification of the manner of motion.[6]

(13) a. Brody poured himself a cup of coffee, *walked* into his office, and began to flip through the morning papers …

(P. Benchley, *Jaws*: 18)

b. Burodi-wa koohii-o sosogi jibun-no heya-ni
Brody-Top coffee-Acc pour oneself-Gen office-to
hait-te chookan-o yomi hajime-ta. (27)
enter-Past morning-paper-Acc read begin-Past
'Brody poured himself a cup of coffee, *entered* his office, and began to read the morning papers.'

---

[6] Henceforth, in each passage, the underlined part shows the word or phrase that denotes the goal or the direction of the movement.

c. Brody se servit   une tasse de café,   *entra*   dans son
   Brody helped-himself a   cup of coffee, entered   in his
   bureau et   commença   par jeter   un coup d'oeil sur
   office and began   by throw   a   glance   at
   les journaux … (24)
   the journals
   'Brody helped himself to a cup of coffee, *entered* his office and began by throwing a glance at the journals.'

d. Brody schenkte sich   eine Tasse Kaffee ein,   *ging*
   Brody poured   himself a   cup   coffee in   walked
   in sein Büro   und sah   flüchtig die Morgenzeitungen
   into his office and looked quick   the morning-papers
   durch … (21)
   through
   'Brody poured himself a cup of coffee, *walked* into his office, and looked through the morning newspapers quickly.'

e. 布罗迪   倒   了   杯   咖啡,   端着   *走*   *进*
   bùluódí   dào   le   bēi   kāfēi   duānzhe   zǒu   jìn
   Brody   pour Perf cup   coffee   hold-Manner   walk   enter
   他的 办公室,   开始   翻阅   当天   的
   tā-de bàngōngshì,   kāishǐ fānyuè   dàngtiān   de
   his   office   begin   flip through that day   of
   报纸… (17)
   bàozhǐ
   newspaper
   'Brody poured a cup of coffee and, holding it, *walked* into his office, and began flipping through the day's newspapers.'

In the German and Chinese translations, the phrase *walk into his office* is accurately translated as *in sein Büro gehen* "to walk into his office" and 走进他的办公室 *zǒu jìn tāde bàngōngshì* "to walk into his office," respectively. In them, the verbs *gehen* and 走 *zǒu* correspond to the verb *walk*, and the German preposition *in* and the Chinese directional complement 进 *jìn* parallel the preposition *into*, encoding a movement to the inside of a place. In Japanese and French, on the other hand, the whole motion is expressed by *jibun-no heya-ni hairu* "to enter one's own office" and *entrer dans son bureau* "to enter his office," respectively. In these phrases, the verbs *hairu* "to enter" and *entrer* "to enter" are both verbs of directed motion, and denote a movement into a place without referring to a particular manner of motion. In other words, the manner of motion lexicalized by *walk* is left out of the Japanese and French translations.

A similar observation applies to the next set of examples:

(14) a. Vaughan *walked* into Brody's office and sat down.
(P. Benchley, *Jaws*: 37)
   b. Vôn-ga   Burodi-no   heya-ni   hait-te   ki-te
      Vaughan-Nom Brody-Gen   office-to enter   come
      koshi-o   oroshi-ta. (50)
      back-Acc   lower-Past
      'Vaughan *entered* Brody's office and lowered himself.'
   c. Il *entra*   dans le   bureau   et   s'assit. (43)
      he entered   into the office   and oneself-seated
      'He *entered* the office and seated himself.'
   d. Vaughan *trat*   in   Brodys Büro   und setzte   sich. (39)
      Vaughan stepped into   Brody's office and seated   oneself
      'Vaughan *stepped* into Brody's office and seated himself.'
   e. 沃恩   走   进   布罗迪的   办公室   坐   了
      wōēn   zǒu   jìn   bùluódí-de   bàngōngshì   zuò   le
      Vaughan walk into Brody's   office   sit   Perf
      下来。(35)
      xialai
      down
      Vaughan *walked* into Brody's office and sat down.

In Chinese, the verb phrase *walk into Brody's office* is translated as 走进布罗迪的办公室 *zǒu jìn bùluódí-de bàngōngshì* "to walk into Brody's office," and the verb 走 *zǒu* and the directional complement 进布罗迪的办公室 *jìn bùluódí-de bàngōngshì* are semantically analogous to the main verb "to walk" and the prepositional phrase "into Brody's office," respectively. In French, the same phrase is translated as *entrer dans le bureau* "to enter the office," omitting the information that the manner of entering is "walking."

In German, the translation is word for word, but it is intriguing that the manner of motion verb *walk* is translated as the verb *treten* "to step." As Beavers (2002: 15) states, the event of walking into a place has "an extremely short duration," and walking with an extremely short duration can be reinterpreted as stepping. This is thought to be why the German translator uses *treten* "to step."

In a similar way to the French version, the manner information is dropped from the Japanese version, but this is not the only change the translator makes. Here, in a similar manner to (7b), the deictic information not described in the original English text is inferred from the context, and the verb *kuru* "to come," which lexicalizes it, ousts the verb *hairu* "to enter" from the main verb position. As a result, the two directed motion verbs, that is, *hairu* "to enter" and *kuru* "to come" are juxtaposed, and the former occurs as a subordinate *-te* construction. This fact is interesting in its own right, and it would be fruitful to consider how it relates to Talmy's typology or the revised system espoused by this book. As space is limited, however, we will leave it for future investigation.

Let us turn to the third group of examples, in which the patterns of translation do not perfectly match Talmy's original typology.

(15) a. He *walked* into her bedroom and stood there watching her.
(S. Sheldon, *A Stranger in the Mirror*: 202)

b. Kare-wa Kanojo-no shinshitsu-ni *hairi* mado-no
he-Top she-Gen bedroom-to enter window-Gen
soba-ni tatte kanojo-o mimamot-ta. (178)
side-at stand she-Acc watch over-Past
'He *entered* her bedroom and stood by the window, watching over her.'

c. Il *fonça* droit à la chambre de la jeune femme
he rushed straight to the bedroom of the young woman
et l'observa. (218)
and her-observed
'He *rushed* straight to the bedroom of the young woman and watched her.'

d. Er *betrat* ihr Schlafzimmer und musterte sie. (174)
he entered her bedroom and watched her
'He *entered* her bedroom and watched her.'

e. 他　　走　　进　　她　　的　　卧室。　站　　在　　那儿
   tā　　zǒu　 jìn　 tā　　de　　wòshì　zhàn　zài　 nàr
   he　 walk enter she　 of　 bedroom stand at　 there
   注视　　　着　　　她。(180)
   zhùshì　 zhe　　 tā
   stare　 Imperf　 her
   'He *walked* into her bedroom and stood there watching her.'

In the Chinese translation, as with (13e) and (14e), the verb *walk* and the preposition *into* are literally translated as 走 *zǒu* and 进 *jìn*, respectively. Since Chinese is a satellite-framed language, this translation confirms the theoretical prediction. In German, however, as in Japanese, the manner of motion denoted by *walk* in the English original is unexpressed and the verb of directed motion *betreten* "to enter" depicts the motion, as the Japanese counterpart *hairu* "to enter" does.[7] This shows that satellite-framed languages allow verb-framed lexicalization when they have verbs to express the concept, and that Talmy's dichotomy should be superseded by the ubiquity of verb-framed lexicalization.

Furthermore, contrary to what we expect, the French translator uses the verb *foncer* "to rush" in order to express the speed of movement gleaned from the context. Intriguingly, this verb does not lexicalize a directed motion event, and is not a typical example of lexicalization in French, a verb-framed language. A more systematic consideration of this verb awaits future research.[8] This type of "enriched" translation appears in various books and so is not uncommon.

Finally we should consider the last and most interesting set of examples:

---

[7] The German verb *betreten* is derived from one of the manner of motion verbs in German, namely the verb *treten* "to step." However, *betreten* is usually glossed as "to enter," and not as "to step into or step on(to)," and therefore, we regard it as a directed motion verb. In fact, it seems that some German *be*-verbs lexicalize a manner of motion, such as *besteigen* "to climb," *befahren* "to drive on or across," *begehen* "to walk along or across," but this is too involved a subject to be treated here in detail.

[8] Like the French verb *se promener*, which is defined in (10) and (11), the French verb *foncer* "to rush" might also be a purpose verb, because it specifies the purpose of getting somewhere very soon, but does not lexicalize a specific manner of motion.

(16) a. The moment Jill *walked* into the room, her nostrils were assailed by the familiar stench of sickness.
(S. Sheldon, *A Stranger in the Mirror*: 284)

b. Soko-e   hait-ta   shunkan   itsumo-no   byoushuu-ga
there-to enter-Past   moment   usual   odor-of-sickness-Nom
kanojo-no   bikou-o   tsui-ta (247)
her   nostril   sting-Past
'The moment she *entered* there, the usual odor of sickness stung her nostrils.'

c. Dès   l'entrée,   l'odeur   familière   de   la   maladie
from   the-entrance   the-odor   familiar   of   the sickness
assaillit   ses   narines. (306)[9]
assailed   her   nostrils
'The moment she entered, the familiar odor of sickness assailed her nostrils.'

d. Als   sie   den Raum   *betrat*,   drang   ihr   der
when   she   the room   entered   penetrated   her   the
bekannte   Gestank   in   die   Nase. ... (241)
well-known   stench   into   the   nose
'When she *entered* the room, the well-known stench penetrated into her nose.'

e. 吉尔   刚   一   进门,   病房   里   那   种
Jí'ěr   gāng   yī   jìnmén   bìngfáng   -li   nà   zhǒng
Jill   as   just   enter-door   sickroom   -in   that   kind-of
熟悉的   难闻的   气味   就   直   冲
shúxi-de   nánwén-de   qìwèi   jiù   zhí   chōng
well-known   stinking   smell   just   direct   hit
她的   鼻孔   (252)
tā-de   bíkǒng
her   nostril
'Just as Jill *entered the door*, the kind of well-known stinking in sickrooms directly hit her nostrils.'

---

[9] Here the French translation uses the noun *entrée* "entrance" instead of the verb *entrer* "to enter," and so we do not discuss it, because this book is concerned with the lexicalization patterns of verbs.

In Japanese, conforming to its characteristic lexicalization pattern, the manner of motion is not expressed in the translation, and the directed motion verb *hairu* "to enter" describes the motion. In German, as with (15d), the manner of motion is left out and the verb of directed motion *betreten* "to enter" describes the movement. Furthermore, more interestingly, the Chinese translator uses the idiomatic phrase 进门 *jìnmén* "to enter the door," which encodes a directed motion event, not specifying a particular manner of motion. The German and Chinese translations clearly show that, even in satellite-framdded languages, verb-framed encoding is possible when lexical resources are available. This does not match what Talmy's binary opposition expects, and in turn justifies considering verb-framedness to be basic and ubiquitous.

Next we consider five sets of examples in which the verb *walk* is accompanied by a goal phrase headed by the preposition *to*. We start by examining the following examples:

(17) a. He ... *walked* to his car. (P. Benchley, *Jaws*: 132)
 b. Kare-wa ... jibun-no   kuruma-ni   *mukat-ta.* (179)
    he-Top   oneself-Gen   car-to   head-for-Past
    'He *went* to his car.'
 c. Hooper ... *se dirigea*   vers   sa voiture. (137)
    Hooper   directed-himself   toward   his car
    'Hooper *headed* for his car.'
 d. Er ... *ging*   zu   seinem Wagen. (124)
    he   walked   to   his car
    'He *walked* to his car.'
 e. 他⋯   朝   他的   汽车   走   去。(132)
    tā   cháo   tā-de   qìchē   zǒu   qù
    he   toward   his   car   walk   away
    'He *walked* toward his car.'

The whole phrase *walk to his car* is literally translated as *zu seinem Wagen gehen* "to walk to his car" in German, but all the other renditions of the sentence are not faithful. In Japanese and French, the manner of motion is expectedly lost in translation. But there are more changes made by the translators.

In the Japanese translation, the main verb is *mukau* "to head for," which does not entail an arrival at a destination, but only signifies a movement toward it. Additionally, the phrase *jibun-no kuruma-ni* "to one's own car" elaborates on the destination. In French, the phrase *walk to* is idiomatically translated as *se diriger vers*, which strictly means "to direct oneself toward" but is usually translated as "to head for." Indeed, this expression is characteristically used in French in order to denote the motion described by the phrases *walk to* and *walk toward(s)* in English. Moreover, in Chinese, *walk* is translated as the phrase 走去 *zǒuqù* "to walk away," which consists of the verb 走 *zǒu* "to walk" and the directional complement 去 *qù* meaning that the movement is away from the speaker's position.[10] The prepositional phrase *to his car* is roughly translated as 朝他的汽车 *cháo tā-de qìchē* "toward his car," in which the character 朝 *cháo*, which corresponds to the English preposition *toward*, signifies a movement in the direction of something. All these translations make it clear that an arrival at a place is sometimes crudely described as motion toward it. We will return to this point when we discuss the translation of *walk toward*.

Let us now turn to the second set of examples:

(18) a. He ... *walked* to the door.
    (J. le Carré, *The Spy Who Came in from the Cold*: 126)
 b. Toguchi-ni mukat-te *aruki* dashi-ta. (166)
   door-to head-for walk begin-Past
   'He began to *walk* toward the door.'
 c. Il ... *se dirigea*   vers la porte (167)
   he directed-himself toward the door
   'He *headed* for the door.'
 d. Er ... *ging*   zur Tür. (133)
   he walked to the door
   'He *walked* to the door.'

---

[10] In Chinese, the character 去 *qù* is used in two ways. When it appears as a main verb, as in (7e), it corresponds to the English verb *go*. On the other hand, when it follows another verb as in (17e), (18e), (21e), (22e), (23e), (24e) and (25e), it functions as a directional complement, which is analogous to the English particle *away*.

e. 他⋯ 向　　　门口　　走　去。(141)
　　tā　xiàng　ménkǒu　zǒu　qù
　　he　toward　entrance　walk　away
　　'He *walked* away to the entrance.'

Here the phrase *walk to the door* is translated word for word only in German, in which the verb *gehen* and the prepositional phrase *zur Tür* correspond to the verb *walk* and the prepositional phrase *to the door* in the original English sentence, respectively.

In Japanese, the verb *walk* is literally translated as the verb *aruku* "to walk," but the prepositional phrase *to the door* is roughly translated as the expression *toguchi-ni mukat-te* "toward the door," which consists of the verb *mukau* "to head for" and the goal phrase *toguchi-ni* "to the door." In French, *walk to* is again loosely translated as *se diriger vers* "to head for," a typical collocation in French. In the Chinese translation, as with the Japanese case, the verb *walk* is faithfully translated as the verb 走 *zǒu*. But the goal prepositional phrase *to the door* is paraphrastically translated as the directional phrase 向门口 *xiàng ménkǒu*, which literally means "toward the door." Similar to 朝 *cháo*, the character 向 *xiàng* is equivalent to the English preposition *toward*, and the directional complement 去 *qù* "away" is also added in a similar way to (17e).[11]

In the examples below, we can observe other translational variations:

(19) a. Tremlett *walked* to the table.
　　　　　　　　　　　(P. D. James, *The Lighthouse*: 201)
　　b. Toremuretto-wa　teeburu-ni　*chikazuite*　kita. (176)
　　　 Tremlett-Top　table-to　approach　come-Past
　　　 'Tremlett came *approaching* the table.'
　　c. Tremlett　*se dirigea*　vers　la　table. (223)
　　　 Tremlett　directed-himself　toward　the　table
　　　 'Tremlett *headed* for the table.'

---

[11] In Chinese, the directional complement 去 *qù* "away" is often used additionally after the main verb. In order to avoid further complications, the addition of 去 *qù* is henceforth not mentioned unless necessary (see also note 10 above).

d. Tremlett *kam* zum Tisch. (203)
   Tremlett came to the table
   'Tremlett *came* <u>to the table</u>.'
e. 特拉姆莱   走   到   桌子   边… (118)
   tèlāmlái   zǒu   dào   zhuōzi   biān
   Tremlett   walk to   table   side
   'Tremlett *walked* <u>to the side of the table</u>.'

Here the phrase *walk to the table* is literally translated only in the Chinese version, in which the verb 走 *zǒu* and the directional complement 到桌子边 *dào zhuōzi biān* correspond to the verb *walk* and the prepositional phrase *to the table*, respectively. In Chinese, the combination of 走 *zǒu* "to walk" and 到 *dào* "to" is sometimes used to translate the phrase *walk to* in English.[12] In French, similar to (17c) and (18c), the expression *walk to* is idiomatically translated as *se diriger vers* "to head for."

In Japanese, the walking manner is not described. What is interesting is that the translator uses the phrase *chikazui-te kuru*, which is comprised of the verb *chikazuku* "to approach" and the verb *kuru* "to come." The first verb *chikazuku* "to approach" denotes a movement toward something and does not entail an arrival at a goal, which is usually encoded by the preposition *to* in English. In addition, the use of the second verb *kuru* "to come" shows that the deictic information not explicit in the original text is inferred in a similar way to (7b) and (14b).

Finally, let us examine the German translation. Intriguingly, though the prepositional phrase *to the table* is exactly translated as *zum Tisch*, the manner of motion verb *walk* is translated as the verb of directed motion *kommen* "to come." This means that, in a similar fashion to (7d), the deictic information not found in the English version is inferred from the context, and verbalized as a directed motion verb. As a consequence, the manner of motion is unexpressed and the motion is depicted in a verb-framed manner even in German, a satellite-framed language. This demonstrates that verb-framed

---

[12] In Chinese, the character 到 *dào* is also used in two ways. When it is used as a main verb, it is roughly equivalent to the English verb *arrive*. In contrast, when it follows another verb as a directional complement, it is analogous to the English preposition *to*.

encoding is more common than satellite-framed encoding.

Let us consider the fourth group of examples, in which appears another possible way of translation into Japanese.

(20) a. He *walked* down the hall to the elevator, …
    (J. Archer, *Shall We Tell the President?*: 245)

  b. Kare-wa   rouka-o   erebeta-no   mae-made   *arui*-te
     he-Top   corridor-Acc elevator-Gen   front-until walk
     iki … (295)
     go
     'He walked down the corridor as far as the front of the elevator.'

  c. Il *se dirigea*   vers   l'ascenseur, … (245)
     he directed-himself   toward   the-elevator
     'He headed for the elevator.'

  d. Er *ging*   durch   die Halle   zum   Fahrstuhl, … (256)
     he walked   through   the hall   to-the elevator
     'He walked through the hall to the elevator.'

  e. 他   穿过   走廊,   走   向   电梯, … (204)
     tā   chuānguo   zǒuláng   zǒu   xiàng   diàntī
     he   pass through corridor   walk   toward   elevator
     'He passed through the corridor and walked toward the elevator.'

Here the phrase *walk … to the elevator* is translated in a similar way to (17) and (18) in French and German. More specifically, the French translator employs the idiomatic phrase *se diriger vers* "to head for," and the German translator uses the verb *gehen* "to walk" and the prepositional phrase *zum Fahrstuhl* "to the elevator."

In Chinese, the main verb 走 *zǒu* "to walk" is followed by the directional complement 向电梯 *xiàng diàntī* "toward the elevator." In this case, the 向 *xiàng* "toward" phrase does not precede the main verb as in (18e), and 走 *zǒu* "to walk" is not accompanied by the deictic complement 去 *qù* "away." The difference in position of the 向 *xiàng* phrase might have considerable significance for the analysis of motion expressions in Chinese, but delving deeply into this issue goes beyond the scope of this study.

Finally, let us look at the Japanese translation, in which the phrase *arui-te iku* "to go (by) walking" is used. Similar to (7b), the verb of directed motion *iku* "to go" is the main verb, and the manner of motion is expressed by a subordinate *-te* construction. What is striking here is the way the prepositional phrase *to the elevator* is translated into Japanese. Here, the goal preposition *to* is reinterpreted as denoting the range of movement, and is expressed by the postpositional word *-made* "as far as or until." This shift in perspective is often observed in translation into Japanese, and is a topic worth exploring further, but its fuller study lies outside the scope of this book.

Let us consider the last set of examples containing a goal prepositional phrase.

(21) a. ... they *walked* together to the front door.
      (J. le Carré, *The Spy Who Came in from the Cold*: 165)
   b. Futarishite genkan-e   mukat-te   aruki   dashi-ta. (216)
      together   front door-to   head for   walk   start-Past
      'They started walking to the front door together.'
   c. ... ils   gagnèrent   le perron. (215)
           they   reached   the steps to the front door
      'They reached the steps to the front door.'
   d. ... sie   gingen   gemeinsam   zur   Eingangstür. (170)
           they   walked   together   to-the   front door
      'They walked together to the front door.'
   e. ... 他们   一起   向   前门   走   去。 (177)
          tāmen   yīqǐ   xiàng   qiánmén   zǒu   qù
          they   together toward   front-door   walk   away
      'They walked together toward the front door.'

An explanation similar to that of the examples (18) applies here, except for the French case. In Japanese, the verb *walk* is translated as the verb *aruku*, and the prepositional phrase *to the front door* is loosely translated as the phrase *genkan-e mukat-te* "toward the front door." The verb *mukau* "to head for" is again used to denote a movement toward a goal. In German, the verb *gehen* and the prepositional phrase *zur Eingangstür* correspond to the verb *walk* and the prepositional phrase *to the front door*, respectively. In

Chinese, the verb *walk* is literally translated as the verb 走 *zǒu*, and the prepositional phrase *to the door* is translated as the directional phrase 向前门 *xiàng qiánmén* "toward the door."

Interestingly, the French translator uses the verb *gagner*, which basically means "to win, to gain," but metaphorically denotes "to reach" when it takes a direct object referring to a place. But *gagner* is not so frequently used to translate the phrase "walk to," because French translators are assumed to employ the idiomatic phrase *se diriger vers* "to head for," which entails an approach and not an arrival, because of its familiarity and idiomaticity.

5.3. When Verb *walk* Takes Directional Prepositional Phrase

The verb *walk* sometimes appears with a prepositional phrase headed by the preposition *toward*, which denotes that an entity moves in the direction of another entity. In this case, it is predicted that the manner of motion verb can be followed by a prepositional phrase or its counterpart even in verb-framed languages, since satellite-framedness is relevant only to goal prepositional phrases, which cause event coidentification.

To begin with, let us consider the following examples:

(22) a. ... Brody *walked* <u>toward his car</u>. (P. Benchley, *Jaws*: 260)
    b. ... Burodi-wa   jibun-no   kuruma-ni   *mukat-ta*. (351)
         Brody-Top   oneself-Gen   car-to   go-Past
        'Brody *went* <u>to his car</u>.'
    c. ... Brody   *se dirigea*   <u>vers</u>   <u>sa voiture</u>. (265)
         Brody   directed-himself   toward   his car
        'Hooper *headed* <u>for his car</u>.'
    d. ... *ging*   Brody   <u>zu</u>   <u>seinem Wagen</u>. (240)
         walked   Brody   to   his car
        'He *walked* <u>to his car</u>.'
    e. 布罗迪   朝着   他的   汽车   走   去。(260)
         bùluódí   cháo-zhe   tā-de   qìchē   *zǒu*   qù
         Brody   toward   his   car   walk   away
        'He *walked* <u>toward his car</u>.'

What is intriguing here is that the verb phrase *walk toward his car* is translated in much the same way as the verb phrase *walk to his car* in the example (17a). Though the manner of motion verb *walk* does not take a goal prepositional phrase, the manner of motion is lost in translation into Japanese and French. The main verb in Japanese is *mukau* "to head for," which does not entail an arrival at a destination but an approach to it, and is therefore semantically closer to the preposition *toward* than the preposition *to*. In addition, the phrase *jibun-no kuruma-ni* "to one's own car" gives more details about the destination. In French, the idiomatic phrase *se diriger vers* "to head for" is again used, denoting a movement toward something. In German, the verb *walk* and the prepositional phrase *toward his car* are translated as the verb *gehen* "to walk" and the prepositional phrase *zu seinem Wagen* "to his car," respectively. The German preposition *zu* denotes an arrival at a place and is usually glossed as "to." In the German case, therefore, the motion toward a destination portrayed in the English original is metonymically reinterpreted as the arrival at it.[13] Finally, in Chinese, the verb *walk* in English is translated as the verb 走 *zǒu* followed by the directional complement 去 *qù*, and the prepositional phrase *toward his car* is accurately translated as 朝着他的汽车 *cháo-zhe tā-de qìchē* "toward his car," in which 朝着 *cháo-zhe* denotes a movement in the direction of something.[14]

To sum up, all the translations in (17) and (22) indicate that an arrival at a place and a movement toward a place are sometimes used interchangeably to refer to the same situation. Then what motivates this interchangeability? One reasonable answer is that the two concepts are highly associated. More specifically, an arrival at a place and motion toward the place are related by spatio-temporal contiguity, and therefore one is easily reinterpreted as the other by metonymic inference.

A similar style of translation is observed in the examples below (except

---

[13] It is assumed that this stems from the fact that German has no single preposition equivalent to the English preposition *toward*. This is interesting but we leave the more detailed consideration of the differences between English and German as a topic for further research.

[14] According to *Shogakukan Chinese English Dictionary* (second edition), 着 *zhe* is used to make it clear that the previous character functions as a preposition (or to put it more accurately, a Chinese equivalent to an English preposition). Therefore, 朝 *cháo* and 朝着 *cháo-zhe* have almost the same meaning.

for the Japanese version):

(23) a. She turned and *walked* toward the door.

(P. Benchley, *Jaws*: 101)

b. Kanojo-wa kibisu-wo kaesu to doa-ni mukat-te
she-Top heels-Acc turn and door-to go
aruki dashi-ta. (135)
walk start-Past
'She turned on her heel and started *walking* to the door.'

c. Elle fit demi-tour et *se dirigea* vers
she made half-turn and directed-herself toward
la porte. (107)
the door
'She turned back and *headed* for the door.'

d. Sie drehte sich um und *ging* zur Tür. (97)
she turned oneself around and walked to the door
'She turned around and *walked* to the door.'

e. 她 转身 向 门口 走 去。(101)
tā zhuǎnshēn xiàng ménkǒu zǒu qù
she turn around toward entrance walk away
'She turned around and *walked* away toward the entrance.'

In Japanese, unlike (22b), the manner of motion is retained in translation and expressed by the manner of motion verb *aruku* "to walk." The direction of motion, on the other hand, is depicted by the phrase *doa-ni* "to the door" and the verb *mukau* "to head for." This is consistent with the theoretical prediction that the manner of motion is not lost in translation into verb-framed languages when the manner of motion verb takes a directional phrase, and not a goal phrase.

In all the other three languages, the sentence is translated in a similar way to (22). In Chinese, the verb *walk* is literally translated as the verb 走 *zǒu* "to walk," and the directional phrase *toward the door* is also accurately translated as 向门口 *xiàng ménkǒu* "toward the entrance," in which the character 向 *xiàng* corresponds to the preposition *toward*. In French, *walk toward* is translated as *se diriger vers* "to head for," a typical collocation in French. What is more, in German, though the verb *walk* is translated as the verb *gehen* "to walk," the directional phrase *toward the door* is translated as the goal phrase *zur Tür* "to the door."

Let us look at a third group of examples, in which the Japanese and German versions exhibit an interesting pattern of translation.

(24) a. Mark *walked* <u>towards the elevator</u> ...
(J. Archer, *Shall We Tell the President?*: 272)

b. elebeetaa-no hou-ni *aruki* ... (304)
elevator-Gen direction-in walk
'He *walked* <u>in the direction of the elevator</u>.'

c. Mark *se dirigea* <u>vers l'ascenseur</u> ... (252)
Mark directed-himself toward the-elevator
'Mark *headed* <u>for the elevator</u>.'

d. Er *ging* <u>auf den Fahrstuhl</u> *zu* ... (264)
he walk to the elevator in the direction
'He *approached* <u>the elevator</u>.'

e. 马克 朝 电梯 走 去… (210)
mǎkè cháo diàntī zǒu qù
Mark toward elevator walk away
'He *walked* <u>toward the elevator</u>.'

In Chinese, *walk* is translated as 走 *zǒu* "to walk," and the directional phrase *toward the elevator* is translated as 朝电梯 *cháo diàntī* "toward the elevator," in which 朝 *cháo* "toward," as in (17e), plays a role parallel to the preposition *toward* in English. In French, in the same way as (22c) and (23c), the typical collocation *se diriger vers* "to head for" is used to express the motion.

In Japanese, the verb *walk* is literally translated as the verb *aruku* "to walk," and the prepositional phrase *towards the elevator* is translated as the phrase *elebeetaa-no hou-ni* "in the direction of the elevator," in which the noun *hou* means a direction. The Japanese phrases *-no hou-ni* and *-no hou-e* are semantically and syntactically equivalent to the English phrase *in the direction of*, and are sometimes chosen to translate the preposition *toward*.

In German, the translator employs the separable verb *zu|gehen*, which is translated as "to approach somebody or something" in *Oxford German*

Dictionary (Third Edition).[15] The separable verb prefix *zu* originates as the particle *zu*, which etymologically and semantically corresponds to the English preposition *to*. The prefix now denotes "to be in the direction of something or to approach something." When it is attached to a verb, the resulting separable verb is idiomatically used with the preposition *auf* taking an accusative object, which elaborates on the direction or the destination.

Let us examine a fourth set of examples, in which the Japanese version has a unique feature:

(25) a. They *walked* towards Seal Cottage.
          (P. D. James, *The Lighthouse*: 211)
 b. Futari-wa Shiirusou-made *arui*-ta. (185)
  two persons-Top Seal Cottage-until walk-Past
  'They *walked* as far as Seal Cottage.'
 c. Ils *se dirigèrent* vers Seal Cottage. (234)
  they directed themselves toward Seal Cottage
  'They *headed* for Seal Cottage.'
 d. Sie *gingen* zum Combe House. (214)
  they walked to the Combe House
  'They *walked* to the Combe House.'
 e. 他们 向 海狮 别墅 走 去。(125)
  tāmen xiàng hǎishī biéshù zǒu qù
  they toward sea-lion villa walk away
  'They *walked* away toward Sea-Lion villa.'

It should be noted that, in Japanese, the directional phrase *towards Seal Cottage* is reinterpreted as specifying the range of movement, and is translated as *Shiirusou-made* "as far as or until Seal Cottage." This is surely the

---

[15] The German separable verb *zu|gehen* is derived from one of the manner of motion verbs in German, namely *gehen* "to walk." Nevertheless, *zu|gehen* is defined as "to approach," and not as "to walk toward," in *Oxford German Dictionary*. Therefore, similar to the aforementioned verb *betreten* "to enter," it can be regarded as a directed motion verb. It seems that when the manner of motion verbs *gehen* "to walk" and *treten* "to step" are prefixed, their manner of motion is sometimes semantically "bleached." It should be further investigated how the verb classification and the semantics of prefixes are related in German.

same as the case of (20b), but here, the English prepositional phrase *towards Seal Cottage* denotes a direction, and not a goal as that in (20b). This also illustrates the interchangeability of an arrival at a place and a movement toward it.

In the other three languages, the way of translation is far from unique. The original English text is translated similarly to (22) and (23). In Chinese, the verb *walk* is translated as the verb 走 *zǒu* "to walk" and the directional phrase is translated as 向海狮别墅 *xiàng hǎishī biéshù* "toward Seal Cottage." In French, as usual, the phrase *walk towards* is translated as the characteristic collocation *se diriger vers* "to head for." Furthermore, in German, the verb *walk* is faithfully translated as the verb *gehen* "to walk," but, in a similar way to (22d) and (23d), the directional phrase *towards Seal Cottage* is paraphrastically translated as the goal phrase *zum Combe House* "to the Combe House [i.e. Seal Cottage]."

Let us examine the final set of examples, which illustrate other possible ways of translation into Japanese, French, and German.

(26) a. Alice Tanner ... *walked* toward him.
                      (S. Sheldon, *A Stranger in the Mirror*: 68)
   b. Arisu Tanaa-wa ... kare-no hou-e   yat-te ki-ta. (58)
      Alice Tanner-Top his   direction-in over come
      'Alice Tanner *came over* toward him.'
   c. Alice Tanner ... *marcha* vers   lui. (70)
      Alice Tanner   walked toward him
      'Alice Tanner *walked* toward him.'
   d. Alice Tanner ... *ging* ihm entgegen. (56)
      Alice Tanner   go   him to meet
      'Alice Tanner went to meet him.'
   e. 阿丽思・坦纳… 向   托比 走 来。(51)
      ālìsī tǎnnà   xiàng tuōbǐ zǒu lái
      Alice Tanner   toward Toby walk up
      'Alice Tanner *came walking* toward Toby.'

In Chinese, similar to (23e) and (25e), the verb *walk* is translated as the verb 走 *zǒu* "to walk," and the prepositional phrase *toward him* [i.e. Tody] is translated as the directional phrase 向托比 *xiàng tuōbǐ* "toward

Toby." However, the directional complement following the main verb is not 去 *qù* "away", but 来 *lái* "up, toward the speaker's location" in this case.[16]

In Japanese, the prepositional phrase *toward him* is translated as the phrase *kare-no hou-e* "in his direction or toward him," in which the noun *hou* means a direction. Interestingly, the verb *walk* is translated as the verb phrase *yat-te kuru* "to come over," which is thought to be a directed motion verb.[17] As a result, the manner of motion is lost in translation. Here, similar to (7), the deictic information not explicit in the English version is inferred from the context, and verbalized as a directed motion verb.

Unlike the foregoing examples (22c), (23c), (24c) and (25c), the verb *walk* and the prepositional phrase *toward him* are translated word for word in French as the verb *marcher* "to walk" and the directional prepositional phrase *vers lui* "toward him," respectively. Surprisingly, of all thirty seven examples of the collocation *walk toward(s)* taken from novels, this is the only example in which the phrase is translated as *marcher vers* "to walk toward" in French. In fact, in seventeen out of the thirty seven examples, the idiomatic phrase *se diriger vers* "to head for" is utilized in French.

It is important to note that a manner of motion verb followed by a directional preposition, like *marcher vers* "to walk toward," is supposed to be theoretically possible in verb-framed languages. As we have seen in the preceding chapters, satellite-framed lexicalization comprises a manner of motion verb and a goal prepositional phrase following it. It is this formation of phrases that is not allowed in verb-framed languages.

Nevertheless, the phrase *marcher vers* "to walk toward" is rarely used in French. Therefore, it is reasonable to assume that although this expression is not prohibited by the language system itself, the typical collocation *se diriger vers* "to head for" is much more familiar in French.

Lastly, in German, the separable verb *entgegen|gehen* "to go (somewhere) to meet someone" is used. Interestingly, this verb does not lexicalize a manner of motion nor a directed motion, but the purpose of meeting someone. This is a free translation of the text, and so is difficult to evalu-

---

[16] In Chinese, the character 来 *lái* is also used in two ways. When it occurs as a main verb, it corresponds to the English verb *come*. But when it follows another verb as in (26e), it functions as a directional complement, which is analogous to the English particle *up* and shows that the movement is toward the speaker's location.

[17] It is beyond the scope of this book to analyze the verb phrase *yat-te kuru* in depth.

ate. But it seems that the existence of this kind of verb shows that some motion verbs might be classified under the category of purpose verbs proposed by Fellbaum (2013).

5.4. When Verb *walk* is Followed by Particle *away*

Finally, let us consider three sets of examples in which the verb *walk* takes the particle *away*, which describes the deictic information that the motion is away from the speaker's position. In the examples below, the French and Chinese translations dovetail exactly with what is expected from Talmy's original typology, whereas the Japanese and German cases do not:

(27) a. He *walked* rapidly away.
(G. Greene, *Our Man in Havana*: 219)
b. Kare-wa   sassa-to   *aruki*   dashi-ta. (220)
   he-Top   quickly   walk   begin-Past
   'He began to *walk* quickly.'
c. Wormold   *s'éloigna*   d'un pas rapide. (259)
   Wormold   moved-himself-away   at-a rapid pace
   'Wormold *moved away* at a rapid pace.'
d. Er   *ging*   schnell   weg. (227)
   he   went   rapidly   away
   'He *left* rapidly.'
e. 他   快步   走   开   了。(229)
   tā   kuàibù   zǒu   kāi   le
   he   at a quick pace   walk   away   Perf
   'He walked away at a quick pace.'

As theoretically predicted by Talmy's classification, in French, the movement and the deictic information are lexicalized into the single directed motion verb *s'éloigner* "to move away," and the manner of motion "walking" is lost in translation. In sharp contrast, the verb *walk* and the particle *away* are translated word for word as the verb 走 *zǒu* "to walk" and the directional complement 开 *kāi* "away," respectively, in Chinese.[18]

In Japanese, *walk ... away* is freely translated as the phrase *aruki dasu* "to begin to walk," which is made up of the verb *aruku* "to walk" and the auxiliary verb *dasu* "to begin." In this case, the deictic information is not explicit in the translation, but is assumed to be implied by the inchoative aspect denoted by *dasu* "to begin." Moreover, in German, *walk away* is translated as the separable verb *weg|gehen*, which is defined as "to leave, to go out, to move away" in *Oxford German Dictionary* (Third Edition). Here, the manner of motion is not presented in the translation, and we can assume that the sentence is translated in a verb-framed manner even in German, a satellite-framed language.[19]

In the following examples, intriguingly, the manner of motion denoted by the verb *walk* is not expressed in all the four translations, whether the target language is satellite-framed or verb-framed.

(28) a. "Thank you, I don't drink." Jill smiled and *walked* away.

(S. Sheldon, *A Stranger in the Mirror*: 210)

b. "Arigatou, demo atashi-wa nom-e-nai no," Jiru-wa
thank you but I-Top drink-cannot it is that Jill-Top
bishoushite *tachisat-ta.* (184)
smile leave-Past

'"Thank you, but I can't drink." Jill smiled and *left*.'

c. —Je vous remercie, je ne bois pas, dit-elle
I you thank I ne drink not said-she
en souriant avant de *s'éloigner.* (226)
in smiling before moved-herself-away

'"Thank you, but I don't drink," she said smiling before *moving away*.'

---

[18] In Chinese, the character 开 *kāi* primarily means "to open," but when it is used as a complement to a motion verb, it denotes a separation, which bears a close resemblance to the particle *away*.

[19] In the case of the separate verb *weg|gehen*, similar to the case of the phrase *zu Fuß gehen* "to go on foot," the basic verb stem *gehen* is thought to express not a manner of motion, but a directed motion lexicalized by the verb *go* in English. Therefore the separate verb is presumed to be not defined as "to walk away" but as "to leave, to go out, to move away" in *Oxford German Dictionary*.

d. »Herzlichen Dank, ich trinke nicht.« Jill lächelte und
   sincere   thanks   I   drink   not   Jill   smiled   and
   verschwand. (181)
   disappeared
   '"My sincere thanks, I don't drink," Jill smiled and *disappeared*.'

e. "谢谢   您,   我   不   喝   酒。"   吉尔   微微
   xièxie nín wǒ   bù   hē   jiǔ   Jí'ěr   wēiwēi
   Thank you   I   not drink alcohol Jill   slightly
   一   笑   就   走   了。(188)
   yī   xiào   jiù   zǒu   le
   soon smile just   leave Perf
   '"Thank you, I don't drink alcohol." Jill *left* as soon as she smiled slightly.'

In Japanese and French, the manner of motion is not preserved in translation, and this fits the lexicalization typology formulated by Talmy. More specifically, the motion event in these examples is depicted by the verb *tachisaru* "to leave" in Japanese and by the verb *s'éloigner* "to move away" in French, and both are directed motion verbs. This just exemplifies the typical omission of manner of motion in verb-framed languages. Surprisingly, however, the manner of motion is not verbalized even in satellite-framed languages in these examples. The German verb *verschwinden* "to disappear" and the Chinese verb 走 *zǒu* "to leave" are both verbs of directed motion and do not specify a manner of motion.[20] This clearly demonstrates that when the manner of motion does not matter or is easily inferable from the context, it can remain unexpressed, and concomitantly the motion is expressed in a verb-framed way even in satellite-framed languages. Therefore, these examples also validate the pervasiveness of verb-framed encoding.

Let us look at the last set of examples of the collocation *walk away*, in which, again, the German and Chinese translations do not follow Talmy's

---

[20] In Chinese, the character 走 *zǒu* has two meanings. The first meaning denotes a manner of motion, and in this case, the character roughly corresponds to the English manner of motion verb *walk*. Intriguingly, the second meaning encodes a directed motion event, which is lexicalized by the verb *leave* in English. Here the character 走 *zǒu* is used in the second meaning.

original typology.

(29) a. … with a big smile all over her face, she *walked* <u>away</u>, …
(J. Archer, *Shall We Tell the President?*: 251)
b. … manmen-ni   emi-o   ukabe-nagara …
   all over her face smile-Acc   have-while
   ayum-i <u>sat-ta</u>. (281)
   walk   leave-Past
   'Having a smile all over her face, she left walking.'
c. La femme …, la mine   épanouie, *s'éloigna*, … (233)
   the woman   the expression beaming   moved-herself-away
   'The woman, with a beaming expression, went away.'
d. … die Frau … *ging*   mit   strahlendem Lächeln
     the woman   went   with   beaming   smile
   <u>fort</u>, … (214)
   away
   'The woman, with a beaming smile, *left*.'
e. 那   女人…   满面   笑容   地
   nà   nǔrén   mǎnmiàn   xiàoróng de
   that woman   all over her face smile   with
   <u>离开</u> 了, … (193)
   líkāi   le
   leave   Perf
   'That woman *left* smiling all over her face.'

In Japanese, the main verb is the directed motion verb *saru* "to leave," which corresponds to the particle *away* in the original text. The verb *walk* is translated as the literary manner of motion verb *ayumu* "to walk." In this example, *ayumu* occurs in the adverbial form, modifying the main verb *saru* "to leave," and this pattern of expression conforms to Talmy's remarks on verb-framed languages. In French, as with (27c) and (28c), the manner of motion is lost in translation, and the verb *s'éloigner* "to move away" denotes the movement and the deictic information.

In German, *walk away* is translated as the separable verb *fort|gehen*, which is, as with the separable verb *weg|gehen*, defined as "to leave, to go away" in *Oxford German Dictionary* (Third Edition). This shows that the manner of motion is not lexicalized in the meaning of this verb, which in turn means that this is an instance of verb-framed encoding. Furthermore, in Chinese, *walk away* is translated as the phrase 离开 *líkāi*, which literally means "to leave away," but is usually glossed as "to leave." More specifically, the directed motion verb 离 *lí* "to leave" encodes a separation, and the directional complement 开 *kāi* "away" also lexicalizes a separation, as we have seen in (27e). This means that 离开 *líkāi* contains no element expressing the manner of motion at all, and is therefore regarded as an example of verb-framed encoding. To sum up, the lexicalization style in these German and Chinese translations exhibits verb-framed behavior, and substantiates the ubiquity of verb-framedness.

Before concluding this section, we can pause to glance at the examples in which *leave*, one of the typical verbs of directed motion, is used in the English original. In this case, no manner is added in the translations into the other four languages.

(30) a. Clifton *left* Jill's cabin …
                     (S. Sheldon, *A Stranger in the Mirror*: 315)
    b. Kurifuton-wa Jiru-no Senshitsu-o *deru* to … (273)
       Clifton-Top Jill-Gen cabin-Acc leave and …
       'Clifton *left* Jill's cabin …'
    c. En *sortant*, … (339)
       in leaving
       '*Leaving*, …'
    d. Clifton *verließ* Jills Kabine … (268)
       Clifton left Jill-Gen cabin
       'Clifton *left* Jill's cabin …'
    e. 克里夫敦 离开 吉尔 的 舱房, … (279)
       kèlǐfūdūn líkāi Jí'ěr de cāngfáng
       Clifton leave Jill of cabin
       'Clifton *left* Jill's cabin …'

Here the Japanese verb *deru*, the French verb *sortir*, the German verb *verlassen* and the Chinese verb 离开 *líkāi* are all semantically analogous to the English *leave*, and are therefore categorized as verbs of directed motion. This demonstrates that verb-framed expressions should be thought to be possible in all the languages we consider in this book, and in turn justifies the conclusions we have presented as (2) at the outset of this chapter.

5.5. Conclusion

We have begun this chapter by outlining the claim made at the end of chapter 2 that verb-framed lexicalization is observed in almost all languages whereas satellite-framed conflation is an add-on to it. In section 5.1, we have considered examples in which the verb *walk* takes no prepositional phrase. We have observed that, in this case, *walk* can be translated as a semantically corresponding manner of motion verb in all the four languages. Moreover, we have looked at examples in which the English original is translated in a verb-framed fashion in all the translations, and have stated that this indicates the availability of verb-framed encoding options in satellite-framed languages. In section 5.2, we have examined cases in which *walk* is followed by a goal prepositional phrase headed by the preposition *into* or *to*. We have revealed that the manner of motion can be lost when the English original is translated not only into verb-framed languages such as Japanese and French, but even into satellite-framed languages like German and Chinese. In section 5.3, we have discussed examples in which *walk* appears with a directional prepositional phrase headed by the preposition *toward*. Since the acceptability of directional prepositional phrases following manner of motion verbs is not influenced by whether the target languages are satellite-framed or not, all the translations are theoretically predicted to contain a manner of motion verb. Quite unexpectedly, the directed motion verb *se diriger* "to direct oneself" is used in many of the French translations, probably because of its conventionality. This means that we should be aware of this kind of lopsidedness when we use translations as data. We have also shown that some of the German translations can be regarded as examples of verb-framed lexicalization. Finally, in section 5.4, we have looked at how the phrase *walk away* is translated. We have demonstrated that the manner of motion can be omitted in translation into all the languages we have dealt with in this chapter. This supports our conclusion that verb-framed encoding is not unavailable even in satellite-framed languages, and so is judged not to be strictly prohibited by their grammatical systems.

It is true that the same collocation is variously translated because of the translators' personal preference and the idiomaticity of the relevant languages. This is shown by the famous Italian proverb "translators are traitors." But what is important is this: satellite-framed languages such as German and Chinese sometimes use verb-framed encoding options to translate satellite-framed expressions in English. We assume that this strongly corroborates the basicness and ubiquity of verb-framed lexicalization. In other words, the data in this chapter clarifies and exemplifies the asymmetry of Talmy's binary opposition between satellite-framed and verb-framed lexicalization patterns.

In this chapter, we have examined a limited number of examples. Without doubt, more research is needed on a variety of data. However, by scrutinizing the available data, we have sufficiently reinforced the conclusion we have reached in chapter 2. We hope that we have achieved the primary purpose of this book.

Chapter 6

Conclusion

This work has been primarily concerned with explicating the lexicalization of motion events in terms of scale-based event structure templates.

In chapter 2, we have argued that Talmy's well-known dichotomy between satellite-framed and verb-framed languages should be superseded by the view that verb-framed encoding is all-pervasive and thus in principle possible in almost all languages unless they lack vocabulary to encode it, whereas satellite-framed lexicalization is made possible by an add-on module that is included only in so-called satellite-framed languages. More specifically, in section 2.3.6, we have put out the following three statements: (i) verb-framed expressions are linguistically more basic than satellite-framed ones; (ii) more basic verb-framed lexicalization options are observed in almost all languages; (iii) satellite-framed conflation is an add-on to basic verb-framed lexicalization ubiquitous in the language system; thus it is possible only in certain languages conventionally characterized as satellite-framed. In brief, we have clarified the asymmetry between satellite-framed and verb-framed lexicalization patterns, and have proposed a viable alternative.

In chapter 3, we have chronicled the advancements in Levin and Rappaport Hovav's theory in terms of event structure templates. First, after covering the basics of aspectual classification and the origin of lexical decomposition, we have introduced the original version of event structure templates proposed by Rappaport Hovav and Levin (1998). Next, we have reviewed the divergence of their theory from aspectual notions. We have seen that Levin and Rappaport Hovav have advanced the concepts of scalar and non-scalar changes as viable alternatives to aspectual characterization of event structure templates. Finally, we have suggested that by identifying manners with non-scalar changes consisting of complex changes, it is deduced that manners can be informationally richer than results, which encode a simple scalar change in the values of an attribute, and that less informative results can be incorporated or integrated into more informative manners, but not vice versa.

In chapter 4, we have associated event structure templates with motion macro-events proposed by Talmy (1991, 2000) by using as a catalyst the process of event coidentification advanced by Levin and Rappaport Hovav (1999) and Rappaport Hovav and Levin (2001). After introducing the Unaccusative Hypothesis proposed by Perlmutter (1978), we have redefined event structure templates in terms of the hypothesis. Next, we have looked back at Levin and Rappaport Hovav (1992), a paper published before the advent of event structure templates and dealing with verbs of manner of motion and directed motion. We have argued that it is difficult to incorporate its findings into event structure templates. Then we have scrutinized the process of event coidentification, which explains the semantic amalgamation between manner of motion verbs and goal prepositional phrases. After that, we have created the event structure representation of goal prepositional phrases, and have integrated the concept of scalarity into the process of event coidentification. Given these, we have proposed an event structure template representing the resultant coidentified event. Furthermore, we have connected event coidentification with the configuration of Talmy's motion macro-events, and have shown that event coidentification is conceptually equivalent to the structuring function carried out by framing events. Finally, we have demonstrated that event coidentification is more favorable than lexical subordination in terms of event structure templates.

In chapters 5, we have examined how the verb *walk* in English novels is translated into Japanese, French, German and Chinese. First, in section 5.1, we have confirmed that when *walk* occurs with no prepositional phrase, it can be in principle translated as a semantically similar manner of motion verb in all the languages mentioned above. In section 5.2, we have considered cases in which *walk* takes a goal prepositional phrase headed by the preposition *into* or *to*. Then in section 5.3, we have looked at examples in which *walk* is followed by a directional phrase headed by the preposition *toward*. Finally in section 5.4, we have studied how the phrase *walk away* is translated. Adding everything up, we can say that the manner of motion tends to get lost in translation into verb-framed languages, and in addition that even in satellite-framed languages, the manner of motion is sometimes not preserved in translation. This supports the conclusion we have reached at the end of chapter 2, namely that verb-framed expressions are possible even in satellite-framed languages, because satellite-framed conflation is an add-on to basic verb-framed lexicalization ubiquitous in the language system. Or to put it another way, this chapter illustrates the asymmetry of Talmy's bipartite opposition between satellite-framed and verb-framed lexicalization patterns.

There are four main conclusions to be drawn from the discussions in the previous chapters. The first conclusion is concerned with the modification of Talmy's famous typological dichotomy between satellite-framed and verb-framed languages, and it can be summarized as follows:

(1) (i) Verb-framed expressions are linguistically more basic than satellite-framed ones.
   (ii) More basic verb-framed lexicalization options are observed in almost all languages.
   (iii) Satellite-framed conflation is an add-on to basic verb-framed lexicalization ubiquitous in the language system, and is therefore limited to the languages traditionally classified as satellite-framed.

The second conclusion refers to the differences in mapping between satellite-framed and verb-framed expressions. In particular, we have argued that only satellite-framed languages have the mechanism that makes possible a non-isomorphic mapping between macro-events and syntax. This can be described in the following way:

(2) (i) In the case of verb-framed expressions, the configuration of macro-events is isomorphic to the syntactic structure.

(ii) In the satellite-framed pattern, the components of macro-events are related but not isomorphic to the syntactic constituents.

(iii) Satellite-framed languages have a special conceptual apparatus that can simplify the structure of macro-events so as to make possible a more straightforward mapping. The apparatus is the process of event coidentification, which alters the hierarchical structure of macro-events by embedding the framing event in the subordinate event as a path scale.

The third conclusion is about the mechanism of event coidentification. More specifically, we have argued that the concepts of scalarity and the amount of information are involved in this process. This is given essentially as follows:

(3) (i) In the process of event coidentification, the scalar change denoted by the goal subevent gives a scale to the non-scalar change encoded by the running subevent.

(ii) When two types of changes are combined, the simple scalar change is associated with one of the multiple changes comprising the non-scalar change.

(iii) The goal subevent, which contains only abstract information, is overshadowed by and absorbed into the running subevent, which encodes substantial information.

The fourth conclusion has to do with the relation between event coidentification and Talmy's motion macro-events. Contrary to Talmy's characterization of framing events, we have argued that framing events lose their privileged status when event coidentification occurs. We can express this in the following way:

(4) (i) The subordinate event and the framing event in Talmy's macro-events roughly correspond to the running subevent and the goal subevent in the process of event coidentification, respectively.

(ii) Event coidentification is a scale addition, and can be regarded as an instantiation of the structuring function the framing event exercises over the subordinate event.

(iii) When event coidentification is applied to motion macro-events, counter to Talmy (2000), the framing event loses its status as a discrete semantic entity and is integrated into the subordinate event, which in turn is mapped isomorphically onto syntactic structure. In other words, the process of event identification removes irregularity by subordinating the framing event to the (ex-)subordinate event.

The proposed theory undermines Talmy's typology of binary opposition between satellite-framed and verb-framed lexicalization. The conventional view, which was put forward by Leonard Talmy more than twenty years ago, has gained recognition among linguists (in particular, cognitive linguists and lexical semanticians) and has been applied to multifarious languages. It has created a cornucopia of linguistic findings for linguists who are interested in language typology based on lexicalization patterns. However, mutually exclusive dichotomies have been challenged in many places, and sometimes they have been shown to be untenable.

As we have seen in section 2.3.6, both Talmy (1985: 75) and Beavers et al. (2010: 350–351) inadvertently refer to the inherent asymmetry between satellite-framed and verb-framed encoding patterns, and it is lamentable that they have not made this irregularity more explicit. But whether they delve more deeply into the issue or not, we cannot ignore the fact that verb-framed expressions are much more prevalent in the whole language system. And this is just what this study takes as its point of departure. But where do we go from here?

The overall picture of motion verbs is still incomplete. In particular, a further study of verbs of directed motion, or the *arrive* verbs, should be conducted. We tentatively assume that the *arrive* verbs and goal prepositional phrases are semantically amalgamated not by the process of "event coidentification," but by the process named "event elaboration." The latter does not involve a complicated mechanism of scale addition, but just fleshes out the unspecified destination of the directed motion denoted by the *arrive* verbs. In addition, it is necessary to provide a systematic and detailed analysis of motion verbs that are assumed to denote neither manner nor direction of motion, such as *move, travel, shift*, and of so-called purpose verbs briefly mentioned in chapter 5. The findings would not only contribute to our understanding of motion verbs, but also to the research into manner/result complementarity.

References

Aske, Jon (1989) "Path Predicates in English and Spanish: A Closer Look," *BLS* 15, 1-14.
Beavers, John (2002) "Aspect and the Distribution of Prepositional Resultative Phrases in English," *LinGO Working Paper* No. 2002-07, CSLI, Stanford University, Stanford.
Beavers, John., Beth Levin and Shiao Wei Tham (2010) "The Typology Of Motion Expressions Revisited," *Journal of Linguistics* 46, 331-377.
Becker, A. L. and D. G. Arms (1969) "Prepositions as Predicates," *CLS* 5, 1-11.
Binnick, Robert (1968) "On the Nature of the 'Lexical Item'," *CLS* 4, 1-13.
Demizu, Takanori (2001) "Nishurui no Accomplishment Verbs: Jootaihenka to Idoosuishin-Doosa no Goigainen Koozoo (Two Kinds of Accomplishment Verbs: Lexical Conceptual Structures of "Change-of-State" and "Motion-promoting Activity")," *KLS* 21 (*Proceedings of the 25th Annual Meeting of Kansai Linguistic Society*), 128-138.
Demizu, Takanori (2013) "Do Event Semantics Dream of Active Zone?" *Kyoto Working Papers in English and General Linguistics* 2, 127-142.
Dowty, David (1979) *Word Meaning and Montague Grammar: The Semantics of Verbs and Times in Generative Semantics and in Montague's PTQ*, D. Reidel, Dordrecht.
Erteschik-Shir, Nomi and Tova R. Rapoport (2004) "Bare Aspect: A Theory of Syntactic Projection," *The Syntax of Tense*, ed. by Jacqueline Guéron and Jacqueline Lecarme, 217-234, MIT Press, Cambridge, MA.
Erteschik-Shir, Nomi and Tova R. Rapoport (2005) "Path Predicates," *The Syntax of Aspect: Deriving Thematic and Aspectual Interpretation*, ed. by Nomi Erteschik-Shir and Tova R. Rapoport, 65-86, Oxford University Press, Oxford.
Fellbaum, Christiane (2013) "Purpose Verbs," *Advances in Generative Lexicon*

Theory, ed. by James Pustejovsky et al., 371–384, Springer Science+Business Media, Dordrecht.
Filip, Hana (1999) *Aspect, Eventuality Types and Nominal Reference*, Garland, New York.
Filip, Hana (2004) "The Telicity Parameter Revisited," *SALT* 14, 92–109.
Geis, Jonnie Elinor (1970) *Some Aspects of Verb Phrase Adverbials in English*, Doctoral dissertation, University of Illinois at Urbana-Champaign. University Microfilms, Inc., Ann Arbor.
Goldberg, Adele E. (1995) *Constructions: A Construction Grammar Approach to Argument Structure*, University of Chicago Press, Chicago.
Goldberg, Adele E. (2006) *Constructions at Work: the Nature of Generalization in Language*, Oxford University Press, Oxford.
Grimshaw, Jane (2005) *Words and Structure*, CSLI Publications, Stanford.
Gruber, Jeffrey S. (1976) *Lexical Structures in Syntax and Semantics*, North-Holland, Amsterdam.
Hoekstra, Teun (1984) *Transitivity: Grammatical Relations in Government-Binding Theory*, Foris, Dordrecht.
Kageyama, Taro (1996) *Dooshi Imiron: Gengo to Ninchi no Setten* (*Verb Semantics: The Interface of Language and Cognition*), Kurosio, Tokyo.
Kageyama, Taro and Yoko Yumoto (1997) *Gokeisei to Gainen Koozoo* (*Word Formation and Conceptual Structure*), Kenkyusha, Tokyo.
Kearns, Kate (2000) *Semantics*, Macmillan, Basingstoke.
Kopecka, Anetta (2006) "The Semantic Structure of Motion Verbs in French: Typological Perspectives," *Space in Languages: Linguistic Systems and Cognitive Categories*, ed. by Maya Hickmann and Stéphane Robert, 83–101, John Benjamins, Amsterdam.
Lakoff, George (1968a) "Some Verbs of Change and Causation," *Mathematical Linguistics and Automatic Translation to the National Science Foundation: Report No. NSF*-20, III-1-III-27.
Lakoff, George (1968b) "Instrumental Adverbs and the Concept of Deep Structure," *Foundations of Language* 4, 4–29.
Levin, Beth (1999) "Objecthood: An Event Structure Perspective," *CLS* 35: *The Main Session*, 223–247.
Levin, Beth (2000) "Aspect, Lexical Semantic Representation, and Argument Expression," *BLS* 26, 413–429.
Levin, Beth and Tova R. Rapoport (1988) "Lexical Subordination," *CLS* 24 (Part One: The General Session), 275–289.
Levin, Beth and Malka Rappaport Hovav (1991) "Wiping the Slate Clean: A Lexical Semantic Exploration," *Cognition* 41, 123–151.
Levin, Beth and Malka Rappaport Hovav (1992) "The Lexical Semantics of Verbs of Motion: The Perspective from Unaccusativity," *Thematic Structure: Its Role in Grammar* ed. by I. M. Roca, 247–269, Foris, Berlin.
Levin, Beth and Malka Rappaport Hovav (1995) *Unaccusativity: At the Syntax-Lexical Semantics Interface*, Linguistic Inquiry Monograph 26, MIT Press,

Cambridge, MA.

Levin, Beth and Malka Rappaport Hovav (1999) "Two Structures for Compositionally Derived Events," *SALT* 9, 199–223.

Levin, Beth and Malka Rappaport Hovav (2005) *Argument Realization*, Cambridge University Press, Cambridge.

Levin, Beth and Malka Rappaport Hovav (2013) "Lexicalized Meaning and Manner/Result Complementarity," *Studies in the Composition and Decomposition of Event Predicates*, Boban Arsenijević, Berit Gehrke and Rafael Marín, 49–70, Springer, Dordrecht.

Matsumoto, Yo (1991) "On the Validity of the Restructuring Account of Purposive and Similar Complex Predicates in Japanese," *BLS* 17, 180–191.

Matsumoto, Yo (1996) *Complex Predicates in Japanese: A Syntactic and Semantic Study of the Notion 'Word'*, CSLI Publications, Stanford.

Matsumoto, Yo (2003) "Typologies of Lexicalization Patterns and Event Integration: Clarifications and Reformulations," *Empirical and Theoretical Investigations into Language*, ed. by Shuji Chiba et al., 403–418, Kaitakusha, Tokyo.

McCawley, James D. (1968) "Lexical Insertion in a Transformational Grammar without Deep Structure," *CLS* 4, 71–80.

McCawley, James D. (1973) *Grammar and Meaning: Papers on Syntactic and Semantic Topics*, Taishukan, Tokyo.

Perlmutter, David M. (1978) "Impersonal Passives and the Unaccusative Hypothesis," *BLS* 4, 157–189.

Perlmutter, David M. and Paul M. Postal (1984) "The 1-Advancement Exclusiveness Law," *Studies in Relational Grammar 2*, ed. by David M. Perlmutter and Carol G. Rosen, 81–125, University of Chicago Press, Chicago and London.

Pinker, Steven (1989) *Learnability and Cognition: The Acquisition of Argument Structure*, MIT Press, Cambridge, MA.

Randall, Janet H. (2010) *Linking: The Geometry of Argument Structure*, Springer, Dordrecht.

Rappaport, Malka and Beth Levin (1988) "What to Do with θ-Roles," *Syntax and Semantics* 21: *Thematic Relations*, ed. by Wendy Wilkins, 7–36, Academic Press, San Diego.

Rappaport Hovav, Malka (2008) "Lexicalized Meaning and the Internal Temporal Structure of Events," *Theoretical and Crosslinguistic Approaches to the Semantics of Aspect*, ed. by Susan Rothstein, 13–42, John Benjamins, Amsterdam.

Rappaport Hovav, Malka and Beth Levin (1998) "Building Verb Meanings," *The Projection of Arguments: Lexical and Compositional Factors*, ed. by Miriam Butt and Wilhelm Geuder, 97–134, CSLI Publications, Stanford.

Rappaport Hovav, Malka and Beth Levin (2001) "An Event Structure Account of English Resultatives," *Language* 77, 766–797.

Rappaport Hovav, Malka and Beth Levin (2010) "Reflections on Manner/Result Complementarity," *Lexical Semantics, Syntax, and Event Structure*, ed. by Malka Rappaport Hovav, Edit Doron and Ivy Sichel, 21–38, Oxford University Press,

Oxford.
Rosen, Carol G. (1984) "The Interface between Semantic Roles and Initial Grammatical Relations," *Studies in Relational Grammar 2*, ed. by David M. Perlmutter and Carol G. Rosen, 38-77, University of Chicago Press, Chicago and London.
Rothstein, Susan (2004) *Structuring Events: A Study in the Semantics of Lexical Aspect*, Blackwell, MA.
Schäfer, Florian (2009) "The Causative Alternation," *Language and Linguistics Compass* 3:2, 641-681.
Smith, Carlota S. (1997) *The Parameter of Aspect*, 2nd ed., Kluwer, Dordrecht.
Talmy, Leonard (1975) "Semantics and Syntax of Motion," *Syntax and Semantics 4*, ed. by John P. Kimball, 181-238, Academic Press, New York.
Talmy, Leonard (1985) "Lexicalization Patterns: Semantic Structure in Lexical Forms," *Language Typology and Syntactic Description: Volume III Grammatical Categories and the Lexicon*, ed. by Timothy Shopen, 57-149, Cambridge University Press, Cambridge.
Talmy, Leonard (1991) "A Typology of Event Conflation," *BLS* 17, 480-519.
Talmy, Leonard (2000) *Toward a Cognitive Semantics: Volume II: Typology and Process in Concept Structuring*, MIT Press, Cambridge, MA.
Tenny, Carol (1994) *Aspectual Roles and the Syntax-Semantics Interface*, Kluwer, Dordrecht.
Vendler, Zeno. (1957) "Verbs and Times," *Philosophical Review* 66, 143-160.

Works Cited

Archer, Jeffrey. *Shall We Tell the President?* London: Pan Books, 2003. (First published in 1977 by Jonathan Cape Ltd.)
    Japanese: Shinpan: *Daitooryoo ni Shirasemasuka* (*Should we Let the President Know? (New Editioin)*). Toyko: Shincho, 1987.
    French: *Faut-il le Dire à la Présidente?* (*Is it Necessary to Say it to the President?*) Translated by Dominique Wattwiller. Paris: France Loisirs, 1986.
    German: *Das Attentat* (*The Assassination Attempt*). Translated by Ilse Winger and Margarete Venjakob. Köln, Deutschland: Bastei Lübbe, 2003.
    Chinese: 要不要报告总统? *yàobuyàobàogàozǒngtǒng* (*Do we Need to Report to the President?*) Translated by 江唐 jiāngtáng. 北京 Běijīng: 中国华侨出版社 Zhōngguóhuáqiáochūbǎnshè, 2012.
Benchley, Peter. *Jaws*. New York: Ballantine Books, 1991. (First published in 1974 by Doubleday)
    Japanese: *Joozu* (*Jaws*). Translated by Keigo Hirao. Tokyo: Hayakawa, 1981.
    French: *Les Dents de la Mer* (*The Teeth of the Ocean*). Translated by Michel Deutsch. Paris: Librairie Hachette, 1975.
    German: *Der weiße Hai* (*The While Shark*). Translated by Egon Strohm. Frankfurt am Main: Verlag Ullstein, 1977.

Chinese: 大白鲨 *dàbáishā* (*The Big White Shark*). Translated by 赵学熙 zhàoxuéxī, 乐眉云 lèméiyún and 张柏然 zhāngbǎirán. 南京 Nánjīng: 译林出版社 yìlínchūbǎnshè, 2000.

Greene, Graham. *Our Man in Havana*. London: William Heinemann and the Bodley Head, 1970. (First published in 1958 by William Heinemann Ltd.)

Japanese: *Habana no Otoko* (*A Man of Havana*). Translated by Seijiro Takana. Tokyo: Hayakawa, 1979.

French: *Notre Agent à La Havane* (*Our Agent at the Havana*). Translated by Marcelle Sibon. Paris: Robert Laffont, 2001.

German: *Unser Mann in Havanna* (*Our Man in Havana*). Translated by Dietlind Kaiser. München: Deutscher Taschenbuch Verlag, 1995.

Chinese: 哈瓦那特派员 hāwǎnātèpàiyuán (a Havana Correspondent). Translated by 吴幸宜 wúxìngyí. 南京 Nánjīng: 译林出版社 yìlínchūbǎnshè, 2008.

James, P. D. *The Lighthouse*. London: Penguin Books, 2006.

Japanese: *Toodai* (*The Lighthouse*). Translated by Hisae Aoki. Tokyo: Hayakawa, 2007.

French: *Le Phare* (*The Lighthouse*). Translated by Odile Demange. Paris: Librairie Arthème Fayard, 2006.

German: *Wo Licht und Schatten ist* (*Where Light and Shadow is*). Translated by Ulrike Wasel and Klaus Timmermann. München: Th. Knaur Nachf. GmbH & Co., 2007.

Chinese: 灯塔 *dēngtǎ* (*The Lighthouse*). Translated by 沈亦文 shěnyìwén. 北京 Běijīng: 人民文学出版社 rénmínwénxuéchūbǎnshè, 2008.

le Carré, John. *The Spy Who Came in from the Cold*. London: Hodder & Stoughton Ltd, 2009. (First Published in 1963 by Victor Gollancz Ltd.)

Japanese: *Samui Kuni kara Kaette Kita Supai* (*The Spy Who Came Back from the Cold Country*). Translated by Toshiyasu Uno. Toyko: Hayakawa, 1978.

French: *L'Espion qui Venait du Froid* (*The Spy Who Came from the Cold*). Translated by Marcel Duhamel and Henri Robillot. Paris: Éditions Gallimard, 1964.

German: *Der Spion, der aus der Kälte kam* (*The Spy Who Came out of the Cold*). Translated by Manfred von Conta. Berlin: Ullstein Buchverlage, 2003.

Chinese: 柏林谍影 *bǎilíndiéyǐng* (*A Spy in Berlin*). Translated by 刘险峰 liúxiǎnfēng. 上海 Shànghǎi: 上海人民出版社 Shànghǎirénmínchūbǎnshè, 2008.

Sheldon, Sidney. *A Stranger in the Mirror*. New York: Grand Central Publishing, 2005. (First published in 1976 by William Morrow)

Japanese: *Kagami no Naka no Tanin* (*A Stranger in the Mirror*). Translated by Yutaka Takahashi. Tokyo: Hayakawa, 1979.

French: *Toby* (*Toby*). Translated by Simonne Huinh. [Paris?:] Éditions Alta, 1977.

German: *Ein Fremder im Spiegel* (*A Stranger in the Mirror*). Translated by Egon Strohm. Frankfurt am Main: Verlag Ullstein, 1977.

Chinese: 镜子里的陌生人 *jìngzilidemòshēngrén* (*A Stranger in the Mirror*) Translated by 孙家新 sūnjiāxīn and 马清文 mǎqīngwén. 南京 Nánjīng: 译林出版社 yìlínchūbǎnshè, 2007.

Index

Name Index

Beavers et al. 2, 9, 34, 47–57, 60, 61–62, 231
Demizu 7, 8, 155–156, 185
Dowty 4, 66, 70, 88, 109, 113–118, 122, 145
Filip 69, 112–113
Goldberg 85–86, 97–98
Grimshaw 83–85, 101–102, 129
Kearns 120
Kopecka 34, 44–47
Levin 103–109, 153 (*See also* Levin and Rappaport Hovav *and* Rappaport Hovav and Levin)
Levin and Rappaport Hovav 3–5, 26, 39, 64, 80, 91, 103, 105, 115, 124, 133, 135, 141–153, 157–161, 175, 178, 227–228
Matsumoto 5, 41, 44
McCawley 76–78, 87–88, 95, 110

Perlmutter 136–140, 228
Pinker 80, 82–83, 86, 109, 151–152, 158
Rappaport Hovav 4, 109–110, 115–125, 127–128, 132, 140, 154, 161, 171 (*See also* Rappaport Hovav and Levin *and* Levin and Rappaport Hovav)
Rappaport Hovav and Levin 3–5, 7, 15, 17, 26, 39, 64, 66, 80–82, 83–85, 87–105, 108, 112, 113, 115, 122–123, 128–130, 131–133, 148, 157–163, 166, 173–174, 176, 178, 227–228
Rothstein 115–116, 119, 121–122
Smith 70–76, 89, 94, 154–156
Talmy 1–2, 5, 9–43, 57–58, 61, 62–64, 73, 124, 132, 135, 150, 151, 167, 175–183, 196, 204, 205, 207, 220, 222, 223, 226, 227–229, 230–231
Vendler 66–71, 88–89, 103, 109, 131

Subject Index

accomplishment 3-4, 7, 65-76, 89, 94-95, 98-99, 102, 104-107, 108, 113-122, 129, 132-133, 145
achievement 3-4, 65-76, 88, 93-95, 103-106, 108, 113-114, 118, 126, 132, 139
ACT 3, 88-90, 93-94, 96-101, 103-107, 114, 116, 118-122, 126-127, 130, 137, 141, 147, 149-150, 152-155, 161-162, 169-174, 177-178, 180-187
activity 3, 7, 29, 65-76, 88, 90, 93-102, 104-107, 108, 112, 115-116, 118, 128-130, 132, 137-138, 145-147, 155-156, 176, 178, 185
agent 13, 98-101, 144, 149, 152, 159-160
ambiguity of *again* 117-119
Argument-Per-Subevent Condition 4-5, 105-107, 141, 153-154, 156-158, 184
aspectual 4, 29, 65-76, 88-89, 94-96, 108-112, 114, 120, 122, 130-132, 145, 155, 161, 176, 178, 186, 227-228
atelic 4, 70-71, 75-76, 112-114, 119-120, 132, 145
BECOME 3, 76-79, 88-90, 93-94, 98-99, 103-106, 114-121, 125-126, 130, 141, 148-150, 152-155, 161-174, 177-178, 180-187
causative 7, 95, 101, 104, 106, 107, 114, 126, 130, 137, 141, 151, 155, 165, 186-187
CAUSE 3, 76-79, 89-90, 93-94, 98-99, 103-106, 114, 116, 118-121, 126, 130, 141, 150, 152-155, 161, 165, 184-187
change of state 4, 21, 70-74, 84-85, 94, 95, 98, 101-102, 107, 114-116, 124, 125-126, 140, 149, 155, 162-163, 166, 167
coerced interpretation 119-120, 155-156, 185
co-event 28-31, 35-43, 63, 91, 177-183
conflation 14-21, 32, 36, 43, 61-63, 73, 190-191, 225, 227-229
dichotomy 2, 9, 31-64, 87-108, 132-133, 143, 161, 189, 205, 227, 229
directed motion 4-7, 17, 91-95, 124-128, 137, 140, 142-143, 148-150, 162-163, 165-166, 168, 170, 179, 187, 190-225, 228, 231
displacement 92, 147
durative 68-69, 71
dynamic 70, 72, 122, 133, 171
event coidentification 5, 26-28, 39, 64, 82, 133, 135, 157-183
event structure template 3, 87-108, 114, 116, 118-122, 125-127, 130-131, 149-155, 160-162, 166-174, 176-187
figure 10-23, 31-32, 38-39, 47, 63, 124, 150, 167, 177-181
for-adverbial 68, 75-76, 119-120, 154-156, 184-185
framing event 5, 9, 21-32, 34-45, 63-64, 175-183, 196, 228-231
ground 10-24, 30-39, 47, 124, 150, 167, 172, 177-181
idiosyncratic component/part 3, 80-88, 93, 95, 102, 123-124, 142-143
in-adverbial 68, 75
intransitive 107, 114, 136, 138-139, 153-154, 157, 168
lexical decomposition 3, 65, 76-88, 109-122, 131, 133, 149, 227
lexicalization 1-3, 7, 9-21, 31-32, 34, 38, 49-64, 189-226, 227-229, 231

macro-event 9, 21-32, 36-43, 45, 63, 135, 151, 174-183, 228-231

manner of motion 4-7, 15, 18, 47, 51-56, 72-73, 81, 91-95, 128-129, 133, 135, 138, 141-144, 147, 149-150, 176, 183, 187, 190-225, 228-229

manner/result complementarity 91, 94, 129, 132, 143, 232

manner verb 2, 46, 50-51, 57, 60, 65, 87, 90-103, 108, 111-122, 125, 129-133, 169, 174, 176, 189

non-causative 139, 158, 166-167

non-scalar change 5, 122-123, 128-131, 132-133, 137, 139, 141, 162, 169-170, 172-173, 176-183, 185-187, 228-230

path 1, 3, 5, 10-13, 16-19, 20-21, 23-24, 31-32, 37-39, 44-63, 72, 124-127, 133, 150-185, 190-191, 230

purpose verb 129, 199, 205, 220, 231

repair reading 120, 154-155

result verb 65, 87, 90-96, 102, 108, 111-122, 130-133, 174

satellite 31-36, 40-49, 57-60

satellite-framed 2-7, 9, 34-64, 91, 133, 175, 179-183, 189-226, 227-231

scalar change 5, 11, 122-127, 129-131, 132-133, 138-139, 141, 159, 162, 166-170, 172-173, 176-183, 185-187, 228-230

scale 5, 11, 29, 63, 109, 122-130, 133, 159, 161, 162, 167-172, 174, 176-186, 227, 230-231

semantic content 21, 28, 43, 84-85, 102, 174-175, 182

structural component/part 3, 80-88, 136, 143

subevent 103-107, 152-153, 157-161, 163, 169-170, 172-187, 230

telic 4, 70-71, 75-76, 112-117, 120, 132, 145, 155

temporal(ly) 21, 25-26, 29-30, 45, 65-66, 69-74, 94-95, 109, 114, 120, 131, 141, 158-159, 214

theme 11, 13, 99. 115, 118, 124-127, 129, 140, 144, 149, 152, 159-160, 167

transitive 95-96, 101-102, 104-107, 113, 114, 118, 137-138, 141, 153, 163, 168, 186-187

translation 5-6, 18, 42, 58-59, 189-226, 229

unaccusative 4, 85, 136-140, 141, 143-150, 162, 166, 168, 172, 186-187

Unaccusative Hypothesis 4, 135, 136-140, 187, 228

unergative 4, 136-140, 141, 143-150, 162, 172, 186-187

verb-framed 2-7, 9, 34-64, 91, 133, 179-183, 189-226, 227-231

Lexicalization Typology and Event Structure Templates: Toward Isomorphic Mapping between Macro-event and Syntactic Structures

著作者　出 水 孝 典

発行者　武 村 哲 司

2015年3月19日　第1版第1刷発行©

発行所　株式会社 開 拓 社　　〒113-0023 東京都文京区向丘1-5-2
　　　　　　　　　　　　　　　電話 (03)5842-8900 (代表)
　　　　　　　　　　　　　　　振替 00160-8-39587
　　　　　　　　　　　　　　　http://www.kaitakusha.co.jp

印刷　株式会社 あるむ　　　　　ISBN978-4-7589-2209-8　C3080